The Irish Vampire

The Irish Vampire

From Folklore to the Imaginations
of Charles Robert Maturin,
Joseph Sheridan Le Fanu
and Bram Stoker

SHARON M. GALLAGHER

McFarland & Company, Inc., Publishers
Jefferson, North Carolina

ISBN (print) 978-1-4766-6580-1
ISBN (ebook) 978-1-4766-2796-0

LIBRARY OF CONGRESS CATALOGUING DATA ARE AVAILABLE

British Library cataloguing data are available

Front cover images © 2017 iStock

Printed in the United States of America

*McFarland & Company, Inc., Publishers
Box 611, Jefferson, North Carolina 28640
www.mcfarlandpub.com*

To my husband, Drew,
for all his support, patience, understanding,
and love throughout the entire process,

and

in memory of
Anthony C. Gallagher (1960–2004)
(You were right!)

Acknowledgments

So many people helped make this book possible that it would be difficult to list everyone, but there are some who must be named. First, my dissertation adviser, Dr. James Cahalan, who saw me through the long process from initial ideas to final manuscript. While the contents have been developed and expanded in the dozen years since my dissertation defense, this book would not have been possible without your guidance.

This extensive revision of my dissertation would not have been possible without the librarians at Penn State Behrend, Penn State Berks, and Penn State University Park campuses who were invaluable in their tireless efforts to find every odd text that I requested. A special thank you to Matthew Knight, Assistant Director of Special Collections, Assistant Librarian at the University of South Florida Libraries who provided me with a transcript of Dion Boucicault's rare 1852 play, *The Vampire, A Phantasm*. Also special thanks to Michael Osborne for allowing me to share his meticulous research on Charles Robert Maturin's ancestors.

I want to thank Dr. Eric Corty at Penn State Behrend for recognizing that a non-tenure track faculty member like myself would greatly benefit if she had more time during the semester to work on this project—the course release was greatly appreciated and well-utilized.

Of course, I am grateful for all my family and friends who supported me in a variety of ways as my dissertation evolved into this present text. I could not have done this without you and all your prayers, patient listening, and positive thoughts. Your faith in me and our faith in God has allowed me to realize one of my dreams.

Finally, I wish to thank all those who are cited in this text—and there are a lot of you! Without all your hard work, this book would not have been possible.

Table of Contents

Preface

"The belief in the existence of vampyres is one of the most extraordinary and most revolting superstitions which ever disturbed the brains of any semi-barbarous people. It is the most frightful embodying of the principle of evil, the most terrific incarnation of the bad demon, which ignorance and fanaticism ever suggested to the weak and the deluded. It displays superstition in its grossest and most unrelieved horrors."

—D, "On Vampyrism," January 1823[1]

"Some years ago I set out to answer a single, seemingly limited question—what was the relationship, if any, between the bog bodies of Northern Europe and the vampires of the Slavs—and blundered into an ambush of far more complicated and hostile questions."

—Paul Barber,
Vampires, Burial, and Death: Folklore and Reality, 1988[2]

I readily empathize with Paul Barber's dilemma. In the late 1990s, after finishing my doctoral coursework and exams, I faced the problem of settling upon a topic for my dissertation. My broad area of study was nineteenth-century British literature, but my area of specific focus was Irish literature. I had a long-standing acquaintance with W. B. Yeats and the Irish Literary Renaissance; one of my graduate classes had featured Bram Stoker's *Dracula*, which several of my fellow classmates were surprised to learn was written by an Irishman; and I was a huge fan of Joss Whedon's *Buffy the Vampire Slayer* (1997–2003). Somehow these three unrelated facts converged into the idea that it would be innovative and original to argue that the modern vampire emerged from a nineteenth-century Irish literary tradition. Like Barber, my "seemingly limited" area of focus quickly proved to be otherwise. They say ignorance is bliss; my bliss lasted as long as it took me to walk to the library to begin the research for my working bibliography. It quickly became evident that other researchers—more knowl-

1

edgeable, experienced, and published—had already not only delved into nineteenth-century Irish literature, Stoker, and the vampire, but there were many interesting facets to the topics, among which were two other earlier Irish authors—Charles Robert Maturin (1780–1824) and Joseph Sheridan Le Fanu (1814–1873)—and the relatively new notion (then) of an Irish Gothic literature. Gothic literature was not a genre that had appeared in any titled course offerings in my undergraduate or graduate education, but its texts, like many of Edgar Allan Poe's works and Mary Shelley's *Franken-stein*, were often required reading in some classes.

Fortunately, the reputation of Gothic literature and the vampire has changed in the professional arena.[3] One need look no further than Patrick Brantlinger's *Rule of Darkness: British Literature and Imperialism, 1830–1914* (1988), Carol A. Senf's *The Vampire in Nineteenth-Century English Litera-ture* (1988), Clive Leatherdale's *Dracula the Novel & the Legend: A Study of Bram Stoker's Gothic Masterpiece* (rev. 1993), Nina Auerbach's *Our Vampires, Ourselves* (1995), David Punter's *The Literature of Terror* (1996), Fred Bot-ting's *Gothic* (1996), Leonard Wolf's *Dracula: The Connoisseur's Guide* (1997), Richard Davenport-Hines' *Gothic: Four Hundred Years of Excess, Horror, Evil and Ruin* (1998), *A Companion to the Gothic* (2000) edited by David Punter, Bruce A. McClelland's *Slayers and Their Vampires: A Cultural History of Killing the Dead* (2006), Matthew Beresford's *From Demons to Dracula: The Creation of the Modern Vampire Myth* (2008), and *The Universal Vampire: Origins and Evolution of a Legend* (2013) edited by Barbara Brodman and James E. Doan to glimpse a few of the significant texts seriously examining the Gothic genre and the vampire. Not surprisingly, W. J. McCormack's "Irish Gothic and After" (1991), Margot Gayle Backus's *The Gothic Family Romance: Heterosexuality, Child Sacrifice, and the Anglo-Irish Colonial Order* (1999), Joseph Valente's *Dracula's Crypt: Bram Stoker, Irishness, and the Ques-tion of Blood* (2002), *The Irish Journal of Gothic and Horror Studies* (first issue 2006), Richard Haslam's "Irish Gothic: A Rhetorical Hermeneutics Approach" (2007), and Jarlath Killeen's *Gothic Ireland: Horror and the Irish Anglican Imagination in the Long Eighteenth Century* (2005), "Irish Gothic: A Theoretical Introduction" (2006), and "Irish Gothic Revisited" (2008) have further focused on the subject of Irish Gothic and greatly enriched the discussion.

Killeen's and Haslam's publications particularly illustrate that the Irish Gothic is a dynamic subject area which offers many opportunities for dis-cussion and debate. Killeen's "Irish Gothic: A Theoretical Introduction" provides a useful overview of Irish Gothic criticism up to 2006 and, as he explains in his first paragraph, "I will try to map the theoretical terrain covered by a number of these critics, and put forward a few hypotheses of my own which try to build on the insights already achieved."⁴ Haslam's "Irish Gothic: A Rhetorical Hermeneutics Approach" is his detailed response to Killeen's essay where he addresses the questions: "Is Irish Gothic better understood as a tradition or a mode? What are its distinctive components? How should we conceptualize interactions between literary texts and historical contexts? Is Irish Catholic Gothic a plausible and relevant sub-category of Irish Gothic?"⁵ Killeen's "Irish Gothic Revisited" is his reply to Haslam.⁶ These three articles not only provide an excellent background to the initial introduction of Irish Gothic as described by W. J. McCormack in his *Field Day* essay⁷ but also show ways in which the criticisms and their texts may be analyzed and debated. For the purposes of this study, the broader "Irish Gothic" will be used when discussing all three writers' works rather than subcategorizing into either Protestant or Catholic.

As may be concluded from this very brief overview and list of some of the texts that examine the topic, there is more to Irish Gothic and its vampires than a momentary shiver of fear. The figure of the vampire has a long and culturally diverse history which includes vampiric characters and elements of Irish oral tradition. The Irish Gothic writers tapped into and used these stories for generations to express the horrors of their national and personal situations. Charles Robert Maturin's *Melmoth the Wanderer* (1820), Joseph Sheridan Le Fanu's *Uncle Silas* (1864) and "Carmilla" (1872), and Bram Stoker's *Dracula* (1897) articulate these experiences particularly well and with a prismatic quality—there are multiple angles from which to view their fiction, but to be caught up in just one means losing the other dimensions that make these writings the complex works that they are.

The one facet that everyone sees in Maturin's, Le Fanu's, and Stoker's works is the popular entertainment value of a well-told and frightening tale, and for Maturin and Le Fanu,⁸ the purpose for writing them was financial. Irish folklore is filled with such tales that served to pass a long winter evening before the hearth, and the Victorian era further popularized these stories. Still, popular writing with supernatural themes is not usually given considerable thought unless it can be transferred to film or television and generate a profit. The limited perception of these popular works prevents readers from benefiting from other aspects of the texts. In the Irish Gothic, what most readers may not see is that the tales and their vampiric characters are the products of specific cultures, times, places, and people. Without those various factors influencing the writings, the resulting stories would have been very different. They would have remained as part of the

English Gothic tradition rather than developed into an Irish Gothic one that produced the Irish vampire.

Even though fellow scholars and critics recognize the importance of the Irish Gothic and engage in active discussion about it, the general reading public who are familiar with the current popular representations of the vampire may not be aware of its Irish influences or the authors and their works that contributed to the development of the modern vampire currently depicted in literature, television, and film. This work hopes to not only add to the present scholarly and professional dialogue analyzing Maturin, Le Fanu, and Stoker for their distinctive roles within and contributions to the Irish Gothic tradition and its most famous creation, the vampire, but to do so in a way that will be interesting to the nonacademic reader and spark his/her desire to read more of these authors' works, learn more about Irish Gothic, and investigate not just Irish folklore but global tales of the vampire.

In an effort to accomplish these ambitious goals, Maturin, Le Fanu, and Stoker's specified works will be examined using criteria inspired by members of the Irish Literary Renaissance in the late nineteenth and early twentieth century. Although much has happened since then with Irish literature, this was the time where Irish writers sought to define what Irish literature was and, as a result, writers like Maturin and Le Fanu, who preceded this period, and those writing during it, like Stoker, were scrutinized for their "Irishness." This analysis may have contributed to Maturin not being included in an early twentieth-century multi-volume collection of Irish literature and in the Irish Gothic contributions of Le Fanu and Stoker to be greatly minimized in their importance.

Interestingly, the criteria for inclusion in the collection was not unified or specified, which shows how Irish writers in this era struggled to articulate what their vision of a national literature encompassed. Yet, elements of a nineteenth- and early twentieth-century Irish national literature not only emerge but assist in supporting the argument for the Irish vampire. This criteria indicated that Irish writers should write about Irish subjects exhibiting passion and originality which would result in them finding their personal as well as a national identity. The lives of Maturin, Le Fanu, and Stoker play an essential role in the analysis of their works in relation to the Irish Gothic vampire as well as the national literature. Their personal lives shaped their identities and their identities directly affected their works. In Ireland during the 132 years encompassing the lifetimes of these three authors, the personal lives were bound with the public issues. I cannot discuss the professional achievements of these men in relation to Ireland without also talking about their lives.

Before I can begin the discussion of the Irish vampire, it will be helpful for the reader to first meet the vampire that was known prior to the nineteenth century as presented in the first chapter. This introduction to vampire folklore will show how Irish folklore fits into global tales and will support arguments made in later chapters by showing how Maturin, Le Fanu, and Stoker transformed the vampire of folklore into an Irish vampire. Following the chapter on folklore will be a chapter presenting an overview of Gothic and Irish literature to complete the foundation for the succeeding chapters devoted to Maturin, Le Fanu, and Stoker. The final chapter will conclude by showing how the Irish vampire has influenced the vampire of the twentieth and twenty-first centuries. However, before I can conclude, I will need to begin.

1

"The facts of vampirism are as old as the world"[1]

The Etymology, Folklore and History of the Vampire

"...our landlord seemed to pay some regard to what Baron Valvasor has related of the Vampyres, said to infest some parts of this country. The Vampyres are supposed to be the bodies of deceased persons, animated by evil spirits, which come out of the graves, in the night time, suck the blood of many of the living, and thereby destroy them."
—"The Travels of Three English Gentlemen,
from Venice to Hamburgh, being the Grand Tour of Germany,
in the Year 1734. MS Never Before Published," 1745[2]

"In a 7,000-year-old town [Thracian] in Bulgaria, over 100 graves have been uncovered, revealing skeletons with stakes through their hearts and mutilated bones.... Thracian ... was only discovered 20 years ago and is home to a number of vampire grave sites. This latest discovery is just one of more than 100 medieval graves that contain the remains of those once suspected of being vampires and that have been unearthed over the past few decades across Bulgaria."
—Nina Strochlic,
"Bulgaria's Vampire Graveyards," 15 Oct. 2014[3]

Most people would agree with the description of the vampire provided by the three travelling English gentlemen from the 1730s and would likewise not be surprised that archaeologists are currently unearthing "vampire" burial sites; current media tells us that vampires leave their graves at night to prey upon unsuspecting victims by sucking their blood and the only way to stop vampires is to stake them. One could further assume that since Strochlic's article also indicated that Bulgaria has been using vampire rising-prevention techniques since the tenth century[4] that the vampire has remained unchanged throughout his/her[5] centuries of immortality. While immortality is often a characteristic associated with the vampire, so is shapeshifting. Providing a comprehensive definition of a creature that shifts its characteristics to suit its current culture or time is a daunting task to achieve in a single chapter, but fortunately, many scholars have conducted thorough research into vampire folklore and their expertise will be drawn upon in order to provide a surprising overview[6] of the vampire's complicated history, beginning with the word itself.

The *Oxford English Dictionary (OED)*[7] indicates that the word "vampire" is derived from a Slavonic language, first appeared in print in English in 1745 in "The Travels of Three English Gentlemen," and is defined as: "A preternatural being of a malignant nature (in the original and usual form of the belief, a reanimated corpse), supposed to seek nourishment, or do harm, by sucking the blood of sleeping persons; a man or woman abnormally endowed with similar habits."[8] While few would dispute the authority of the *OED*, some current research provides an opportunity to further enhance this entry on "vampires."

"The Travels of Three English Gentlemen" is regularly identified as the text where the word "vampyre" first appeared in print in English. Few challenge this claim but, with so many texts becoming scanned and digitally available through a variety of library databases, it is much easier to search hundreds of years of written materials for one word and discover words appearing in print earlier than anticipated. Searching the *British Newspapers 1600–1950* for "vampire OR vampyre" yielded such a result. The March 16, 1732, edition of the *Grub Street Journal* contained the following news item: "Friday, March 10—Medreyga in Hungary, Jan. 7, 1732—Upon a current report, that in the village of Medreyga certain dead bodies (called here *Vampyres*) had killed several persons by sucking all their blood…. These good men [government investigators] say farther, that all such as have been tormented or killed by the *Vampyre*, become *Vampyres* when they are dead."[9] While it cannot be said with certainty that this is the earliest printed appearance of "vampyre" in English,[10] it does precede the 1745 publication of "The Travels of Three English Gentlemen" by thirteen years so it would not be unreasonable to conclude that further database searches could result in the word appearing even earlier in print.[11]

New information about the word "vampire" does not end with when it was first printed in English since the English word was derived from another language. As noted earlier, the *OED* indicates that the word has Slavonic roots, listing: "Magyar *vampir*, a word of Slavonic origin occurring in the same form in Russian, Polish, Czech, Serbian, and Bulgarian, with such variants as Bulgarian *vapir*, *vepir*, Ruthenian *vepyr*, *vopyr*, *opyr*, Russian *upir*, *upyr*, Polish *upior*."[12] However, not all scholars agree upon the Slavonic origins, as researcher Katharina M. Wilson explains:

> There are four clearly discernible schools of thought on the etymology of "vampire" advocating, respectively, Turkish, Greek, Hebrew, and Hungarian roots for the term. The four groups are chronological and geographic entities: the first group is represented by a nineteenth-century Austrian linguist and his followers, the second consists of scholars who were the German contemporaries of the early eighteenth-century vampire craze, the third comprises recent linguistic authorities, and the last is almost entirely limited to recent English and American writers.[13]

Wilson provides a helpful overview of the discussion surrounding the origins of the word "vampire," which continues to be an active topic of discussion among scholars.[14]

In addition to the debate on the origins of the word "vampire," its meaning is not as straightforward as the *OED* would have its readers believe. As will be seen, vampires from folklore possess a wide range of characteristics so any definition that would accurately include all of them would be broad rather than specific and provide a series of definitions to suit certain cultures and time periods. For instance, blood-sucking and being undead are not characteristics that apply to all vampires of folklore, which is supported by the first written use of the word as it appears in an Old Russian text from the mid-eleventh century.[15] It is not used to indicate an undead, bloodsucking creature that attacks people in their sleep but, as Bruce McClelland explains in *Slayers and Their Vampires: A Cultural History of Killing the Dead*, "was a shorthand (and probably pejorative) label for an individual who either belonged to a specific group or practiced a particular belief or ritual … the original vampire was nothing or no one supernatural."[16] So, the first appearance of the written word in any language refers to non–Christian groups rather than the undead.

Even though the meaning of the word "vampire" evolved over time to represent the supernatural creature recognized by modern audiences, this does not mean that vampiric creatures and their attendant folklore are only as old as the undead meaning of the word "vampire." The figure of the vampire in folklore existed long before it was actually called a "vampire" in oral traditions or written records. The difficulty of the vampire is determining when and where it first appeared since many cultures possessed vibrant oral traditions that often would later record stories once writing entered the society. So, old texts could contain an even older story which would be difficult to date. Dudley Wright in *Vampires and Vampirism: Legends from*

Around the World states: "Some writers have ascribed the origin of the belief in vampires to Greek Christianity, but there are traces of the superstition and belief at a considerably earlier date.... The earliest references to vampires are found in Chaldean and Assyrian tablets."[17] Wright more than likely reached his conclusion after reading R. Campbell Thompson's *The Devils and Evil Spirits of Babylonia* (1903–1904),[18] which was also used by Montague Summers in *The Vampire: His Kith and Kin* (1928) when he "suggested that vampires had a prominent place in Mesopotamian mythology.... In particular he spoke of the *ekimmu*, the spirit of an unburied person."[19] J. Gordon Melton explains in *The Vampire Book: The Encyclopedia of the Undead* how Summers actually arrived at an erroneous conclusion:

> It appeared that Summers confused the issue of revenants and the return of the dead who could become vampires with ghosts of the deceased who might simply haunt the land. The ghosts were plainly noncorporeal—they neither ate nor drank, whereas the dead in the underworld had a form of corporeal existence and enjoyed some meager pleasures. The source of this misunderstanding was an inadequate translation of the last parts of the Gilgamesh Epic. The line "The spirit resteth not in the earth," was originally translated in such a way as to leave open the possibility of the dead wandering in the world of human habitation. However, more recent translations and a survey of the context of the last couplets of the Gilgamesh Epic made it clear that the dead who died in the desert uncared for (the *ekimmu*) roamed restlessly not on earth but through the Netherworld.[20]

Melton's analysis diminishes Summers's claim that the vampire was an extensive figure in ancient Mesopotamian mythology, but it does not eliminate it. In fact, the Sumerian *Gilgamesh Epic*'s adventures from around 2000 BCE feature a well-known figure to students of vampire folklore, Lilith.[21] While she is most often identified as Adam's very independent first wife, she is also recognized as a dangerous demon "who brings death to men, mothers, and children. She may have adopted her penchant for destructive deeds from other ancient she-demons, such as the Babylonian Lamashtu, the Canaanite Lil, and the Sumerian Lilitu" whose careers predate her later biblical ones.[22] Like the word "vampire," the perception of Lilith changed over time and cultures. She was a succubus, a mother of demons, a bloodsucker, a predator of babies, and a woman who sought the wisdom of King Solomon and the identity of the Queen of Sheba.[23] It is not surprising to learn that "versions of her appear in Iranian, Mexican, Roman, Greek, Arabic, English, German, Asian, and Native American stories,"[24] which would imply that versions of the vampire likewise appear in these cultures.

Since Lilith appeared in *Gilgamesh* approximately 4,000 years ago and the king who inspired the tale lived around 2650 BCE,[25] it would seem that vampiric stories have a long history, and further evidence suggests that they were not limited to Mesopotamia 4500–4000 years ago. Matthew Beresford in *From Demons to Dracula: The Creation of the Modern Vampire Myth* connects the ancient Egyptians to vampire beliefs by citing several specific spells from the *Book of the Dead*. Among them are spells "for going out into the day and living after death," "for not permitting a man's heart to be taken from him," "for preventing a man's decapitation," "for being transformed into any shape one may wish to take," and "for preventing a man's corpse from putrefying."[26] As explained by Beresford and supported by vampire folklore, each of these spells addresses a specific characteristic of the vampire as depicted in more than one culture: leaving the grave to move about after death, cutting out the heart or cutting off the head to keep a vampire from rising, the vampire's ability to shapeshift, and a corpse's lack of decomposition as a sign of a vampire.

Other vampire signs and methods of dispatching them appear in a text which not only claims to be the transcription from a much older oral tradition, but is from a place not readily associated with vampire folklore— Ireland. Between 1629 and 1631, Geoffrey (Jeoffry) Keating wrote, in Irish, *The General History of Ireland* in an effort to correct "those false and injurious representations, which have been published, concerning the ancient Irish, who for above these three thousand years have inhabited this kingdom."[27] While Keating did not provide a list of his sources, he frequently states them in-text and in his preface explains that "since most of the authentic records of Ireland are composed … in verse, I shall receive them as the principal testimonies to consult in compiling the following history" because verse was used in the composition of the oldest records because they were replicating their spoken origins; verse was easier to commit to memory during Ireland's oral, pre-literate tradition of record-keeping.[28]

Keating's history offers two very interesting contributions to early vampire folklore which connect to other existing cultures of the time. The first story involves one of the early colonizers of Ireland, Partholanus, who, according to the oral traditions that were later written down, landed on Ireland with his followers 300 years after the Flood.[29] He was reportedly a direct descendant of Japhet, son of Noah,[30] whose descendants "are the peoples of the Indo-European languages to the north and west of Mesopotamia and Syria"[31] and "from them sprang the maritime nations."[32] Partholanus seemed to fulfill this description of Japhet's descendants since he and his family resided in Greece, where his parents ruled until he was forced to leave. "The reason why Partholanus left his own country, and undertook this voyage [to Ireland], was, because he slew his father and mother in Greece, in order to obtain the crown, and hinder his elder brother of the succession; but the vengeance of God overtook the inhuman parricide, and destroyed some time after nine thousand of the posterity of his colony by the pestilence: they were carried off within the space of a week, at Binneadair, now called the Hill of Hoath, near Dublin."[33]

While this story seems much more like a Greek tragedy, ending with the gods and goddesses meting out justice reserved for people who murdered their family members, a brief explanation of vampire folklore will show further connections. Partholanus's Greek origins would have bound him to the customs described in John Cuthbert Lawson's *Modern Greek Folklore and Ancient Greek Religion: A Study in Survivals* (1910), which explains the consequences of murder and how one becomes a *vrykolakas* (vampire). Murder "was the gravest possible injury to the man who was slain [and] ... it was a source of 'pollution' ... an abomination to the gods and a peril to living men,"[34] so it is not surprising that the law surrounding murder was "based upon a religious doctrine which Plato esteemed 'old even among the traditions of antiquity.'"[35] Lawson continues by providing the distinctions of murder: "[I]n cases of the utmost enormity, as where a man willfully murdered his father or mother, religion provided no means of purification. Blood-guilt in general was 'hard to cure'; but parricide belonged to the class of sins 'incurable.' Such a murderer therefore must die, for, as Plato says, 'there is no other kind of purification' in this case than the paying of blood for blood."[36] It was commonly believed that this payment was sought by the revenant of the murder victim, but the ancient dramatic literature modified it so that "the instrument of his vengeance is a curse executed by demonic agents."[37]

Partholanus committed the worst type of murder known to the ancient Greeks; he killed his parents. There was no purification. At best, he was cursed; at worst, the revenants of his parents would pursue him and enact their own fitting punishment. So, he chose the best course of action available; he fled across the sea because vampires cannot cross water.[38] Since Partholanus remained in Ireland for thirty years and his death appeared unremarkable,[39] it would seem that he escaped any punishment for his crime. However, it may not be the case when one considers that vampire folklore strongly supports the notion that vampires are made rather than created by other vampires.[40] The circumstances that lead to a person becoming a vampire may be seen across many cultures. These include sudden death (murder or unfortunate accidents), suicide, an animal (often a cat) jumping over a body, improper burials, being a witch, wizard, or werewolf in life, a woman dying in childbirth, or a person dying unbaptized or in the state of excommunication. In addition, the illegitimate child of illegitimate parents[41] and the seventh son of the seventh son were also candidates for vampirism after their deaths.

There are also more culturally specific ways a person becomes a vampire. In Poland, "a person born with teeth" can become a vampire, and in Eastern Europe precautions were taken when alcoholics died.[42] In Russia, the "unholy union between a witch and a werewolf or a devil" will result in the birth of a vampire.[43] "In South Slavic belief, people who die during this period [twelve days of Christmas] invariably become vampires. Also, children who are born or conceived during this period have special powers and may themselves become vampires."[44] This belief seems to have influenced the Greeks, who felt that children conceived or born on a church holiday would be werewolves in life and vampires in death.[45] Vampirism could also result from inattention to food consumption; "[t]hose who have eaten the flesh of a sheep which was killed by a wolf"[46] could also become vampires.[47] The Greeks, like other cultures, also believed that murderers would become vampires upon their deaths.

An argument could be made that Partholanus did not escape punishment for the murders of his parents. Although he lived for thirty years in Ireland,[48] he "died in the plains of Moynealta, where he was buried; the place was called Sean-mhagh-ealta Eadair, because the soil was barren, and not so much as a shrub would grow upon it."[49] There is a story of a Greek Lamiae, a vampiric creature who had an insatiable thirst for blood, who was killed and "when her body was thrown out on a desert plain, no grass would grow where her blood had dripped."[50]

The infertility of Partholanus's final resting place could be a coincidence but after his death all 9,000 of his descendants in Ireland died of a pestilence, the divine punishment for his murders. Inexplicable illnesses are regularly a feature of many vampire stories, especially those from the 1700s. While it may have occurred 270 years after Partholanus's death, he could have been the vehicle for the epidemic which killed everyone, for "the spirits that cause illness, especially fever and ague, are continually recruited on the death of old maids, *murderers*, and those that die a violent death" (emphasis mine).[51]

The case for Partholanus's vampirism may be a bit tenuous; however, future colonists to Ireland provide an undeniable connection. Following the demise of the Partholanians, no human set foot on Ireland for thirty years and then came several waves of settlers: the Nemedians (relatives of Partholanus), the Firbolgs and Firgailiains (from Greece), and the Tuatha de Danans.[52] The Tuatha de Danans also claimed familial ties with

Partholanus through Nemedius's (leader of the Nemedians) son who left Ireland with a group and settled in Achaia.[53] Keating continues to describe an interesting skill of the Tuatha de Danans and how they used it:

> Here [Greece] it was that the Tuatha de Danans learned the art of necromancy and enchantment; and they became so expert in magical knowledge, that they had a power of working wonderful feats, so far as seemingly to raise the dead … the city of Athens, was invaded by the Assyrians, and several battles fought between them, these sorcerers would use their diabolical charms, and revive the bodies of the dead Athenians, and the next day bring them into the field … the Assyrians resolved to take the advice of a druid of great learning among them, and, if possible, discover in what manner they could defeat the skill of those necromancers…. The druid told them, that after a battle was over, they should thrust a club or a stake of quick-beam wood through every one of the dead bodies … if it was the power of the devil by which they were brought to life, this counter-charm would defeat the skill of the enchanters, and the bodies could never more be revived…. The Assyrians, relying upon the advice of the druid, immediately challenged the Athenians to a pitched battle, when they fought with great courage, and obtained a complete victory; and after the fight, they drove stakes through the bodies of the dead Athenians, and so the evil spirits had no more power to take possession of them, and the sorcerers were disappointed. The Tuatha de Danans, perceiving their art to be ineffectual, came to a resolution of quitting the country for fear of falling into the hands of the Assyrians; accordingly set out, and wandered from place to place, till they came to Norway and Denmark, where they were received with great hospitality by the inhabitants, who admired them for their learning and skill in magic, and the wonderful effects of their enchantments.[54]

Few will fail to recognize one of the most common ways to restrain or destroy a vampire—staking. The type of material that comprises the stake may vary across cultures (in Bulgaria, a red-hot iron is favored[55] over the more frequently used wood), as does the question of where to stake the vampire (the heart is the most popular but the stomach,[56] arms and thighs[57] also appear in research), and the technique may also contain specific directions, as in Russia where it is vital "when driving a stake into the body of a vampire, this must be done by one single blow, as a second blow will reanimate the corpse."[58] Other common ways to deal with the undead include beheading, removing the heart, and cremation.[59]

Sometimes when the person who has died has the potential to become a vampire because he/she meets one of the criteria stated earlier, precautions were taken to prevent the corpse from rising. The suspected dead were buried face down in either the coffin or the ground because apparently vampires will dig in the direction they are facing so they will dig themselves deeper into the ground rather than escape by digging up and out of the grave. Placing something in the person's mouth like a coin or a charm is also a common way to keep a vampire from rising because he/she becomes preoccupied with chewing, preventing him/her from leaving the grave and chewing on someone. The ever-popular garlic is placed in graves as well as worn or hung to ward off vampires.[60] Where the body is buried is also of importance. Beresford reports in his article, "The Dangerous Dead: The Early Medieval Deviant Burial at Southwell, Nottinghamshire in a Wider Context," that "quite often the Anglo-Saxon dangerous dead were buried in bogs or waterlogged areas."[61] Water seemed to inhibit the rise of the undead, but Beresford's article also notes that the remains found in these saturated burials were staked, too, perhaps just to be certain that they stayed in their graves.

Placing something on top of the grave is supposed to be equally effective. In Ireland, stones are placed "on top of graves to prevent the deceased returning after death to the world of the living, a practice similar to the construction of cairns in the prehistoric period."[62] McClelland explains that "[t]he most common methods of blocking a vampire's movements involve placing thorns, grains (including grains of sand), or inflammable materials on or near the body or the grave or else pouring various liquids into the grave."[63] Several sources say that if thorns, grains, seeds, sand, etc., are scattered on and around the burial site that the vampire is compelled to stop and count them if he/she leaves the grave. It not only prevents the vampire from claiming any victims, but it greatly simplifies the task of locating and dispatching the vampire for those who are hunting him/her. Another reason for scattering grain was more ceremonial. "Among nomadic peoples, who did not build permanent temples and altars where their sacrifices would be performed, sprinkling grain in a circle around a sacrificial victim was a common method of creating a temporary consecrated space."[64] Pouring libations would likewise create a consecrated area, and vampires were contained in that holy space. The purpose of spreading materials like cotton, gunpowder, or hemp is to have something present in the event there is a need for fire (like a spontaneous cremation).[65]

Another common way of containing the suspected vampire is through various means of "crossing" the corpse. This is as simple as crossing the arms across the chest of the deceased and/or placing a cross or crucifix in the grave, either over the mouth or wrapping the chain or rosary that is affixed to it around the hands. Wright also noted that in Germany, "Crosses are ... frequently erected at the head, or by the side, of graves, even in Protestant cemeteries, in order that their presence may prevent occupants from being controlled by any demon that might, but for the presence of such a charm, take possession of the body."[66] A more labor-intensive method of "crossing" actually predates Christianity but was still legally practiced into the nineteenth century in some countries—burial at the crossroads. Beresford explains:

The practice of burying suspected vampires with crosses or at the junctions of cross-roads is prevalent throughout Europe. Even as far back as the Roman period there is evidence of the dead being buried at crossroads; the reason for this, it is thought, is that if dead criminals or social outcasts were to come back to life, they would be confused by the abundance of paths, and thus be unable to find their way back to their village or town and cause further horror.[67]

When Christianity became widespread, it was standard practice to bury suicides at a crossroads because they were not permitted to be buried in consecrated ground.[68] The symbolism of the cross was felt to restrain the would-be vampire, but many would include the added assurance that the corpse would not rise by driving a stake through the heart. In some countries, this custom became law like when "during the Anglo-Saxon period in England a law was passed that allowed wooden stakes to be driven through any person suspected of being undead ... and that this law was only repealed in 1823."[69]

While the above methods frequently appear throughout many cultures, there are other, more unique ways of dealing with vampires. Wright reports that one way in China is to take the coffin lid far away after the vampire has risen because "[i]t is held that the air thus entering freely into the coffin will cause the contents to decay."[70] Another Chinese method involves an alternative use for the "stake," demonstrated when coffin-bearers "fell upon the vampire with great blows from their brooms, battering it on the bed and then enclosing it in the coffin.... (Note: Ghosts are afraid of brooms made like rods. This belief goes back to high antiquity. The ancient brooms were made of cane; the modern ones are generally in bamboo.)."[71] Vampires in China should also fear machines since running their souls through a winnowing machine will dissipate the soul, making it impossible for the body to rise again.[72] A simpler but equally effective way is performed in Bulgaria, where a witch or wise woman locates the vampire's grave "by a hole in his tombstone or the earth which covers him, and stuffs it with human excrement (his favorite food) mixed with poisonous herbs."[73] A more detailed practice exists in Bulgaria. It involves bottling the vampire with the following method.

The sorcerer, armed with the picture of some saint, lies in ambush until he sees the vampire pass, when he pursues him with his picture. The vampire takes refuge in a tree or on the roof of a house, but his persecutor follows him up with the talisman, driving him away from all shelter in the direction of a bottle specially prepared, in which is placed some favorite food of the vampire. Having no other alternative, he enters this prison, and is immediately fastened down with a cork on the interior of which is a fragment of an eikon or holy picture. The bottle is then thrown into the fire and the vampire disappears forever.[74]

While bottling may not be as familiar to the modern vampire audience, perhaps the most surprising way of dealing with a vampire comes from Scandinavia, where "[i]n some parts ... a singular method was adopted for getting rid of vampires, viz. by instituting judicial proceedings against them."[75]

Knowing that there are a range of options, from legal prosecution to cremation to restraining or eliminating a vampire threat, is useful information to have if one ever encounters a vampire; however, this knowledge is not helpful unless one can recognize a vampire. Knowing the previously stated conditions that could predispose someone to a vampiric afterlife are an excellent starting point, but many cultures provided specific characteristics to help discern the living from the undead, and some cultures even had specially designated members of society who could not only recognize the vampires walking among them but also provided the indispensable service of dealing with the community's problem.

Unlike Buffy Summers, who could spot a vampire in a crowded dance club based on his dated attire,[76] there were other more distinct attributes that indicated the presence of the undead, and many of these may surprise those who are familiar with the vampire of modern cinema. Barber provides an excellent explanation in his book, *Vampires, Burial, and Death: Folklore and Reality*:

> If a typical vampire of folklore, not fiction, were to come to your house this Halloween, you might open the door to encounter a plump Slavic fellow with long fingernails and a stubbly beard, his mouth and left eye open, his face ruddy and swollen. He wears informal attire—in fact, a linen shroud—and he looks for all the world like a disheveled peasant.[77]

Barber's Eastern European folkloric vampire could easily be mistaken for an inebriated peasant who is a bit lax about his personal hygiene. Equally easy to dismiss at first glance were the vampires in Russian folklore who have a sharp, pointed tongue,[78] sharing this feature with those "in Slavonic countries [where] the vampire is said to be possessed of only one nostril, but is credited with possessing a sharp point at the end of his tongue, like the sting of a bee."[79] The Greek "vrykolakas [who] usually appears bald and beardless"[80]; or the West African obayifo who "in everyday life is supposed to be known by having sharp, shifty eyes, that are never at rest, also by showing an undue interest in food"[81] would also be difficult to immediately notice.

However, not all vampires blend in as well with their living neighbors. In China, the vampires "were green, covered with mould, and ... had a propensity to glow in the dark."[82] Glowing in the dark would have saved

many of the victims of the West African asasabonsam, a human-like creature that lives deep in the forests and lies in wait for its victims up in the
trees with its legs dangling "down to the ground and have hooks for feet
which pick up anyone who comes within reach. It has iron teeth and is
both male and female."[83] Another vampire fond of trees is the baital of
India, vividly described by Sir Richard Burton in *Vikram and the Vampire*:

> Its eyes, which were wide open, were of a greenish-brown, and never twinkled; its hair
> also was brown, and brown was its face—three several shades which, notwithstanding,
> approached one another in an unpleasant way, as in an over-dried cocoa-nut. Its body
> was thin and ribbed like a skeleton or a bamboo framework, and as it held on to a
> bough, like a flying fox, by the toe-tips, its drawn muscles stood out as if they were
> ropes of coir. Blood it appeared to have none … its skin, it felt icy cold and clammy as
> might a snake. The only sign of life was the whisking of a ragged little tail much
> resembling a goat's.[84]

The baital blends human and animal forms, but its human elements remain
recognizable. Other vampires retain only necessary human elements which
meant they were even less likely to blend in with the living. The "Malaysian
penanggalen consisted of just a head, stomach, and dangling entrails. It
would soar through the air to pursue its preferred victims: babies or women
in labour."[85]

Perhaps the most visually distinctive descriptions of vampires come
from Bulgaria and Greece, which seem to have influenced each other in
the initial appearance of the vampire.

> Before it assumes animal shape, the Bulgarian vampire is characterized most frequently
> as a "puffed-up bag of blood" that is made of skin. Rather than a nose, he has a sharp
> snout with a hole through which he sucks blood…. Sometimes the vampire is like a
> "buffalo head" or the head of a pig or ox, which rolls along the countryside…. This bag
> can be easily destroyed by no more than a thorn, specifically a hawthorn, which is
> thought to have special properties.[86]

While a sharp, pointy tongue and shifty eyes could go unnoticed by the
everyday public, a puffed-up bag of blood bouncing along the countryside
would gain a lot of attention whether one was a folklore scholar or not.
Leo Allatius's description of a Greek vampire from his mid-seventeenth
century work would likewise draw attention:

> [The vampire] is the body of a man of evil and immoral life—very often of one who
> has been excommunicated by his bishop. Such bodies do not like those of other dead
> men suffer decomposition after burial nor turn to dust, but having, as it appears, a skin
> of extreme toughness become swollen and distended all over, so that the joints can
> scarcely be bent; the skin becomes stretched like the parchment of a drum, and when
> struck gives out the same sound…. Into such a body … the devil enters, and issuing
> from the tomb goes about, chiefly at night, knocking at doors and calling one of the
> household. If such an one answer, he dies next day; but a *vrykolakas* never calls twice,

and so the inhabitants of Chios ... secure themselves by always waiting for a second call at night before replying. This monster is said to be so destructive to men, that appearing actually in the daytime, even at noon—and that not only in houses but in fields and highroads and enclosed vineyards.[87]

While this vampire may appear almost comical in his bloated form, he is dangerous to any of the living who encounter him. This is unlike the Bulgarian vampire in his initial form who "nine days after his burial he returns to upper earth in an aériform shape. The presence of the vampire in this his first condition may be easily discerned in the dark by a succession of sparks like those from a flint and steel."[88] According to S. G. B. St. Clair and Charles A. Brophy in *A Residence in Bulgaria*, this first stage of the vampire is a harmless practical joker, though being lured outside and then beaten black and blue may not seem exactly harmless to everyone.[89]

This brief overview of what the vampire of folklore looks like contains a range of features, except the one that nearly every fan of modern vampire fiction, television, or film would expect—fangs. Unlike many fictional and modern visual representations of the vampire, it is rare for a vampire to have fangs in folklore.[90] In fact, as seen earlier with the vampires distinguished by sharp, pointed tongues, teeth were not needed to draw blood from their victims. Furthermore, not all vampires drained blood from people for nourishment. The Bulgarian vampire preferred human food and only sought out blood if there was a serious shortage of food.[91] Other vampires drained the energy from their victims.

Now that the vampire's various characteristics have been reviewed, this chapter would not be complete without some actual vampire stories that predate the representation of Maturin, Le Fanu, and Stoker. The most logical place to start is the best-known account that launched a vampire-craze in Europe and perhaps introduced the word into English—Arnod Paole. It was the account of Paole (or "Arnold Paul," as his name was reported in English newspapers) that appeared in the March 16, 1732, edition of the *Grub Street Journal*. Although long, the article merits quotation since it may be the first account of a vampire appearing in print, in English, and to the general reading public.

[Government investigators] unanimously declared, that about 5 years ago a certain Heyduke, named Arnold Paul, was killed by the overturning of a cart load of hay, who in his lifetime was often heard to say, that he had been tormented near Cajchaw,[92] and upon the borders of Turkish Servia, by a *Vampyre*; and that to extricate himself, he had eaten some of the earth of the *Vampyres* graves, and rubbed himself with their blood.— That 20 or 30 days after the decease of the said Arnold Paul, several persons complained that they were tormented; and that, in short, he had taken away the lives of four persons. In order therefore to put a stop to such a calamity, the inhabitants of the place, after having consulted their *Hadnagi*, caused the body of the said Arnold Paul to be taken up, 40 days after he had been dead, and found the same to be fresh, and free from all manner of corruption; that he bled at the nose, mouth, and ears, as pure and florid blood as ever was seen; and that his shroud and winding sheet were all over bloody; and lastly, his finger and toe nails were fallen off, and new ones grown in their room.—As they observed from all these circumstances, that he was a *Vampyre*, they, according to custom, drove a stake through his heart; at which he gave a horrid groan, and lost a great deal of blood. Afterwards they burnt his body to ashes the same day, and threw them into his grave.[93]

Whether it was this article or some of the studies that appeared in the eighteenth century, like Dom Augustin Calmet's 1769 publication, *Dissertations Upon the Apparations of Angels, Daemons, and Ghosts and Concerning the Vampires of Hungary, Bohemia, Moravia, and Silesia*, Arnod Paole's story is one of the most well-known and regularly referenced vampire stories.

It is interesting to note that while Paole's story is one of the most famous accounts of a vampire, it is actually one of the more recent in a long history of written tales tracking the vampire much further back in time. Prior to Paole was Peter Plogojowitz from 1725 in Kisilova, Serbia. Fully translated by Barber, Plogojowitz's story is a familiar one. He dies and, ten weeks later, nine people become sick, say that Plogojowitz laid on them as they slept and suffocated them, and all nine die within twenty-four hours of the onset of their illness.[94] It becomes imperative to exhume Plogojowitz's corpse to determine if he is a vampire. The government investigator reported that there was no smell and, aside from his nose, the body was not only intact but fresh and exhibiting the classic signs of a vampire: "The hair and beard—even the nails, of which the old ones had fallen away—had grown on him; the old skin, which was somewhat whitish, had peeled away, and a new fresh one had emerged under it. The face, hands, feet, and the whole body were so constituted … some fresh blood in his mouth, which, according to the common observation, he had sucked from the people killed by him."[95] With such irrefutable evidence of vampirism, the body was staked through the heart and burned to ash.

A little further back in time, the next story originates not in Eastern Europe but from seventeenth century England—"The Vampire of Croglin Grange." When it was first recounted in Augustus Hare's *Peculiar People: The Story of My Life* (1896–1900), several critics felt it was actually inspired by the initial chapters of James Malcolm Rymer's *Varney the Vampire; or, The Feast of Blood* (1847), but the research of both F. Clive Ross and Lionel and Patricia Fanthorpe date the story almost 200 years prior to Rymer's.[96] Hare's story begins with the Cranswell[97] family: two brothers, Michael and Edward, and their sister, Amelia[98]; who rented Croglin Grange. At first, all went well. Winter and spring passed without incident.[99] The Cranswells were well-received by their neighbors, and they were delighted with their lodgings. This changed during the summer on a particularly hot evening. The siblings dined early and retired to their rooms on the ground floor of the single-storied house. Amelia could not sleep and found herself looking out her window, where she saw two lights in the distant churchyard making their way toward her. At first, she was paralyzed with fear but then jumped from her bed to her door in order to unlock it and escape. As she fumbled with the lock, she heard a scratching at the window. She paused and turned to see "a hideous brown face with flaming eyes glaring in at her."[100]

> Suddenly the scratching ceased, and a kind of pecking took place. Then, in her agony, she became aware that the creature was unpicking the lead! The noise continued, and a diamond pane of glass fell into the room. Then a long bony finger of the creature came in and turned the handle of the window, and the window opened, and the creature came in; and it came across the room, and her terror was so great that she could not scream, and it came up to the bed, and it twisted its long bony fingers into her hair, and it dragged her head over the side of the bed, and—it bit her violently in the throat.
>
> As it bit her, her voice was released, and she screamed with all her might and main. Her brothers rushed out of their rooms, but the door was locked on the inside. A moment was lost while they got a poker and broke it open. Then the creature had already escaped through the window, and the sister, bleeding violently from a wound in the throat, was lying unconscious over the side of the bed. One brother pursued the creature, which fled before him through the moonlight with gigantic strides, and eventually seemed to disappear over the wall into the churchyard.[101]

Amelia's wound was terrible, but she was a mentally and physically strong young woman and made a full recovery. Still, her doctors thought a change of scenery would be best, so her brothers took her to Switzerland where they remained until autumn, when Amelia appealed to her brothers' reason, pointing out that they had six more years on their lease and, since subletting the house could take time, they should just return. Her brothers agreed and they enjoyed a quiet winter back at Croglin Grange. Unfortunately, Amelia's assailant reappeared in March, but this time they were ready. Her brothers grabbed their pistols and chased the creature back to the cemetery. One brother managed to shoot it in the leg, but it "seemed to disappear into a vault which belonged to a family long extinct."[102] The following day, they found the creature in that same vault "with the marks of a recent pistol-shot in the leg; and they did—the only thing that can lay a vampire. They burnt it."[103]

Around the time that the events that would eventually evolve into "The Vampire of Croglin Grange" were occurring, Henry More was writing *An Antidote Against Atheism* (1655), which included the story of "The Shoemaker of Breslaw."[104] The shoemaker lived in Breslaw, Silesia, and during the morning of Friday, September 20, 1591,[105] he allegedly committed suicide in his own garden by cutting his throat with his shoemaker knife.[106] Since suicide carried quite a stigma, the family covered up the cause of his death, saying that it was apoplexy, and gave him a Christian burial. Unfortunately for the family, this did not put the situation to rest; rumors, as well as the shoemaker himself, were circulating about town, and the magistrate was required to investigate.

Under persistent questioning, the family admitted that the shoemaker did not die of apoplexy. However, they were not going to admit to suicide, either, saying that someone could have broken in and killed him, or that it had been an accident.[107] Their desperate reasoning seemed to work for a while on the magistrate, who did not order the exhumation of the body. As the court deliberated, the townspeople became increasingly harassed by the shoemaker, who appeared not only at night but also during the day.[108] Night, though, was the worst time for the villagers because they needed to rest after their day's work but could not because of the shoemaker: "For this terrible *Apparation* would sometimes cast itself upon the midst of their beds, would lie close to them, would miserable suffocate them, and would so strike them and pinch them, that not only blue marks[109]; but plain impressions of his fingers would be upon sundry parts of their bodies in the morning."[110]

The situation became so unbearable that people were ready to leave their homes and the village to escape the shoemaker's torments, so finally the magistrate had no choice but to order the exhumation of the shoemaker's body, which was done on April 18, 1592[111]:

> [H]is body was found entire, not at all putrid, no ill smell about him, saving the mustiness of the grave clothes, his joynts limber and flexible, as in those that are alive, his skin only flaccid but a more fresh grown in the room of it, the wound of his throat gaping, but no gear nor corruption in it; there was also observed a Magical mark in the great toe of his right foot, *viz* an Excrescency in the form of a rose.[112]

In an effort to encourage decomposition, the body was left exposed from April 18 to 24, but the disturbances continued. The court then buried the body under the gallows, but this not only seemed to increase the shoemaker's activities but caused him to direct his attentions toward his own family. His widow was so distressed that she actually petitioned the court to take more definitive action. The court did not waste any time. On May 7, they exhumed the shoemaker's corpse again, but this time cut off his head, arms, and legs, took out his heart, burned all of it to ashes, collected the ashes in a sack, and threw them into the river, which solved the problem.[113]

Whether in Silesia or England, burning suspected vampires to ashes always destroys them, and this method appears in stories even older than the one retold by Henry More. William of Newburgh wrote the five books of his *The History of English Affairs* between 1196 and 1198,[114] and included alongside his chronicle of the English kings some curious occurrences among the people. As Andrew Joynes explains in the introduction to "The Restless Dead" section of his anthology:

> The twelfth-century Yorkshire canon William of Newburgh asserted that the *Prodigiosa* which he described—the unnatural marvels which resulted in dead men returning to animate existence—were unique to his own time. Yet his descriptions of the activities of ghosts in Buckinghamshire, Yorkshire and Scotland are virtually identical with Scandinavian accounts of dead men who leave their tombs and stagger around on the margins of life. He even has an anecdote about what he describes in Latin as a *sanguisuga*, a vampire or blood-sucking ghost.[115]

"The Ghost of Anant" from William of Newburgh's writing contains many familiar elements associated with vampires. A man of dubious character goes to Anant Castle to seek refuge and finds favor with its owner who hires him, allowing him to marry and settle down.[116] Rather than be grateful with his second chance at a good life, the man grows suspicious of his wife's fidelity and determines to find out if she is seeing someone else. He pretends to leave for several days of business but actually hides on a beam above his wife's bed, where he catches her in the act of adultery with a young neighbor. He is so angry that he falls, badly injuring himself. The neighbor makes a hasty exit and the wife cares for her broken and very angry husband, trying to smoothly convince him that he has imagined the whole thing as the result of delusions that he is suffering from his illness. The priest is called and the man confides in him but does not make his confession. This missed opportunity turns out to have been his last one, and he dies without his final confession.[117] Every night, he leaves his grave and terrifies the community because he infects the very air that they breathe, causing an epidemic that leads to the death of those who are infected. The town's priest calls a meeting and two young brothers who lost their father to the sickness volunteer to dig up the body. When they exhume the corpse, "they realized the creature must have been a vampire, sucking the blood of many people," so they remove its heart, burn the body to ashes, and save the town.[118]

Joynes's account of "The Ghost of Anant" exhibits not only connections with the vampire folklore already presented in this chapter, but it also supports the connection that he made to Sir Walter Scott's translations of the Icelandic *Eyrbyggia Saga*, written around AD 1000. Scott retells the story of Thorolf Baegifot, who sought the help of his estranged son, Arnkill, in his feud against another. Thorolf is sorely disappointed by his son's refusal, angrily returns home, speaks to no one in his household, refuses to eat, and sits in silence. The next morning, he is in the same position—but dead. Arnkill is sent for and when he arrives, he sees that no one has moved his father; "the terrified family hinted that he had fallen by the mode of death of all others most dreaded by the Icelanders."[119] Arnkill carefully follows the prescribed ceremony for removing the dead from a home and for proper burial, but his father does not remain in the grave. "He appeared in the district by night and day, slew men and cattle, and harrowed the country so much by his frequent apparition and mischievous exploits, that his son Arnkill, on repeated complaints of the inhabitants, resolved to change his place of sepulture."[120] It is an arduous process, complete with "a mound of immense height to be piled above the grave,"[121] but Thorolf Baegifot did not disturb the living again.

Iceland, England, and Eastern Europe were not the only places recording encounters with the undead. Léon Wieger translated many tales for his book, *Chinese Tales of Vampires, Beasts, Genies and Men* (1909), from as early as the eighth century AD.[122] As explained in the introduction to the vampire story section:

> The body has two souls, a superior soul *hounn* or *jen* which survives after death, and an inferior soul *pai* that can in rare cases keep the body going after death. Normally this inferior soul dissipates after death and the body decays. However, when an inferior soul is evil and very strong, it can conserve the body for a very long time, using it for its own ends. These bodies directed only by an inferior soul are horrible, stupid and ferocious vampires that kill and eat men, violate women, etc. In order to avoid these evils, all bodies that do not decompose normally after death, must be incinerated.[123]

Wieger's collection contains several such stories, some alluded to earlier, but "A Vampire Kills Three Sleeping Men" is particularly interesting. It is a tale of four travelers who stop at a full inn and beg the innkeeper for a place to rest.[124] He takes them to a side building that is housing his recently deceased sister-in-law, who is awaiting burial. The men are too tired to be worried, falling asleep immediately. The fourth is almost asleep when he hears a rustling coming from where the body is lying.[125] He is shocked to see the corpse get up, go to the beds of each of his companions, and breathe on each three times.[126] When she arrives at his bed, he hides under the covers and holds his breath. She breathes on him, too, and then returns to her bed. The man checks on his friends by nudging them with his foot, only to discover that they are all dead from the vampire's breath. The vampire seems to hear him for she gets up again and breathes on him. After she returns to her bed, the man barely has time to put on his pants before fleeing the room in search of help. The vampire chases him, and he hides behind a large poplar tree, dodging right and left to avoid the vampire's reach. She makes a determined lunge for him, which he escapes before promptly passing out. Help arrives to see that the vampire has embedded her fingers into the tree so deeply that none can disengage them. The inn-keeper is roused and quite astonished to find the corpse of his sister-in-law clutching a tree and three of his guests dead. The traveler is inconsolable and at a loss to explain what happened when he gets home. "The mandarin wrote him a document containing an authentic account of what had happened, and gave him some money for the journey."[127] This is how the story ends—one assumes that the vampire is still attached to the poplar tree.

While many would believe that vampire tales would end here, since the Chinese have an ancient and well-documented history, some will be surprised to learn that an Irish written text nearly coincides with the time period Wieger determined some of the earliest to be recorded in his collection. *The Book of Armagh* dates its earliest written entries from AD 807 to 808, but it is recognized to be a "transcript of documents of a much older period."[128]

> The word *sidhe* literally means a *blast of wind*, but figuratively a *phantom*, a fairy...
> The oldest authority in which the word *sidhe* occurs is the Book of Armagh. In this work the word *sidhe* is translated *Dei terreni*, or gods of the earth.
> ...The lenan-sidhe [Leanhaun Sidhe] is the fairy *leman*, succubus, or familiar female sprite.[129]

It is not just the Leanhaun Sidhe who exhibit recognizable vampire characteristics, but all the Sidhe: "The fairies, or 'good people'—the *dhoine shee* of the northerns—are looked upon by us ... as the great agents and prime movers in all accidents, diseases, and death, in 'man or baste'; causing ... blighting crops, abstracting infants or young people, spiriting away women after their accouchements, raising whirlwinds and storms, and often beating people most unmercifully."[130]

The stories of the Irish Sidhe and their connections to previously described vampire attributes from several cultures and times is difficult to ignore, especially when the Sidhe were recorded in the early ninth century but claim to be part of an older oral tradition. This would indicate that the vampire had a presence documented well before the preceding stories. It is even more compelling that recent archaeological findings support a fear of the returning dead even earlier than the eighth century. Matthew Beresford discusses in his article the findings of an English dig in relation to others of the Anglo-Saxon period:

It is this early period [AD 500s–600s] that sees stakings, or at least that is what the archaeology seems to reflect, as "some Anglo-Saxon cemeteries of c. AD 550–700 contain corpses treated in curious ways … (that are), by contrast, extremely rare in normal cemeteries of the later Anglo-Saxon period … archaeologists may of course be failing to recognize heart piercings" (Blair 2009, 549). At Southwell, the heart-piercing was indeed noticed, but the importance of it was not. And this practice of heart-piercing, or staking as we might more commonly call it, is a widespread example of a fear of the returning dead throughout history…[131]

So, twenty-first century archeology in England is supporting ancient folklore—and both go further back in time and to Ireland.

Patrick Weston Joyce retells an interesting story in *The Origin and History of Irish Names of Places* (1870) about a certain figure named Abhartach and his association with an Irish landmark.

It is very curious that, in some parts of the country, the people still retain a dim traditional memory of this mode of sepulture, and of the superstition connected with it. There is a place near Garvagh, in Londonderry, called Slaghtaverty; but it ought to have been called Laghtaverty. The *laght* or sepulchral monument of a dwarf named Abhartach [avartagh]. This Dwarf was a magician, and a dreadful tyrant; and after having perpetrated great cruelties on the people he was at last vanquished and slain by a neighbouring chieftain. He was buried in a standing posture, but the very next day he appeared in his old haunts, more cruel and vigorous than ever. And the chief slew him a second time and buried him as before; but again he escaped from the grave, and spread terror through the whole country. The chief then consulted a druid, and according to his directions, he slew the dwarf a third time, and buried him in the same place, with his head downwards; which subdued his magical power, so that he never again appeared on the earth. The *laght* raised over the dwarf is still there, and you may hear the legend with much detail from the natives of the place, one of whom told it to me.[132]

Bob Curran further adds to Abhartach's tale by stating that he ruled during the fifth and sixth centuries: "Some say that he was a dwarf, others that he was deformed in some way, but most agree that he was a powerful wizard and was extremely evil."[133] Curran further details that the terror which Abhartach inspires in his subjects is partly due to demanding "a bowl of blood, drawn from the veins of his subjects, in order to sustain his vile corpse,"[134] and in addition to burying him "head downwards," with a heavy stone on top, "Abhartach must be slain with a sword made from yew wood … thorns and ash twigs must be sprinkled around him…. Only then could the wizard be restrained in his grave. Should the stone be lifted, however, the vampire would be free to walk the earth once more."[135]

Abhartach contains many familiar elements of vampire folklore, and if his story does date from AD 400 to 500, it is quite an old one that was well-preserved over the centuries, complete with a physical site that could be excavated. However, even if the Slaghtaverty site were excavated and evidence found to corroborate the folklore, Abhartach would not be the oldest vampire evidence. Beresford, in his article, mentions another interesting archaeological discovery. "Oldcroghan Man, an Iron Age bog body from Ireland found in 2003 and dating to c. 362–175 BC, had both his upper arms pierced with a sharp implement, after which hazel rods were inserted through the holes. Finally, his head had been cut off and he had been partially dismembered…. Clearly someone wanted to prevent him from returning after death."[136] On its own, this is an exciting discovery, but to someone making a connection between Ireland and vampires, it is serendipitous. However, this brief overview of vampires cannot end in Ireland, 362–175 BC, especially when earlier in the chapter clear connections between the ancient Egyptians and neighboring civilizations of 4500–4000 years ago were presented. While Keating's recounting of the Partholonians in Ireland nearly 4,000 years ago places a vampire connection in roughly the same time period, it is tenuous at best. Less disputable evidence is required to narrow the significant gap that exists between 362–175 BC and the *Gilgamesh Epic* of around 2000 BC. Fortunately, there was another archaeological discovery.

The title of Eoin Burke-Kennedy's article, "4,000-Year-Old Laois Bog Body Turns Out to be World's Oldest," says it all. Burke-Kennedy recounts that the body of a young man discovered in a Laois bog two years ago yielded some unexpected results that dates it to 2000 BC, predating the Egyptian Tutankhamun by 700 years, making it the oldest bog body ever discovered.[137] Further details about the discovery are included: "radiocarbon tests on the body, the peat on which the body was lying and a *wooden stake* [emphasis mine] found with the body, date it to the early Bronze Age, about 2,000 BC."[138] While researchers believe that the body is the result of a ritual sacrifice, the wooden stake, along with other information in the article, could support another conclusion: "[the] man's arm was broken by a blow and there were deep cuts to his back which appear to have been inflicted by a blade…. Unfortunately, the areas that would typically be targeted in a violent assault, namely the head, neck, and chest, were damaged by the milling machine when the body was discovered, making it impossible to determine the exact cause of death."[139]

Given all the information Beresford provides in his article about the "dangerous dead," it is easy to conclude that this Bronze Age bog body could be evidence of what evolved into vampire folklore across time and countries. Perhaps the Irish literary vampire has a much longer history than ever considered.

2

Gothic and Irish Literature
"The uncreated conscience of my race"[1]

"...literary Ireland consists of many fragments, very far apart and very strange to one another. Even our leading literary societies, working for the same purposes, are not yet like the wings or sections of the same organization. Literary Ireland in fact does not know itself."
—William Patrick Ryan, *The Irish Literary Revival: Its History, Pioneers, and Possibilities* (1894)[2]

"I could not now write of any other country but Ireland, for my style has been shaped by the subjects I have worked on, but there was a time when my imagination seemed unwilling, when I found myself writing of some Irish event in words that would have better fitted some Italian or Eastern event, for my style had been shaped in that general stream of European literature which has come from so many watersheds, and it was slowly, very slowly, that I made a new style. It was years before I could rid myself of Shelley's Italian light, but now I think my style is myself. I might have found more of Ireland if I had written in Irish, but I have found a little, and I have found all myself. I am persuaded that if the Irishmen who are painting conventional pictures or writing conventional books on alien subjects, which have been worn away like pebbles on the shore, would do the same, they, too, might find themselves."
—William Butler Yeats, "Ireland and the Arts" (1901)[3]

In 1901, when William Butler Yeats (1865–1939) wrote this, he was addressing the importance of using Irish subjects for Irish writers so that they may develop their own original style which would lead them to discover their personal Irish identities. Seven years earlier, William Patrick Ryan (1867–1942), who was also deeply involved in the Irish literary movement, indicated that there was no consensus for its members about what defined Irish Literature. It is unlikely that either would have dreamed that

28

his words would preface a chapter discussing Irish Gothic literature as not only separate from English Gothic writings, but also as an important genre in the development of the Irish vampire.

Both Ryan and Yeats worked with a larger group of Irish Literary Society members from London and Dublin to publish the ten-volume work, *Irish Literature*, in 1904. It contained 350 Irish authors,[4] spanning nearly 2,000 years.[5] A review of the alphabetically listed authors reveals that Joseph Sheridan Le Fanu is listed with some decidedly Irish (but perhaps not well-known to twenty-first century audiences) poetry, an excerpt from *House by the Churchyard* (1863), and the short story "The Quare Gander." These selections are surprising since his one-page biography declares: "His chief power was in describing scenes of a mysterious or grotesque character, and the mystery in some of his stories is kept up with considerable skill to the end. The supernatural and the weird were a fashion in fiction in his day, and in this peculiar vein his work has hardly been bettered."[6] *Uncle Silas* is listed among his works but neither "Carmilla" nor the short story collection in which it appeared, *In a Glass Darkly*, are included. Stoker also appears in the alphabetical listing. Though his biography is quite brief, it does include *Dracula*; however, the selected representative text is "The Gombeen Man"[7] from his novel, *The Snake's Pass*.

The greatest surprise when reviewing the list of authors included in *Irish Literature* is that Maturin is not among them. His last name appears twice—once in Volume V in Maurice Francis Egan's essay "Irish Novels": "The influences that have touched on such diverse personalities as Miss Edgeworth and Miss Laffan, Samuel Lover and Charles Kickham, Gerald Griffin, Lady Morgan, Maturin, and Charles Lever, are not the influences that move Lady Gregory, Mr. William Butler Yeats..."[8]; and in Lady Wilde's biography: "she was related to Maturin, the author of 'Bertram.'"[9] The use of only Maturin's last name, especially among the list of authors with both first and last names, implies that either Maturin was so well-known that no first name was required—which would beg the question of why he was not included if he was so well-known?—or perhaps, in the eighty years since his death and the publication of the collection, his first name was forgotten. Maturin did not have a relative who was a member of the Irish Literary Society in London, as Le Fanu did[10] (and who probably served as an advocate for his father's inclusion). Maturin was also not great friends with the collection's editor-in-chief, Justin McCarthy, as Stoker was,[11] which probably aided in his inclusion, too.

To those unfamiliar with Irish history and literature, Maturin's omission from *Irish Literature*, and Le Fanu's and Stoker's inclusion, may seem to be terrible oversights. However, when traditional Gothic literature is considered alongside the criteria of passion, Irish subjects, original style, and an Irish personal identity, one may better understand these decisions as they relate to the task of forming an Irish national literature.

The Gothic genre's popularity had peaked and fallen long before the Irish revivalists were born; its brief moment in the limelight was not surprising, by literary standards. The typical Gothic publication was formulaic popular fiction dominated by ancient ruins, naïve heroines, and some less-than-religious Catholic clergy. Many critics would agree with Raymond T. McNally's detailed outline of the most common elements found in Gothic writing.

1. the ominous, vast, ancient castle as the setting with its long deserted wings and damp corridors;

2. the darkly handsome, tyrannical, dangerous evil nobleman as the seeming villain;

3. the insipid, virginal, and generally naïve heroine who is pursued by the handsome villain who appears to threaten her "with a fate worse than death";

4. the valiant hero who ultimately saves the girl and generally also solves the entirely awkward situation;

5. the convention of foreign names for many of the characters, thereby adding an exotic, alien atmosphere to the story; and

6. the miraculous occurrences, as lamps suddenly go out, trap doors are found, and secret passageways appear as props.[12]

These predictable plots were marketed to the emerging English middle class with the leisure time to read them. It did not require extensive contemplation to realize that there was nothing Irish or original about a genre that followed such a predictable plot line and allied itself with English writers such as Horace Walpole (1717–97), Ann Radcliffe (1764–1823), and Matthew "Monk" Lewis (1775–1818). Walpole, Radcliffe, and Lewis set the standard for what constituted a well-written Gothic tale. Many of their contemporaries tried to reach their level of storytelling and financial success, but few actually succeeded. This did not deter subsequent aspiring authors even after the genre reached its peak of popularity. Maturin was among this group of optimistic authors who looked to the success of a prior generation of English Gothic novelists for literary models, which was not original, Irish, or conducive to any epiphanies of one's identity.

As a result, Irish Gothic writers such as the ones examined here— Charles Robert Maturin, Joseph Sheridan Le Fanu, and Bram Stoker—

are names not generally encountered in a discussion of nineteenth-century Irish national literature, or literature in general, and the texts focused upon here—*Melmoth the Wanderer, Uncle Silas,* "Carmilla," and *Dracula*—certainly do not appear to possess any Irish characteristics that would lead to a case for an Irish vampire. Aside from Stoker's *Dracula* and Le Fanu's "Carmilla," these authors and their collective works are not even commonly known outside literary circles and, even then, some are surprised to learn that Stoker was Irish, not English. Stoker aspired to become a financially secure writer in his post–Lyceum years but was never quite successful during his lifetime. According to Leonard Wolf in *Dracula: The Connoisseur's Guide,* "Though it [*Dracula*] had a steady small sale, in Stoker's lifetime, it did not earn enough to change the Stokers' standard of living."[13] Perhaps one reason was that he used the Irish models of Maturin and Le Fanu, who were also not enormously successful during their lifetimes.

Maturin imitated the popular successes of his day. He was not interested in contributing to a new genre or mythology to further a national agenda. His first priority was to supplement his inadequate curate's income so he could better provide for his family, and he was interested in doing this in a way that would exceed the basic necessities, for he loved to entertain and enjoyed being stylish. He had success on the English stage with one play, and his novel, *Melmoth the Wanderer* (1820), earned him an advance of £500. It is this novel that attracts the most critical and varying attention. Leven M. Dawson in "*Melmoth the Wanderer*: Paradox and the Gothic Novel" considers *Melmoth* to be distinctly a "Gothic masterpiece,"[14] which is supported by Fred Botting's assertion that the novel is "often considered the last truly Gothic text."[15] However, Muriel Hammond proposes more of a compromise—that if Maturin was "the last of the Gothic, he was also the first of the psychological novelists."[16] Diane D'Amico favors the psychological contributions of *Melmoth*, as she concludes that "Maturin's depiction of human nature has the haunting quality of some dark truth.... In a fallen world, no man is born without a shadow, and to deny its existence leads only to increasing its power."[17] Heinz Kosok asserts that "*Melmoth the Wanderer* contains, in the 'Tale of the Indians,' one of the fiercest attacks on colonialism anywhere to be found in nineteenth century literature."[18] Biographer Dale Kramer decides that "to place Maturin finally in his appropriate niche in the literary history of England or of Western Europe is not yet possible."[19] More recent critics have focused upon some of the Irish aspects of the text. Jarlath Killeen comments:

> Paranoia, Protestantism, anti–Catholicism, desire for the Other—these are all fairly typical of Gothic. There is nothing particularly "Irish" about any of these aspects of the

Gothic oeuvre as a whole, although in *Melmoth the Wanderer* Ireland did produce what is perhaps the most heightened example of traditional Gothic fiction imaginable, a novel which works itself into such a pitch of Gothic excitement that the reader gets lost in the twists and turns of its spectacularly labyrinth structure—so elaborate indeed, that only Varney the Vampire rivals it for formal complexity.[20]

As Christina Morin observes in *Charles Robert Maturin and the Haunting of Irish Romantic Fiction*: "Although the structure of Maturin's (in)famous novel may forever remain contested, there is no doubt that *Melmoth* speaks of the ghosts haunting Maturin as he wrote, including contemporary Ireland and its violent past."[21] Finally, among the many observations made by Jim Kelly in *Charles Maturin: Authorship, Authenticity and the Nation* is: "A conflict between memory and history is at the centre of *Melmoth the Wanderer*."[22] *Melmoth the Wanderer* invites a variety of critical attention that does not form any consensus. However, though interpretations vary, all agree about the need to analyze the work.

Maturin's tale begins in Ireland and centers on John Melmoth, who is an ancestor of the current (and soon to be deceased) Irish landowner. John Melmoth reputedly sold his soul in return for 150 years of life. The only way Melmoth can escape this deal with the devil is to find someone who is willing to change places with him. His quest leads him to England, the Continent, and even a tropical paradise. The people whom he encounters and their resulting experiences make up the tales within tales. Although it is an interesting and sometimes quite disturbing novel, it does not appear to be very original, Irish, or vampiric. The deal with the devil can be traced to Christopher Marlowe's *Dr. Faustus* (1604) and later to Johann Goethe's *Faust* (1808). Both were widely known and readily available to an avid reader such as Maturin. But there is more to this novel, as we shall see.

Joseph Sheridan Le Fanu also approached writing as a means to support a family rather than as a crusade for Irish literature. As a newspaper owner, editor, regular contributor, and businessman, Le Fanu was concerned with the financial profit of writing. He published a variety of writing in his periodicals, including his own works. His *Uncle Silas* (1864) and *In a Glass Darkly* (1872) are compelling examples of his Irish Gothic work. Uncle Silas is a creepy and threatening figure who is submerged in Swedenborgianism and the desire to take control of his niece's inheritance. *In a Glass Darkly* is a collection of short stories, many of which Le Fanu revised throughout the course of his life. One of the most memorable stories of this collection is the vampiric "Carmilla," an original contribution to the vampire literature of the time. Although Le Fanu's works are studies in very abnormal psychology and anticipate Freud by a generation, few of his

Gothic stories involve Irish subjects or settings. Yet he would be very influential on later Irish writers, including James Joyce, who includes him in *Finnegans Wake* (1939).

Whereas Le Fanu's writing contained areas of originality, one cannot make a similar claim for Bram Stoker. He is best known for *Dracula*, a novel so obviously influenced by Maturin and Le Fanu that it could almost be described as plagiarized in some areas, an allegation that will be considered at greater length in the chapter about Stoker. What surprises most modern readers even more is that Stoker published several works both before and after this famous novel. All were written in the spare time he snatched from being famous British stage actor Henry Irving's business manager. *Dracula* appears to be a very English novel that utilizes much of the English Gothic tradition. English characters are pitted against an ancient, foreign threat in English settings. The result is a chase that leads to the Carpathian Mountains and the destruction of Count Dracula, but not before the count has claimed the entire crew of the *Demeter*: the aristocratic Lucy Westenra, Dr. Seward's insane patient Renfield, and the wealthy American adventurer Quincey Morris. The imperial, colonial tone of the novel is often remarked upon by critics, especially those who argue that Stoker was more English than Irish. This important aspect of *Dracula* will be analyzed further in the chapter devoted to Stoker.

Taken together, Stoker, Le Fanu, and Maturin do not seem to provide a compelling case for the Irish Gothic and the creation of an Irish vampire. They appear to be further examples of the type of literature Yeats and his fellow revivalists were reacting against. For Yeats in 1901, when he wrote the text quoted at the beginning of the chapter, the concept of "Irish" writers did not exist, at least not in the same sense that it does today. Ireland was just one of the many colonial holdings of England; the inhabitants of Ireland had been British subjects since Elizabeth I's reign. Three hundred years of English rule had left its imprints on all aspects of Irish life, including literature. Irish writers wrote in English and used English models for their works that resulted in very "English" publications. Many of these Irish authors, such as Jonathan Swift (1667–1745), Laurence Sterne (1713–68), and Richard Brinsely Sheridan (1751–1816), were unsure how to define their nationality. The "eighteenth-century novelists of Irish birth—often exiled, invariably writing for English publishers, and quite torn in their allegiances between Ireland and England—found it difficult to see themselves as writing specifically *Irish* novels, and their contemporaries as well as literary historians since then seldom identified them as Irish novelists."[23]

Instead of exploring this problem facing the definition of an Irish literature prior to the Irish Literary Renaissance, it was almost completely ignored in literary circles. William Patrick Ryan tried to articulate the progress of a decade's work from the point of view of a participant in *The Irish Literary Revival: Its History, Pioneers, and Possibilities* (1894) and revealed ideological differences between the London and Dublin Irish Literary Societies which emerged during the planning stages of publishing Irish literature. Older member and society president Sir Charles Gavan Duffy (1816–1903) presented a publication plan to the London group that recommended the publication of prior Irish writers whose works "were scattered in magazines and annuals, in luckless books over-looked ... in publications the very names of which were forgotten by the present generation,"[24] along with the current Irish authors, and Duffy's only apparent criteria for "Irish" authors was that they had been born in Ireland. His plan was well received by his London audience, but the same could not be said for the Dublin group: "They [Dublin] were the representatives of a new Irish generation, keenly conscious of intellectual wants and wishes of its own, with pronounced ideas on the subject of their fulfillment ... they wanted more control, more position, than seemingly were offered."[25] One of the outspoken leaders of this Dublin group was Yeats, who expressed his objections in the press: "Some hard words were said on both sides.... The claim that the hopes and aspirations of the risen generation should not be ignored for antique reprints of Young Ireland aftermaths, was emphasized in several quarters."[26]

In the decade that followed, relationships appeared to have been repaired, but there still did not seem to be complete agreement upon how to define "Irish Literature." The evidence lies with the *Irish Literature* collection. Both Ryan and Yeats worked with a larger group of Irish Literary Society members from London and Dublin to publish the ten-volume work. Its editor-in-chief, Justin McCarthy, M.P., described the collection's purpose in his opening essay, "Irish Literature," in the first volume:

> The object of this library of "IRISH LITERATURE" is to give the readers of all countries ... an illustrated catalogue of Ireland's literary contributions to mankind's intellectual stores. The readers of these volumes can trace the history of Ireland's mental growth from the dim and distant days of myth and legend down to the opening of the present century.... this library may well help the intelligent reader to appreciate the spirit of Irish nationality.... I desire especially to call the attention of readers to the fact that throughout that long course of Irish literature it has always retained in its brightest creations the same distinct and general character of Irish nationality.[27]

McCarthy's managing editor, Charles Welsh, adds to this purpose in his Foreword following McCarthy's essay, stating: "The world has never yet fully recognized the fact that Ireland has produced a literature of her own, fitted to take rank with that of any other nation…. Because it has been so obscured is one reason why Ireland has not been looked upon by thinkers with the respect which she deserves; but this condition of things will, it is hoped, be forever removed by the publication of this work."[28] Welsh adds that many of the Irish writers included "have never been credited with their work as Irish, but have ever been classified under an alien name."[29] So Welsh, McCarthy, and their long list of fellow collaborators, which included Lady Gregory, Standish O'Grady, D. J. O'Donoghue, Douglas Hyde, G. W. Russell (A. E.), T. W. Rolleston, and, of course, Ryan and Yeats, sought to reclaim Irish writers for Ireland and show through the selected literature that Ireland had a well-established literary tradition that demonstrated the deeply intellectual as well as distinctly national nature of her people. They wanted to eliminate the damaging, negative stereotypes that currently existed about the Irish in order to gain global support for their national cause.

One would assume that such an ambitious agenda would require scrupulous selection of which works to include based upon very specific and agreed-upon criteria. However, the only specified criteria seems to be Welsh's pause to explain "by 'Irish literature' we mean the literature which is written by Irish men and women"[30]; otherwise, the contents of the various essays written especially for the collection and the included (and excluded) authors and representative works seem to indicate that an extremely flexible method of selection was used. Welsh provides some insight into the selection process in his Foreword, saying:

> The work of assembling the contents of this library is not that of one man. It is the outcome of the combined wisdom, taste, literary judgement, and editorial skill of a group of the foremost living Irish scholars and critics….
>
> … the whole field of Irish literature in the English language from the seventeenth century down to our own day, including the works of the translators from the ancient Irish, was carefully surveyed, and a mass of material was collected sufficient in quantity for two or three such libraries as this. Lists of these authors and of these examples of their work were then prepared and forwarded to each member of the Committee of Selection, who subjected these lists to a most careful and critical process of winnowing and weeding. The results of their independent recensions were then carefully brought together, compared, and combined. A new list of authors and their works based upon this was made, and this was in turn finally examined and passed upon by the Editor-in-Chief, Mr. Justin McCarthy, and the eminent critic, Mr. Stephen Gwynn, in personal conference.
>
> Only by such effort could a selection have been made which would be thoroughly representative, and in which the people would have confidence that it really represented the best work of the best Irish writers. Popular taste, national feeling and sentiment, and scholarly requirements have been consulted and considered….
>
> The selection has been made without bias, religious, political, or social, and without

fear or favor.... Literary merit and human interest have been the touchstones employed in choosing the contents of the library; at the same time care has been taken to avoid anything which could wound the feelings or offend the taste of any class or creed.[31]

It was a monumental task, and with so many differing opinions, details would inevitably be missed and some authors or works included that did not enjoy unanimous agreement.[32] The included authors are arranged alphabetically rather than chronologically, so, if the purpose of the collection was to allow the reader to gain an appreciation for the history and development of Irish literature from early oral to present time, the reader would need existing knowledge of Irish history to properly place the author's dates within the correct historical timeframe. Additionally, the special articles written for the collection on topics like "Irish Literature," "Irish Novels," "Early Irish Literature," and "Ireland's Influence on European Literature" are inserted at the beginning of each volume without any apparent connection to the contents of the volume.

While the organization of the material is not in keeping with the purpose of the collection (to expose unfamiliar readers to Irish literature, demonstrating its development over time), the special articles lack a unifying theme or ideology concerning the authors and texts included in the ten volumes. For example, McCarthy links Irish history to a progressively developing nationalism in Irish literature that made it distinctive from English literature. McCarthy states:

> One of the immediate results of the Act of Union and the suppression of the Irish National Parliament was to bring about a sharp and sudden reaction against the growing tendency to make Irish literature merely a part of the literature of England. From that time, it may be said with literal accuracy, there came into existence the first school of really able Irish authors who, although writing in the English language, made their work distinctively and thoroughly Irish.[33]

McCarthy follows with the names of Banim, Carleton, and Gerald Griffin as listed examples but begins with Lady Morgan, whom he obviously does not consider in the same league: "Take even the novels of Lady Morgan, with all their flippancy, their cheap cynicism, their highly colored pictures of fashionable life in Dublin, their lack of any elevated purpose whatever—even these novels were ... unquestionably Irish,"[34] because she realistically describes Irish scenery and peasant life. Lady Morgan and her works are included in the collection despite this less-than-ringing endorsement of her "Irishness." The essay continues in the same vein, citing the era of Daniel O'Connell and the literature of that time as the next step in the Irish literature progression, ending with the current time period.

Maurice Francis Egan also makes some curious statements in his essay, "Irish Novels," where he claims:

In the new movement [current time] art counts for much,—and there is the old yearning for the mysticism of the past. In the older movement mysticism counted for little and conscious art for less. All the Irish novelists, except Miss Laffan and Mrs. Tynan-Hinkson ... seem to regard the laws of literary proportion,—in another phrase, the art of construction,—as if they had no relation to the gift of story-telling.

There is another very distinct difference between the writers in the new Irish movement and the older novelists. Carleton and Griffin, Lover and Lever, even the Banims, cannot somehow prevent themselves from seeing their own people from the outside.[35]

Egan's subsequent examples seem to indicate that, when he says "seeing their own people from the outside," he means that the characters lack complex psychologies; their presentations to their readers are superficial, implying that the Irish people are equally simple. Lover and Lever seem to be the greatest offenders in this criticism, but he finds the exceptions in Maria Edgeworth, "a novelist with a purpose,"[36] and Gerald Griffin, who "had more art, more refinement, more sense of the perspective of life than the Banims or Carleton."[37]

The scattered criteria for an Irish literature continues to emerge in Douglas Hyde's essay, "Early Irish Literature," where he demonstrates a distinctive bias toward his subject. Hyde cites many distinctive merits to early Irish literature that offer certain connections to the current subject. He states that early Irish literature distinguishes itself because of its very early beginnings and its absolute originality.[38] The Annals of Ulster date from 444,[39] and one aspect of originality rests in the early literature's "very wildness of flavor and strange extravagance of manners are likely sometimes to render it of only moderate interest to the ordinary reader of English."[40] Although several observations made by Hyde about early Irish literature pertain to characteristics of Irish Gothic writing of the nineteenth century, he concludes his essay on a shocking note:

Irish literature never quite ceased to be written, but the nineteenth century produced little worth remembering. It is only within the last few years that a new and able school of Irish writers has sprung up, with a sympathetic public to encourage it, and bids fair to do something once again that may be worthy of the history of our island—once one of the spots most desirous of learning and of literature to be found in the whole world. The tenth volume of "IRISH LITERATURE" contains some specimens of this new school with translations.[41]

Hyde begins the second volume of *Irish Literature* with an assertion that dismisses the writing of an entire century, advising the reader to skip right to the tenth volume. His remark undermines the entire group's work and may have contributed to over fifty years of neglect of these authors.

Fortunately, in 1959, Thomas Flanagan published *The Irish Novelists 1800–1850* and noted in his preface, "Despite the attention which Irish literature has received, no scholar or critic has concerned himself with the general subject of the novelists who interpreted the life of Ireland during the years of its emergence into the modern world."[42] Flanagan proceeded to analyze the works of Maria Edgeworth (1768–1849), Lady Morgan (1776–1859), John Banim (1798–1842), Gerald Griffin (1803–1840), and William Carleton (1794–1869). His selection of two Anglo-Irish Protestant women, two middle-class Catholics, and one Irish Gaelic peasant who converted to Protestantism implies that Flanagan's definition of an "Irish novelist" encompassed a broader array of authors than originally considered: "This book ... may properly be called a study of five Irelands, for each writer had his own intense understanding of the country which he had taken as his subject."[43] The common thread uniting the five authors was history and identity. "However tedious this preoccupation with history became to others, however much it limited his own work, the Irish writer was yoked to it forever. His search for identity drove him relentlessly into the past."[44]

Flanagan explored this relationship between history and identity within the works of these writers. After a detailed analysis, though, he arrived at a conclusion as stunning as Hyde's: "it matters not at all that there were Irish novelists before Joyce, for their work was entirely useless to him. They had established no conventions by which the actualities of Irish life could be represented."[45] Flanagan further claimed,

> The fact remains, general beyond the point of coincidence, that no writer of ability before Joyce found possible a sustained and successful career in Irish letters....
>   To be sure, there are specific grounds upon which the collapse at mid-century of the Irish literary movement may be explained—the devastating effects of the Famine; the political inertia, born of both despair and cynicism, which followed upon the '48 Rising; the reshaping of the implacable barriers of caste and creed. Yet one can only assume that a literature so dependent upon circumstance had at best had a precarious tenure.[46]

Flanagan effectively dismissed the work of the two generations preceding Joyce. Fortunately for Irish scholars, Flanagan's study was critically received as an initial look into the Irish writers rather than the definitive treatise of Irish novelists and their place in Irish literature.

More recently, James M. Cahalan's *Great Hatred, Little Room: The Irish Historical Novel* (1983) does not dismiss the Irish novelists prior to James Joyce, but defines and demonstrates the importance of a specific subgenre, the Irish historical novel. Among the fifteen authors whom he discusses, Cahalan looks not only at John Banim but also Michael Banim (1796–1874), Sheridan Le Fanu, William Carleton (1794–1869), Standish O'Grady (1846–1928), and William Buckley—all writers who precede Joyce with significant publications. These writers were influenced by Sir Walter Scott's work but, like the Irish Gothic writers, soon developed their own distinct styles in the subgenre of the historical novel. Within his study, Cahalan notes the connection between the Gothic and historical novels as illustrated through a discussion of Scott. "For Scott, Gothicism was part of being historical, rather than an avocation to be pursued for its own sake. Gothicism was part of Scottish history and was to be understood in terms of that history. In short, Scott's Gothicism was an organic Gothicism."[47] Cahalan significantly notes that among the authors he discusses, Le Fanu is an interesting exception.

> The Irish historical novelist has explored his history in order to understand it and to define a mature, contemporary nationalism according to which modern Irish history is seen as the story of the struggle to overcome British domination. The only Irish novelist I discuss who cannot be called a nationalist, Joseph Sheridan Le Fanu, eventually retreated altogether from history to Gothicism, rejecting politics…. He moves from history to Gothicism rather than from Gothicism to history.[48]

Cahalan's *Great Hatred, Little Room* prompted a broader analysis of Irish writers in his subsequent book, *The Irish Novel: A Critical History* (1988). Cahalan explains the need for such a study in his introduction: "As a distinct subject the Irish novel has had to overcome the tendencies of critics to ignore it entirely, to lump it together with the British novel, or to attend only to the works of its most celebrated practitioner, James Joyce."[49] Even Flanagan undermined his own work on the Irish novel by dismissing the authors at the end, saying that nothing of importance was written before Joyce's work. Cahalan counters these claims and agrees with the criticism of Gerald Dawe and Edna Longley, who "emphasize that W. B. Yeats (who, ironically, was a Protestant) did much to encourage a critical code that celebrates southern Catholic writers as Irish at the expense of northern Protestant ones."[50] Their position agrees with that of W. J. McCormack that "critics of Anglo-Irish literature have derived their techniques from Yeats, and so have entered into a conspiracy with that formidable reviser of history."[51] The results of such an approach minimized the importance of Anglo-Irish works like Maturin's *Melmoth the Wanderer*, Le Fanu's *Uncle Silas* and "Carmilla," and Stoker's *Dracula*.

Yeats and his fellow revivalists elevated some Irish writers and their writings at the expense of those of their own class. Yeats was a member of the Anglo-Irish Ascendancy, yet he had more of an affinity for Ireland than for England. Despite his social position and his lack of fluency in the Irish language, he played an integral role in the preservation of the Irish language through his encouragement of those better qualified in that language and

through his contributions in defining and forming an Irish national literature at a time when there appeared to many readers to be no national
body of literature to distinguish Irish writers from English ones. As Yeats
gained in reputation, he also gained in influence. He developed specific
ideas about what he believed constituted a national literature. He ruled out
a great deal of previous Irish literature because he felt that it did not possess
an Irish past, a sense of passion, and discovery of a personal identity through
a national one. He dismissed much of the literature of the prior generation
due to its portrayal of the Irish as vehicles only for comic relief. He felt
that two of the greatest offenders in perpetuating the "stage Irishman" in
fiction were Samuel Lover (1797–1868) and Charles Lever (1806–1872).
Yeats saw this depiction as not only degrading, but very limiting to what
he saw inherent in the Irish character:

> The impulse of the Irish literature of their [Lover and Lever's] time came from a class
> that did not—mainly for political reasons—take the populace seriously, and imagined
> the country as a humorist's Arcadia: its passion, its gloom, its tragedy, they knew noth-
> ing of. What they did was not wholly false; they merely magnified an irresponsible
> type, found oftenest among boatsmen, car men, and gentlemen's servants, into the type
> of a whole nation and created the stage Irishman.[52]

It would be difficult to be taken seriously as an Irish writer when English
publishers were accustomed to seeing the Irish only as sources of comic
relief—characters who more often than not came directly from popular
Anglo-Irish writers such as Lover, Lever, Maria Edgeworth's Thady Quirk
in *Castle Rackrent* (1800), and Somerville and Ross's *Some Experiences of
an Irish R. M.* (1899).

   Yeats and his fellow revivalists felt that the Irish needed to write about
other subjects to be taken seriously as writers and to dignify their people.
Yeats's solution was to rediscover Ireland's glorious past in Celtic legends
and local folktales, an idea he adopted through the influence of Standish
O'Grady, Douglas Hyde, and Lady Augusta Gregory, who were already
active in the collection and publication of such stories. The Irish fairy folk
who had appeared in generations of oral tales soon emerged as a pantheon
of Celtic gods and goddesses in the late nineteenth and early twentieth
centuries. Lady Gregory's 1902 book *Cuchulain of Muirthemne* was a landmark in the rediscovery of Celtic myth. She researched numerous documents written in Irish and worked them into one seamless text, written in
English, but using the Kiltartan dialect to preserve the Irish nature of the
tales. "The publication of *Cuchulain* affected not only Yeats, but almost
every important writer of the period."[53] From this book's enormous cast of
characters, Cuchulain, Emer, Conchubar, Deirdre, Fergus, and Maeve were

a few who distinguished themselves from local folktales and became the subjects of writing for other Irish authors. The result was that a far greater number of Irish writers chose to write about distinctly Irish themes rather than rely on the Greek and Roman myths or recycle themes and styles of the English poets. The Irish past became a much more common source for literary inspiration after Gregory's publication than it had been prior to it.

With the rediscovery of an Irish past, writers were given Irish subjects, and the emergence of an Irish style soon followed. It was imperative for an Irish writer to find his own voice (and ultimately himself) through writing a national literature. This issue of identity seems to be central to both Yeats's and McCarthy's definition of a national literature. An Irish writer needed to connect with Ireland's past, discover his own writing style, and determine who he himself was in order to be worthy of the name of "Irish author."

Along with identity, there was passion. Many writers found that passion in the past, in folktales, and in love. Passion consumed its subjects, sometimes destroying them, as Yeats pointed out: "Love was held to be a fatal sickness in ancient Ireland, and there is a love-poem in the *Love Songs of Connacht* that is like a death-cry: 'My love, O she is my love, the woman who is most for destroying me, dearer is she for making me ill than the woman who would be for making me well ... the woman who left no strength in me."[54] Passion did not exclusively stem from love where Yeats was concerned. He sought passion that could transcend and transform its subject—a spiritual, otherworldly experience. Any emotion or occupation that could drive its subject into a single-minded, obsessive pursuit of it could be classified as "passion." As he stressed in "The Celtic Element in Literature," "Certainly a thirst for unbounded emotion and a wild melancholy are troublesome things in the world, and do not make its life more easy or orderly, but it may be the arts are founded on the life beyond the world, and that they must cry in the ears of our penury until the world has been consumed and become a vision."[55]

The combined results of Yeats and his revivalist colleagues support a criteria for an Irish national literature that includes: passion, Irish subjects, originality and style, and an Irish as well as personal identity. Given these requirements and prior discussion of standard Gothic fare and its connection to actual history, one is not surprised that Gothic novels received little attention in the quest for a national literature. Although Gothic literature possessed passion, it was an established and formulaic genre and, therefore, not original. It also had distinct English associations so it would not be a viable choice for an Irish writer who wished to find his personal and national identity. However, Maturin, Le Fanu, and Stoker selected the Gothic genre when writing *Melmoth, Uncle Silas,* "Carmilla," and *Dracula,* and transformed it into Irish Gothic. They are Irish Gothic writers, separated from the standard Gothic tradition. Collectively, they exceeded national literary expectations by creating a universal vampire myth, culminating in Stoker's novel, which shows every sign of persisting in the twenty-first century: the myth of Dracula.

In three distinct ways, Yeats actually supports the argument for the Irish vampire. When revising a passage about the importance of passion in "The Celtic Element in Literature," Yeats added an interesting footnote in 1924: "I will put this differently and say that literature dwindles to a mere chronicle of circumstance, or passionless fantasies, and passionless meditations, unless it is constantly flooded with the passions and beliefs of ancient times [added footnote in 1924: I should have added as an alternative that *the supernatural may at any moment create new myths,* but I was timid] (emphasis mine)."[56]

The addition of the supernatural is not an unreasonable leap of logic. The folktales and other stories that Yeats collected with Lady Gregory were full of supernatural tales. "[F]antasy always was a traditionally strong element in most Irish story telling since time immemorial."[57] Yeats was not an exception in using fantasy, supernatural, or Gothic devices in his writing. One need not look any further than Yeats's *The Celtic Twilight* (1893) for evidence of Gothic elements. There were fairies, pookas, leprechauns, banshees, changelings, legendary heroes, tragic heroines, and ghosts galore. Many also appeared in *Fairy and Folk Tales of the Irish Peasantry* (1888).

Surprisingly, neither of these collections included two well-known and sometimes closely related figures of Irish folklore—Oliver Cromwell and the vampire. Since his savage leveling campaign of Ireland in 1649, Cromwell has been the evil villain of many Irish tales. Even though his death and subsequent burial in England were unremarkable and historically documented,[58] the Irish version is quite different.[59]

> "He is generally said to have killed himself either by cutting his own throat or casting his body against a spear," according to O'Suilleabhain ... "some accounts even say that he met his death in Ireland." Several versions explain that after its burial in Ireland, Cromwell's corpse was rejected by the Irish soil and the coffin was found back above ground each morning.[60]

The above quotation shows that these stories share a distinct similarity to other Irish tales involving a very particular supernatural being: "the neamh-mhairbh [the undead] ... [or] dearg-diulai, a drinker of human blood. He cannot actually be slain—but he can be restrained."[61] In imagined suicide,

Cromwell would become a vampire and, as an Englishman, he would be unable to find refuge in Irish soil. The story also shares similarities with the story of Abhartach, presented in the first chapter.

As may be readily seen in this chapter, the task of defining a national literature is a monumental one that usually ends with some writers being left out or their body of work not being thoroughly represented. The reasons that prompted the initial omission of Maturin, the exclusion of examples of Le Fanu's supernatural and weird fiction, and the inclusion of Stoker's gombeen man, instead of his vampire in the *Irish Literature* collection, are no longer used to prevent them from being named in the long list of Irish authors or the inclusion of their Irish Gothic works. A steadily growing interest in these writers among literary scholars has prompted republications of their writings and a revived interest in Irish Gothic works, allowing a new generation of critics to study the authors and their texts. Noted biographer and Le Fanu scholar W. J. McCormack uses the phrase "Irish Gothic" in his essay "Irish Gothic and Beyond" in the influential *The Field Day Anthology* (1991), which aims to be a revisionist Norton-styled anthology of distinctly Irish canons. Among the many authors included in the Irish Gothic section are Maturin, Le Fanu, and Stoker, writers whom McNally calls "the Unholy Trinity of Irish Gothic."[62]

Though the concept of the Irish Gothic does not originate with this work, the subsequent pages provide an original contribution to the discussion of it. This study brings all three authors together for an extended analysis of the progression and development of the Irish Gothic genre as illustrated through their writings. The analysis utilizes the criteria of originality, Irish subject, personal/Irish identity, and passion to provide a framework for the discussion of "Irish" as it was being used within the ongoing discussions of the authors' own times and to connect it to the development and particular significance of a distinctly Irish vampire emerging from the Irish Gothic tradition.

In the following chapters, each author will be discussed in detail relating to his role in the development of the Irish Gothic and the vampire, his specific contributions to it, and how he influenced future writers with his work. Maturin naturally begins the exploration into the Irish Gothic vampire. He is not the first Irish writer to use themes of Gothicism in his novels, but he is an originator in regard to how he utilizes it. Maturin borrows from a range of previous works, including Irish ones, to create *Melmoth the Wanderer*. The eclectic use of resources combined with his own family tales of persecution, his personal story of eccentricity and frequent hardship, and the Irish history unfolding around him meld together to form something unique in the character of Melmoth and the novel in which he appears.

The publication of *Melmoth the Wanderer* influenced the writing of Le Fanu, who was then a young boy of six enjoying an idyllic childhood in Dublin's Phoenix Park, and only ten when Maturin died under debated circumstances at the age of forty-four. Still, Maturin's book would prove influential in Le Fanu's own writing career. In the fourth chapter, Le Fanu's novel *Uncle Silas* and novella "Carmilla," appearing in his collection *In a Glass Darkly* are analyzed in reference to the whole of his Irish Gothic writing. Le Fanu was inspired by Maturin's novel but did not strictly adhere to some of Maturin's innovations. Le Fanu further develops the Irish Gothic genre and the Irish vampire, significantly and influentially adding more to it that serves to separate it further from the English Gothic. His innovations also come from prior publications, his own difficult life, and the changing atmosphere in Ireland. Le Fanu writes in the midst of conflict, and his fiction reflects this.

Le Fanu died at the age of fifty-nine in 1873, just a year after publishing one of his best-known works, "Carmilla."[63] Stoker was then a young man of twenty-six living in Dublin, working as a civil servant during the day, and writing theater reviews at night, when Le Fanu died. Stoker's life-altering dinner with actor Henry Irving had not yet occurred, but one essential influence for the future *Dracula* had happened: Stoker had read "Carmilla" and was greatly influenced by it. The works of Le Fanu and Maturin are as critically important to the creation of Stoker's writing as his own research, life experiences, and Irish national history. It is necessary to first see the connections between Stoker and his influential predecessors, Le Fanu and Maturin, before even delving into *Dracula*. Where Stoker directly uses the ideas of the writers, he establishes his connection to the Irish Gothic; however, the ways in which he deviates from the tradition created by these two Irish writers shows the full manifestation of the Irish Gothic and the Irish vampire and the most recognized figure to emerge from it, Count Dracula. In order to clearly demonstrate this connection and its importance, Le Fanu and Maturin are discussed in detail again in Chapter 5, in reference to Stoker. That discussion and the particularly compelling nature of *Dracula* make that chapter the longest one. The additional analysis provides the needed link to show that all three writers, not just Stoker, were essential in the creation of the Irish Gothic tradition.

3

Charles Robert Maturin
Stirring the Imagination
of an Irish Vampire

"...repeated disappointments have destroyed my self-confidence—I
have been too much neglected by the world to think there is any thing
in me worth the world's notice..."
—Charles Robert Maturin in a letter to Sir Walter Scott,
27 October 1813[1]

Charles Robert Maturin (1780–1824) would be surprised, and probably
quite pleased, at the interest taken in his life and work. No doubt he would
be very disappointed in some critics for their prying and speculation about
his mental state, but with someone like Maturin, rumors and legends are
difficult to separate from facts. The man is as interesting as his characters,
sometimes even more so. Looking at the man and the writer is a study of
paradox that only seems appropriate for someone best known now for *Melmoth the Wanderer* (1820). This book is known for several reasons among
twentieth and twenty-first century critics—as the last Gothic novel, as a
transitional piece between the old and new Gothic, and as changing the
nature of the genre. It is also where this discussion of the Irish Gothic
vampire begins. Despite Maturin's adherence to Gothic conventions and
his open borrowing from numerous texts, he exhibits an original style, utilizes Irish subject matter, overflows with passion, and, most importantly,
shows evidence of searching for both an Irish and personal identity. Without Maturin as a model, the writings of Joseph Sheridan Le Fanu and
Bram Stoker would have been quite different.

Before beginning a discussion of *Melmoth the Wanderer*, it is necessary
to present a detailed account of Maturin's life for three reasons. Much of
the Maturin's biography was written in the early twentieth century in

carefully researched works like Niilo Idman's *Charles Robert Maturin: His Life and Works* (1923), Bernard Nicholas Schilling's *Charles Robert Maturin: A Biographical and Critical Study* (1928), Willem Scholten's *Charles Robert Maturin: The Terror Novelist* (1933), *The Correspondence of Walter Scott and Charles Robert Maturin* (1937), and John B. Harris's *Charles Robert Maturin: The Forgotten Imitator* (1965, 1980). With the exception of *The Correspondence*, copies of these works are not readily accessible to the ordinary reader except through special interlibrary loan requests or purchasing rare, out-of-print texts at a significant cost. So, aside from those who have researched Maturin, the details of his life may not be as well-known as those of Le Fanu and Stoker. Additionally, some of the known events of Maturin's life are contradictory, so presenting them and attempting to reconcile them will be useful in separating as much fact from fiction as possible. The final reason for presenting Maturin's biography is that, contrary to how the author felt about separating his work from his person,[2] many aspects of his life pertain to the argument being made for originality, Irish subjects, personal and Irish identity, and passion, especially when looking at *Melmoth*.

Maturin's life contained a great deal of paradox. He was Anglican and born into a long line of Protestant clergymen originating in France, where a significant and often retold story of Gabriel Maturin, the great-great grandfather of Charles Maturin, occurred. The first written version appeared while Maturin was still alive in William Monck Mason's *The History and Antiquities of the Collegiate and Cathedral Church of St. Patrick, near Dublin, from Its Foundation in 1190, to the year 1819* in a footnote that was attributed to be a direct quote from Maturin. Gabriel was a foundling in France who was taken in by a noble woman of Louis XIV's court. "As the lady was a devotee, she brought him up a strict catholic, and being puzzled for a name for him, she borrowed one from a religious community, *les Maturins* ... who were then of sufficient importance to give their name to a street in Paris, La Rue des Mathurins."[3] He grew up to be a Protestant minister in a country where Catholicism was the dominant and ruling religion. Gabriel "was imprisoned in the Bastille for a number of years, and was released only when he was weak and crippled. In spite of his infirmities he led the faithful remainder of his flock to Ireland in the pursuit of religious freedom."[4]

Maturin strongly identified with this family story and had always felt that the lady who had adopted his ancestor was actually the child's mother and "devotedly cherished the thought that his ancestry, to whom he assigned places of rank and distinction, and whom he invested in his poetic ardour with all the pomp and paraphernalia of chivalry, would ultimately be discovered."[5] Maturin's clear investment in the family story demonstrated his romantic and imaginative nature. This story is also often cited as the root for the anti–Catholic tone that runs throughout most of his work,[6] especially *Melmoth*. The Maturin legend of persecution parallels the trials of several characters found in the novel and, like Gabriel Maturin, the characters persevere despite the obstacles. Ironically, this influential family legend appears to contain more fiction than fact. The 1892 edition of *Melmoth* included a "Memoir of Charles Robert Maturin" which cited Lady Wilde and Oscar Wilde "for several details with regard to Maturin's life."[7] The foundling story is recounted but included the comment: "There is little reason for doubting that it [foundling story] was anything but one of his [Maturin's] delightful romances."[8] The Wildes' belief is supported by the actual genealogy and history of the Maturins that was documented by Michael Osborne.[9] Osborne's research reveals that Gabriel Maturin (1638–1718) was born in France, became a Protestant minister, married, had a family, and left France for Holland when the Edict of Nantes was revoked in 1685. A few years later, Gabriel and five other ministers secretly returned to France to serve those Protestants left behind, which was a very risky mission since the penalties for being caught were severe. Gabriel and his fellow courageous missionaries were arrested in 1690 and sentenced to life in solitary confinement at one of the royal prisons on the île Sainte-Marguerite.[10] The prisoners never left their small cells and were not permitted to communicate with anyone. Gabriel's wife, Rachel, was not idle during his imprisonment, working tirelessly to obtain his freedom, which probably happened through some of the influential people whom their son, Peter, knew.[11] By the time Gabriel's release was successfully negotiated[12] as part of the terms of the Treaty of Utrecht, twenty-five years had passed and four of the five missionaries arrested with him had died—one had actually gone insane and died within a year of his incarceration.[13] Gabriel had retained his mind but not his health. Still, he managed to join his family—now in London—in late 1714 or early in 1715.[14] They did not remain there long because Peter, an English regimental chaplain, was assigned a post in Dublin, Ireland, which is where the family moved in 1715 and where Gabriel died in 1718.[15]

It is unclear whether Maturin ever knew the real story of Gabriel; perhaps he had known just enough to provide him with the material to embellish his family's origins since he would have found the actual story even more engaging to his romantic sensibilities than the one that has endured for over two centuries. Maturin certainly believed the foundling story, and Gabriel actually did suffer tremendously for his religious beliefs. Such biographical aspects of Maturin's life are woven into his writing, frequently appearing as themes. This technique lends an originality to his work, while it also assists in the quest for a personal and Irish national identity.

Ireland received the Maturins in a much more hospitable manner than its French neighbors. The French Huguenot refugees settling in Ireland toward the end of the seventeenth and start of the eighteenth century experienced the hopes and challenges faced by most immigrant groups but eventually successfully assimilated into Dublin society.[16] The Maturins were one of these early groups who succeeded in Ireland. Even though Protestants were a minority in Ireland, they were the ruling minority, the Anglo-Irish class. Thus, the Anglican ministry was a secure occupation to pursue; the Maturins seemed to encourage it within the family. Maturin's father, William, deviated from the ministerial course, first aspiring to a career in literature which was curtailed by the death of his patron and then settling for the steadier course of government employment in the postal service.[17]

It would not be surprising that William shared his love of literature with his children, though the number of those children whom he and Fidelia Watson had who lived to maturity is one of those debatable facts within the author's story. Some sources note that Maturin was the youngest and only surviving child of his parents.[18] Yet other biographical accounts contradict this information.[19] In "Memoir of the Rev. C. R. Maturin," published when Maturin was still alive, Alaric Watts[20] briefly discusses Maturin's father who, "during the course of a long and respectable life, had brought up and maintained a numerous family; he had married his daughters, and established his sons," which suggests that Maturin had siblings who survived childhood. Being the only surviving child of doting parents would certainly appeal to Maturin's romantic and tragic sensibilities; however, several family genealogies, with a variety of supporting documentation from Michael Osborne's website and matching information on Ancestry. com, indicate that Maturin did have five other siblings—Fidelia, Emma, Alicia, William, and Henry. Fidelia and Emma both married in the 1790s,[21] and Alicia and William married in the early 1800s,[22] which means at least four of his siblings lived to be adults.

The genealogical sources also show that Maturin was the oldest son, not the youngest, as is sometimes indicated in his biographical accounts, so it seems more likely that Maturin received greater attention from his parents as the first-born male. His reportedly vulnerable health and precocious nature further increased his parents' attention and affections. According to an anonymous biographer who wrote a series of articles in the *New Monthly Magazine and Literary Journal* a few years after his death, "[Maturin was] treated with extraordinary fondness, and every new instance of ability was fresh notice to that natural and lavish affection: his appearance, too, was a justification of their anxiety, for his frame was delicate and fragile, and a cast of melancholy and reserve overspread his features."[23] Not surprisingly, he was "spoilt on account of his delicate health and looked up to for his cleverness,"[24] growing up in a home where "literary inclinations were cherished and encouraged.... Charles Robert's childhood poems and youthful addictions to play writing and acting were looked upon as indications of genius."[25] During these early years, Maturin demonstrated a particular affinity for drama; "here he was the director, the manager, the prompter, the arranger of scenes, and the overseer of the wardrobe,"[26] and his siblings all played their assigned roles.[27]

When he was fifteen, he entered Trinity College in Dublin. According to Muriel E. Hammond: "There he seems to have been remarkable for considerable academic capabilities, combined with an even greater lack of application."[28] However, Fannie E. Ratchford and William H. McCarthy note in their biographical account of Maturin that precedes his correspondence with Scott that the author possessed academic accomplishments. Maturin earned a scholarship, participated in the Historical Society, and "won two medals for composition and a premium for extempore speaking."[29] These contradictory reports of Maturin's scholarly industry are best reconciled in Watts's biographical sketch first printed in the *New Monthly Magazine and Universal Register* in 1819 and reprinted at least three times with little revision in 1819 (the *Antheneum, or the Spirit of the English Magazine*), 1820 (*La Belle Assemblee or Court and Fashionable Magazine*), and 1824 (the *Kaleidoscope, or Literary Scientific Mirror*):

> [Maturin's] academical progress was marked not only by the attainment of premiums and a scholarship, but of prizes for composition and extempore speaking in the theological class, and of the medals bestowed by the (now abolished) Historical Society, on those who distinguished themselves by rhetorical productions. Though his collegiate life was thus not without its honors, we understand from the friend who communicated the materials for this memoir, that its subject was considered, both by his tutors and his companions, as more remarkable for indolence and melancholy than for talent.[30]

Twenty-two years after his death, a friend of Maturin's recalled that "he was not the deep student of derivations and editions, nor the pedant of Greek metres ... he was also extensively read in old French history and literature."[31] Maturin seemed to focus his energy on studying those subjects that interested him most, giving superficial attention to those that did not.

Maturin's selective approach to his studies did not prevent him from graduating from Trinity in 1800 and following the family tradition of the ministry because it suited his romantic imagination, his desire for social position, and his need for an audience in the form of dedicated parishioners at his sermons. He was appointed to Loughrea, County Galway, in 1803, and then married the love of his life, Henrietta Kingsbury, whose brother was the archdeacon of Killala.[32] Henrietta was "well known for her beauty and social graces, particularly for her fine voice,"[33] and "Mrs. Maturin and her two sisters, Mrs. Elgy and Lady Ormsby, were all remarkable for their beauty."[34] She was also "the first love of boyhood, and full of ardour and truth."[35] Theirs was a genuinely loving relationship. Maturin was described by his contemporaries as "the most uxorious man breathing,"[36] and "the conjugal harmony is said never to have been broken."[37] Reportedly, Maturin "retained that sentiment undiminished to the last hour of his life."[38] The importance of a happy and stable home life would be reflected in the originality and passion with which he characterized women in his writing. Maturin devoted a whole sermon to the importance of women, titling it "The Necessity of Female Education" in his *Sermons* (1819), where he stated:

> The destiny of women in all civilized society is of the utmost importance to man. Of what importance then is it that they should be prepared for the part they are to support in it—a part of the most awful consequence to the fates of empires, to the interests of society, and, above all, to the peaceful felicities of domestic life: yes—let me not be thought to make a false climax when I speak of the felicities of domestic life as last and highest in the scale of human existence—they are highest.[39]

Maturin spoke from experience; his wife served as his anchor through all the changes and trials that would test their relationship.

Their first apparent test was the Loughrea parish. It was remote, especially for a young man who grew up in Dublin. Shortly after their marriage, the couple left Loughrea and returned to Dublin in 1806 because Maturin was appointed curate of St. Peter's. They moved in with his parents, where Maturin's first child, William, was born in 1806 and his first two novels were written and published under the pseudonym Dennis Jasper Murphy: *Fatal Revenge; or, the Family of Montorio: a Romance* (1807) and *The Wild Irish Boy* (1808). Unfortunately, domestic bliss did not last long. Maturin's father was dismissed in November 1809 from his position[40] on "suspicion of irregularities in office."[41] The family never recovered from the financial loss (even though his father was cleared years later). Maturin was now in the position of supporting his parents and his small family but found it difficult to live on a minister's salary of £70–£100 a year[42] after being accustomed to his father's generous financial assistance. Maturin tried to supplement his income through tutoring. He rented a large house to take in students as boarders where he prepared them to enter the university, and according to at least one contemporary source, he succeeded until he became responsible for someone else's debt, one source indicating that the debt defaulter was his brother.[43]

> [Maturin] applied himself to his task with industry and hope. For some time he was successful, and we have been informed that "Bertram" was written while the author had six young men residents in his house, and four who attended him for instruction daily, to all of whom his attention was unremitting. At this period he was unfortunately induced to become security for a relation whose affairs were considerably involved: the consequence was—what the consequence usually is—the relation defeated his creditors by taking the benefit of the Act of Insolvency, and left the burthen of his debts on those who had attempted to lighten their pressure on him.[44]

This biographer is supported by Maturin's own report of his income and the financial hardships experienced in assuming another's debt. He tells Scott that his income in 1812 was approximately £1175 and, in mid–July 1813, to be £675.[45] The difference in income between the two years could be attributed to the publication of *The Milesian Chief* (1812), the first work for which he sold the copyright in 1811 for £80[46] and his shifting number of students.[47] While both amounts would allow a family of seven to meet the usual household expenses, Maturin's students would require a certain amount of expense for boarding. Additionally, Maturin was not known for his thrifty nature, so paying off a large debt would cause some strain and the debt appeared to be significant. The debt may be what prompted Maturin to write *Bertram; or, the Castle of St. Aldobrand*, a task which he completed in 1813 although he was unsuccessful in persuading the Crow Street Theatre in Dublin to perform it.[48] Its later great success in London allowed Maturin to clear the debt for which he stood security, his own account claiming that he had little to spare for his own household.[49] Since many sources estimated that Maturin earned approximately £1,000 for his play, he must have owed a great deal on expenses that were not even his own; however, it is more likely that the debt was not that extreme and whatever amount remained was quickly spent; "as soon as he obtained a sum of money either by his writings or by borrowing, he gave great balls and fetes, indulged in eating quantities of Pine Apples, and as soon as possible exhausted his resources."[50]

Maturin's pressing financial obligations and lack of success with the Dublin theater probably served as the incentive for him to write one of the most important letters of his career to Sir Walter Scott. *The Fatal*

Revenge caught the attention of the famous poet who critiqued it in an anonymous 1810 article in the *Quarterly Review*:

> Mr. Murphy [Maturin] possesses a strong and vigorous fancy, with great command of language. He has indeed regulated his incidents upon those of others, and therefore added to the imperfections which we have pointed out, the want of originality. But his feeling and conception of character are his own, and from these we judge his powers. In truth we rose from his strange chaotic novel romance as from a confused and feverish dream, unrefreshed and unamused, yet strongly impressed by many of the ideas which had been so vaguely and wildly presented to our imagination....
>
> If the author of it [*Fatal Revenge*] be indeed, as he describes himself, young and inexperienced, without literary friend, or counsellor, we earnestly exhort him to seek one on whose taste and judgement he can rely. He is now, like an untutored colt, wasting his best vigour in irregular efforts without either grace or object; but there is much in these volumes which promises a career that may at some future time astonish the public.[51]

Maturin was obviously aware of this review, discovered that it was written by Scott, and initiated a correspondence with the famous author on December 18, 1812, which would continue until Maturin's death.[52] Scott, the classic historical novelist, became the mentor and friend to Maturin.

As Scott advised and critiqued Maturin's writing, the minister still sought to better his position in the church, though his eccentricities of character were already well-known. He was "said to display a mixture of placidity and insouciance often united in the literary character, and to be a kind relative, an indulgent parent, and the *most uxorious man breathing* ... [he was also] the gayest of the gay, passionately fond of society, and of all that can exhilarate or embellish it—of music, of dancing, of the company of the youthful, and the society of females."[53] His superiors found it difficult to reconcile Maturin's personal exuberance with his profession as a preacher, but he took his role seriously and tried to keep his literary identity separate from his religious profession. "His being a clergyman induced him to publish his early works anonymously, as they were not of that class which the evangelical critics of Dublin would have deemed strictly professional."[54] Maturin was obviously aware that a clergyman writing Gothic romances would not fare well, so he strove to keep the two worlds separate, though an entry in *A Biographical Dictionary of the Living Authors of Great Britain and Ireland* (1816) lists his pseudonym "Dennis Jasper Murphy" followed by: "Under this name, assumed we believe, by the Rev. Robert Maturin,"[55] indicating that even before *Bertram*, Maturin was known as a writer of Gothic romance.

Still, he maintained a firm and active commitment to his parish in a time "of ecclesiastical torpor."[56] "As a preacher Mr. Maturin was highly

esteemed; his sermons were masterly compositions, his reasoning incon-
trovertible, and his language the most calculated to subdue the heart, and
to demand attention."[57] Another contemporary wrote that: "there was
always something impressive about him—something which clearly shewed
[*sic*] he was no common man. He read the church service in a most perfect
manner, and his sermons were beautifully written, and well delivered."[58]
Whenever Maturin's performance as a minister was addressed by any of
his contemporaries, there was always praise; "he was always the Minister
of Christ"[59];

> [N]o curate in the diocese performed its duties more zealously and irreproachably....
> He was universally beloved by his parishioners, who were proud of having a man of
> such talents in their pulpit, and attracted by the amenity of his manners ... his gaiety of
> manner, fascinating conversation, and his gentle, good-natured disposition, disarmed
> even prudent censure of its bitterness, and often converted blame to admiration.[60]

Among his congregation and the general public, he was quite popular.
"[H]is placidity of temper and easy, gentlemanly manners usually disarmed
the displeasure of those coming into contact with him, and he had, upon
a whole, no personal enemies."[61] He passionately believed that the road to
Irish salvation was to disassociate Ireland from the Roman Catholic
Church. It would seem that his outspoken stance against Catholicism
would have gained him favor within the Anglican hierarchy, but this was
not the case. Unfortunately for Maturin, being a conscientious minister
was not the only criteria for advancement in the church.

   Though no particular individual harbored ill-will against Maturin, his
relationship with his Anglican Church superiors sufficiently made up for
it. Even before they knew of Maturin's publications, they did not approve
of his "eccentricities," nor did they approve of his proclaimed religious
beliefs. Being Protestant did not automatically mean acceptance in the
small world of the Irish Anglican Church. Connections to those with influence often meant the difference between advancement and obscurity in
the church. When Maturin's father lost his influential government position,
any important church connections that he may have had to help his son
were also lost.[62] Maturin also had declared religious views that would have
been unpopular with church officials. He tells Scott in a letter written on
January 11, 1813: "I am a high Calvinist in my Religious opinions, and
therefore viewed with jealousy by Unitarian Brethren and Arminian [*sic*]
Masters."[63] Such a statement of beliefs would naturally concern his Anglican colleagues. John Calvin was a French reformer of the faith, and among
his beliefs was the separation of church and state. The Anglican Church
supported and served the monarch who headed it, not the other way around.

Scott advised "prudence upon your [Maturin's] part and candour and liberality on that of others might prevent their being an effectual bar to your promotion."[64] Scott continued by asking if the Bishop of Meath knew him because the bishop was a good friend of Scott's.

Harris relates that when Scott approached the Bishop of Meath on Maturin's behalf, he was unequivocally turned down: "With the religious tenets he [Maturin] professes he cannot look for preferment in the Church of England, nor ought he, in conscience, to seek employment in it, which he continues to do as a Curate."[65] Maturin was blithely unaware of the bishop's opinion of him since he enthusiastically responded to Scott's suggestion of writing the bishop on his behalf: "I had the honor of being in the Bishop of Meath's diocese for upwards of a year. He knows me well, and can and will I am convinced bear most favorable attestations to my Character, conduct and abilities—... there is no one to whom I would more readily appeal for a Confirmation of all I have presumed to say of myself."[66] Maturin's religious beliefs and their resulting conflict would manifest themselves in the pages of *Melmoth* and would serve to further support originality, Irish subject, and passion.

His superiors were obviously not pleased with him, but, instead of realizing this and tempering his behavior as Scott suggested, Maturin continued to be himself, which means he further alienated himself from the Anglican Church. As Harris reports, one of the main objections of the Church's officials was that Maturin liked to have a good time: "It has often been noted ... that his fondness for dancing, flamboyant clothes, heavy make-up for his wife, and an extravagant bohemian artiness when he was composing quelled his chances of receiving ecclesiastical elevation at the hands of his more conservative church superiors."[67] A clergyman should set an example for his parishioners, but even before his theater success, Maturin's example seemed to partake in more secular pleasures and attention-seeking behaviors than his superiors were willing to overlook. One of his obituaries focused on his "affectation and eccentricity" instead of his religious piety:

> Mr. Maturin was tall, slender, but well-proportioned, and, on the whole, a good figure, which he took care to display in a well-made black coat, tightly buttoned, and some odd light-coloured stocking-web pantaloons, surmounted in winter by a coat of prodigious dimensions, gracefully thrown on, so as not to obscure the symmetry it affected to protect. The Rev. Gentleman sang and danced, and prided himself on performing the movements and evolutions of the quadrille, certainly equal to any other divine of the Established Church, if not to any private lay gentleman of the three kingdoms. It often happened, too, that Mr. Maturin either labored under an attack of gout, or met with some accident, which compelled the use of a slipper or a bandage, on one foot or

one leg, and by an unaccountable congruity of mischances, he was uniformly compelled on these occasions to appear in the public thoroughfares of Dublin, where the melancholy spectacle of a beautiful limb in pain never failed to excite the sighs and sympathies of all the interesting persons who passed, as well as to prompt their curiosity to make audible remarks or inquiries respecting the possessor.[68]

Maturin's concern for appearances also extended to his wife, especially when they were entertaining. "His quadrille parties, where his accomplished and beautiful wife made so charming a hostess, were famous in Dublin, Henrietta Maturin was always dressed in the fashion, even to the extent of rouging. Though she disliked this last—for her unnecessary—practice, her husband insisted on it, and would often send her back to her room on the occasion of parties if he did not think that art had been sufficiently employed."[69]

More than one source observed that Maturin's literary success did not curtail these behaviors (considered "eccentric" by certain critics). The public and financial success of Maturin's play, *Bertram,* led to the inevitable collision between the worlds of the clergyman and the writer. The authorship of *Bertram* was much debated, as evidenced in this surprising firsthand account of a gentleman traveling from Oxford on June 3, 1816, sharing his coach with three other strangers, and participating in

a discussion on the passing events of the day ... a passing observation ... on the subject of the anonymous author of the tragedy Bertram, led to a discussion as to the merit of that celebrated performance, and the great mystery, which seemed to hang over its deserving author. Some one remarked, that he had heard it attributed to a Mr. Maturin; a gentleman, by my side, who hitherto had remained silent, assured him of the correctness of his information, as he himself, was that fortunate individual![70]

This anonymous anecdote supports the memory of a contemporary who knew Maturin, saying that he had to establish his authorship of *Bertram,* but it came with a price.

In 1816, partly in consequence of hearing that several persons were claiming the authorship of "Bertram," Maturin came to London, and from the obscurity and depression of his former life, was suddenly elevated to the most dizzy[ing] and flattering distinction. He was caressed by the first men of the day, recognized by the audience during the performance of his play, and received with acclamations, and in one brief month of brilliant applause, obtained the reward of years of neglect and anguish and distress.... His character, habits, and opinions seemed to undergo a total alteration. He returned to Ireland, gave up his tuitions, indulged in the intoxications of society, and became a man of fashion, living upon the fame of his genius.[71]

Like many people who experience sudden notoriety after toiling for years unnoticed, Maturin became a victim of his own success. As noted by Willem Scholten in *Charles Robert Maturin, Terror-Novelist,* "When he had money he did not always use it as a man in his circumstances should have done; his love of extravagance and display sometimes proved too strong for him."[72] *Bertram's* success definitely proved too strong for him. The unnamed biographer of the above "Recollections," who claimed to be a friend of Maturin's, pointed to this moment in time to be

> the commencement of that folly of which Maturin has been lavishly accused. Whatever might have been the levities of his conduct before, they now certainly became more remarkable ... he now became luxurious in his habits and manners. He was the first in the quadrille—the last to depart. The ball-room was his temple of inspiration and worship. So passionately attached was he to dancing, that he organized morning quadrille parties, which met alternately two or three days in the week at the houses of the favourite members of his coterie.... He was a perfect bigot in his attachment to female society; and generally restless and dissatisfied in the exclusive company of men.[73]

The criticism that emerged from *Bertram* and all subsequent romantic publications of Maturin's linked the content of the works to the character of the man. Maturin lost all hopes of receiving any promotion within the established church, as Idman explains: "The apparent incompatibility of the two [author and preacher] in Maturin's case was continually emphasized by hostile critics, and his eccentric habits, his connection with the theatre and his excessive fondness for dancing was more than the average mind could ever understand in one of his profession; to judge from certain utterances Maturin was, at least in the most rigorous-minded circles, actually considered more or less insane."[74]

The stories of his composing habits and speculations surrounding his death enhanced the perceptions of an unbalanced mind. Many sources tell that Maturin would stick a red wafer on his forehead to indicate to his family that he was writing and wished not to be disturbed. Others relay that he would paste his mouth shut when writing to prevent himself from taking part in conversation, claiming that he would not move to a quieter room because he needed the noise to compose. Idman is quick to offer an explanation for these reported habits, believing that Maturin performed them with less frequency than they were repeated among Dublin society:

> This [the wafer, the paste] ... might have happened once or twice and then been related at the tea-tables of Dublin as a token of the eccentricity of their literary curate. The story of the wafer seems to be contradicted, or at least greatly qualified, by the statements of some other writers. Carleton says that Maturin had composed the greatest part of his earlier romances at Marsh's library in St. Patrick's Close, "on a small plain deal desk, which he removed from place to place according as it suited his privacy or convenience"; and an intimate friend of his has said that he never worked on his two last novels except in the stillness of night, when there was consequently no fear of his being disturbed.[75]

This explanation seems much more likely when considering the following such moment of composition reportedly witnessed by an influential member of the church who visited Maturin with the intent of helping him gain a promotion while Maturin was in the midst of writing *Bertram*. This anecdote is still repeated almost 200 years later. Maturin kept the gentleman waiting for thirty minutes before finally greeting his well-meaning visitor.

> [Maturin] entered the room suddenly, reciting some rapturous passage—a part of the manuscript play in one hand, the pen in the other; his person attired in a theatrical morning-gown—his attitude that of an inspired *provisante*, his arms tossing, and his eyes strained, and thus continued his oration until he wound it up, by flinging himself on the sofa, beside the astonished minister. This unlucky interference of the ruling passion lost to poor Maturin whatever patronage or advantage might have been derived from the intended friendship of his visitor, whose nerves or habits were ill qualified for the grotesque exhibition presented by the Curate of St. Peter's.[76]

While Idman challenged the conclusion that these stories meant that the author was mad,[77] an unidentified friend of Maturin's recalled witnessing him write *Melmoth*:

> Returning late in the evening, it was then after a slight refreshment that his literary task commenced, and I have remained with him repeatedly ... till three in the morning, while he was composing his wild romance of "Melmoth." Moderate, and indeed abstemious in his appetites, human nature, and the over-busy and worked intellect, required support and stimulus, and brandy-and-water supplied to him the excitement that opium yields to others; but it had no intoxicating effect on him: its action was, if possible, more strange, and indeed terrible to witness. His mind travelling in the dark regions of romance, seemed altogether to have deserted the body, and left behind a mere physical organism; his long pale face acquired the appearance of a cast taken from the face of a dead body, and his large prominent eyes took a glassy look; so that when, at that witching hour, he suddenly, without speaking, raised himself and extended a thin and bony hand to grasp the silver branch with which he lighted me downstairs, I have often started, and gazed on him as a spectral illusion of his own creation.[78]

Maturin sounds like a man possessed by the Muse rather than merely inspired by it. This firsthand observation also supports one of Sharon Ragaz's conclusions after analyzing the correspondence between Maturin and his publisher, Archibald Constable: During the writing of *Melmoth*, "after a slow beginning, Maturin was writing compulsively."[79]

While some of Maturin's writing and recreational habits may not have been the best choices for his health or reputation, they are inadequate in proving an unbalanced mind. Maturin himself readily acknowledged that he enjoyed secular pursuits and never tried to deny it or preach in a "do-as-I-say-and-not-as-I-do" vein. In a sermon where he was trying to demonstrate the importance of making God a priority for parents in their children's education, he clarified, "Let me not be supposed here foolishly and fanatically to undervalue human learning and human advantages. No man prizes them more—perhaps too much."[80] Perhaps this is why his parishioners liked him so much; he was not perfect but he was genuine. It could also be why some of his religious colleagues were uneasy and why they felt the need to discredit him in the eyes of the public.

His detractors whispered the most damning rumor against Maturin's sanity in the stories surrounding his death, which imply that he committed suicide. In this time period, the social stigma surrounding even a rumor of suicide was tremendous, as described by Barbara Gates:

[S]uicide in nineteenth-century England was both illegal and touched with the taint of insanity. Until 1823 it was legally possible to bury suicides at a crossroads with a stake through the heart … civil law required not only ignominious burial but also forfeiture of personal and real property to the Crown…. [S]uicide was thought to be the one unrepentable crime against God, life being considered a commission from God and the taking of it God's prerogative only…. Thus suicide was a disgrace.[81]

By some, Maturin was considered insane, so for them it did not require a great leap of the imagination to believe that the author took his own life. At the time of his death, Maturin was ill, financially unsuccessful as a writer, held no expectations as a minister, and had a growing family to support. Maturin requested advances before *Women* (1818), his *Sermons* (1818), and *Melmoth* (1820) were published,[82] indicating his family's need for income. A person who met Maturin around this time, and who became a friend who would write affectionately about him after his death, remembers going to Maturin's home for the first time. He had expected to see a place that reflected the success and reputation of the writer but instead

my feet struck with a lonely sound on the naked flags of the hall, which was barely furnished with two chairs surmounted by his crest, a galloping horse; the stairs were without carpets. On entering the drawing room it almost appeared to be unfurnished. A simple drugget partly covered the floor, and a small table stood in the centre; but the entire end nearest the door was occupied by a divan covered with scarlet, which appeared strangely out of fashion with the general meagerness of the apartment; besides the folding doors was a square piano; at the fire was placed an old armchair in which I afterwards saw him sit for many a weary hour, till three or four o'clock in the morning, while writing the "Albigneses"; on a small work-table between the windows lay a very ancient writing-desk. Such was my first glimpse of the author's domicile, which had once been a witness of very different scenes.[83]

This is where Maturin apparently wrote *Melmoth*, but even the £500 he earned[84] did not ease his financial situation. The situation was so dire that Maturin wrote to the Royal Literary Fund on September 25, 1822, requesting financial assistance, which was granted, and again on October 23, 1823, requesting further help due to his ill health, also granted,[85] even though announcements of *The Albigenses'* November 1823 publication were appearing in literary notices.[86] Maturin's health continued to decline in 1824 but he persevered, as his final volume of sermons seemed to indicate.

The *Five Sermons on the Errors of the Roman Catholic Church* (1824) were published during the summer of 1824[87] and were preached during the prior Lenten season.[88] Maturin concluded Sermon III with a brief allusion to his health: "I had prepared more, much more matter on this subject, my brethren, but I feel myself actually unable to pursue it this night any further. On next Sunday evening I will, if health be spared, renew the subject."[89] A week later, at the end of Sermon IV, Maturin's health seemed to have taken such a serious turn that he felt the need to be more direct when he concluded: "Health long precarious, and now seriously impaired, compels me, not to decline, but to deter my task till I have recovered strength to pursue it; and should I do so, I here pledge myself to renew it with every power of mind and body that God has given me."[90] He sufficiently rallied to deliver a fifth sermon the following week.

Shortly after these sermons were published, Maturin received a visit from William Bewick (1795–1866), an artist who was then traveling through Ireland drawing portraits of many of the country's notable men and women, including Maturin. Bewick kept a journal of his travels where he detailed his impressions of these famous people. He wrote at length about Maturin.

The first remarkable Irishman whom I attempted to portray was the Rev. Charles Robert Maturin, the author of *Bertram, Melmoth, &c.* I had read his works, and was anxious to secure, not only a faithful likeness of him, but ... *the character of his mind,* as it might appear either in his general appearance, in particular configuration, or in his expression when excited by feeling or passion. And accordingly I tried to engage him, whilst he was sitting, in subjects analogous to his strange turn of mind, and to the gloomy tendency of his wild imagination.

From reading his works, and from what I had heard of the idiosyncracy of his very peculiar and original genius, I had formed in my own mind a vague but defined notion of what he was like.... What was my surprise and disappointment when, coming to him by appointment, I found him waiting for me dressed up for the occasion, a courteous and finished gentleman, pacing his drawing-room in elegant full dress, a splendidly bound book laid open upon a cambric pocket-handkerchief, laced round the edges and scented with *eau-de-Cologne,* and held upon both hands; a stylish new black wig curled over his temples, his shirt-collar reaching half-way up his face, and his attenuated cheeks rouged up to the eyes! It was a perfect *make-up,* and my chagrin was accordingly great.... I had expected that the author of *Melmoth* would have received me as an author in his true character; not in the elegance fit for a lady's boudoir, or with the etiquette of the court of George IV....

Before commencing the portrait, I explained to Mr. Maturin what it was I wished to obtain in the drawing,—that I only desired to represent his natural character, and to embody his mental traits. Upon which he seemed satisfied, and begged I would just do as I wished with him. Whereupon I began to disrobe him of his neckcloth and collar, and of every accessory likely to detract from his individual character ... [his family] all expressed their unbounded satisfaction at the perfect resemblance, and Mrs. Maturin was affected to tears; their beautiful daughter sympathizing with a grace and simplicity truly affecting. I was struck with the elegance of this family; while their appreciation, lively affection, and interest in Mr. Maturin, seemed to lend an additional charm to the peculiarities of a genius so original ... [he] begged to be allowed to present me with a copy of his *Five Sermons on the Errors of the Roman Catholic Church*, just published.[91]

Unfortunately, Bewick did not provide a precise date for his visit with Maturin but the early summer of 1824 is estimated since Maturin gave Bewick the "just-published" *Five Sermons*. Although the visit was a few months before Maturin's death, the only indication that he may not have been well during this portrait sitting was Bewick's use of "attenuated" in his description. Coincidentally, Bewick was visiting Scott when they both learned about Maturin's death on October 30, 1824, at his home on 41 York Street in Dublin at the age of forty-four.

The circumstances surrounding his death have been variously interpreted by both his contemporary and current biographers. Harris states: "While suffering from an ailment, he accidentally swallowed poison and died before help arrived. It is not, however, clear whether his death was the result 'of an apothecary's blunder' or his own carelessness in swallowing a 'bottle of embrocation' by mistake."[92] Idman does not readily place credence in tales that allude to suicide, though he falls short of supplying an alternate and more plausible explanation for these stories. Idman tactfully circumvents the notion of suicide, saying, "There was a story afloat of his having caused, or at least precipitate, his death by some mistake about his medication; however this may have been, it is evident ... that the case was sufficiently alarming some four weeks before."[93] While Harris suggests there is a real possibility that Maturin was in some way responsible for his own death, Idman's defense of this interpretation is that Maturin was a very sick man who was not expected to live, so how he died was not as important as the fact that, inevitably, Maturin was going to die soon. Several obituaries appeared after his death and although all agreed that Maturin had died after a lengthy illness, none say that he committed suicide. The death notice in the *Liverpool Mercury* on November 12, 1824, is a typical example:

On Saturday, the 30th ult. In Dublin, after a protracted illness, the Rev. R. C. [*sic*] Maturin, A. M. curate of St. Peter's, and author of the celebrated tragedy entitles "Bertram," and several novels. The immediate cause of Mr. Maturin's death was, we understand, his having taken a lotion [*sic*], containing a large quantity of laudanum, in mistake for medicine intended for the stomach.[94]

Other death notices that mention the cause of Maturin's death essentially state the same information. Almost seventy years later, the story that was apparently passed down through the family adds a little more detail: "He was said to have injured his health, never very robust, some time before [his death] by swallowing a bottle of embrocation by mistake during the night for his medicine. He took the prospect of dying perfectly calmly, and appeared disappointed that the poison did not take effect, as he had already summoned his family and made final farewells."[95] Only the theatrically dramatic Maturin would be disappointed that he did not promptly expire after saying his final farewells to his family.

Maturin's wife, Henrietta, appeared not to have much time to indulge in grief, instead writing letters to those who knew him. Bewick recalls showing Scott the portrait that he drew of Maturin,[96] which naturally prompted a discussion about the author. "A few mornings after this conversation I received a note from Mrs. Maturin informing me in the most affectionate and touching language of the death of her husband, and begging me to let her have the drawing I had made but a short time before of him, it being the most faithful and characteristic likeness ever made of him.... I readily made a copy, and sent it to her; Sir Walter enclosing a five-pound note in the letter I sent in answer to Mrs. Maturin."[97]

Bewick does not include the date or the specific contents of Henrietta's letter but, in a letter to Sir Walter Scott on November 11, 1824, twelve days after Maturin died, she gives some further insight into her husband's death: "He has left me with four children, the youngest of whom is only five years old, totally unprovided for—he laboured with incessant assiduity for his family even after it had pleased the Almighty to deprive him of health—his sufferings with regard to pecuniary circumstances preyed on a constitution naturally delicate, till at last it put a period to his existence."[98] Her letter continues by telling Scott that a subscription for the benefit of the family had been initiated by the pastor of St. Patrick's, and she requests his assistance to initiate one in Scotland for the same purpose.[99] Before even writing to Scott of Maturin's death, Henrietta first sent a letter to the Royal Literary Fund on November 3, requesting their financial assistance.[100] Maturin apparently left his family with nothing but financial concerns.

Maturin suffered many misfortunes, and "melancholy" is frequently a word that appeared when his contemporaries described him. Lord Norbury reportedly told Bewick: "That Maturin, poor devil! Is a moody dog; I never can raise a smile in him, and I suppose, he never could laugh in his life except perhaps it might be at that scarlet dame of Rome whom he hacks and tears at with such seriousness and power."[101] One particular friend recalled that "[t]here was in him a strange vacillation of temperament between gaiety and gloom," followed by a conversational recollection that the writer included in his biographical sketch: "[Maturin] once arguing that suicide was not positively and expressly condemned in any passage of Scripture, and declaring, that he conceived to pass away from the sorrows of earth to the peace of eternity, by reposing on a bed of eastern poppy flowers, where sleep is death, would be the most enviable mode of earthly exit; but this he uttered altogether as a doctrine of opinion, and not of purpose."[102]

It is a curious conversation to report, unless the writer was trying to find a way to inform his readers that Maturin did not purposely take his own life. It is difficult to believe that he committed suicide for several reasons. A man who continued to strive to support his family would be unlikely to kill himself, leaving his beloved family not only unprovided for but the open targets of scandal and rumor since he personally knew the effects of scandal from the circumstances surrounding his father's dismissal; his personal pride would not have permitted it. His parish and his plans to write a sequel to *Melmoth* were further motivations to fight for health.

Finally, his deep and sincere religious beliefs would have prevented him from taking his own life. He did not compromise his beliefs when it meant the possibility of greater social and financial status for his family in the form of promotion within the church, so he would not have dismissed them when eternity was on the line. Evidence from his sermons support this point. During the sermon for his niece, Susan Lea who died at the age of eighteen, he talked about her hope and faith as her health continued to deteriorate.

> I saw her suffer—I saw her die. She lingered through two whole years of torture unexampled and unmitigated. I often saw her lip turn white with agony—I never saw it quiver with a murmur. Her youth struggled hard with death, and her friends clung to hope, while there was a hope to cling to. While she could yet walk, she frequented the house of God: when she could no longer do so, she worshipped him from her bed of suffering. Hope and faith were with her there, and her charity "never failed": her last action was to press with her cold hand into mine her accustomed ample bounty to the poor.[103]

As a minister, this was not the first or last time that Maturin attended someone on their deathbed. While the exact nature of Maturin's illness was unclear, the extent of his niece's suffering is not; even so, she did not despair. Maturin not only witnessed the suffering of this world, but he also experienced some of it. It is what made him such an eloquent preacher, especially when he talked about eternal salvation. In his sermon entitled "Preached on the Sunday After the Death of the Princess Charlotte," he asked: "What is life? A dream to the weak, a jest to the wise, a thing that we struggle with, submit to, groan under, laugh at—a mixture of misery and madness! Life—what is life?" and continued by describing the great joy of eternity.[104] At the end of this rhapsody about eternity, Maturin quite carefully and deliberately stressed the following point: "There is then a pleasure that earth cannot give. Of such a nature be our portion: Oh, that it may! *But no human hand must draw the veil: there is a hand approaching that soon will unclose it to all* (emphasis mine)."[105] Maturin wanted his congregation to understand that no matter how great one's suffering becomes, it is only God who may decide to end a person's suffering by ending his or her life. Maturin exhibited too much of a love for God, for family, for life, and for social position to kill himself.

This extensive review of his life reveals a paradox within the man, though one not difficult to understand. Maturin was passionately devoted to his family, his faith, his congregation, his writing, and his dancing. He also was the favored oldest son of indulgent parents who had means. He had a lifestyle and social position to maintain, one with the advantages he wanted his wife and children to have. What stood in his way was an inability to pretend to be someone whom he was not. "He was a complicated nature, and there was—though certainly much exaggerated by tradition—another side of his character, vain, pleasure-loving and extravagant."[106] His dancing was an "escape from the melancholy that also was a constituent part of his mind."[107] Maturin suffered from some unidentifiable ailment that he coped with perhaps his entire life. His illness may have given him a deeper appreciation for life, and when he was well, he celebrated. He may have been aware that his illness would not permit him to live to see his grandchildren, so he did not allow social conventions to restrict his behavior in any way. He pushed himself much harder to provide for his family so they would have something when he died, and, even though he wrote primarily for income, writing was also his attempt at fame and immortality. With *Melmoth* he created a novel that would directly change the Gothic genre and influence future Irish writers in creating the Irish vampire. He may not have been aware of the literary impact that *Melmoth* would have, but he transformed the solitary act of writing into an event on more than one occasion.

A man so difficult to fathom would naturally write in a complex fashion, which is a significant contributing factor to the originality of Maturin's work. He may not seem original, however, because, as Harris writes in his biography of Maturin, he had a tremendous ability to assimilate the works of others. These influences—termed plagiarism by some critics—regularly appear in the critical reviews of *Melmoth* when it was first published: "Its [*Melmoth*'s] merit is not in the idea, which is compounded from the St. Leon of [William] Godwin and the infernal machinery of [Matthew "Monk"] Lewis"[108]; "The novel is not taken from any sermon, but from the Faustus of Goethe" and Christopher Marlowe's *The Tragical Historie of Doctor Faustus*[109]; and "Melmoth ... wants originality. It frequently and fatally reminds the reader of St. Leon; and is a compound of the legend of the Wandering Jew, and the Vampyre."[110]

Maturin was extremely well-read and could easily recall what he read, evidenced by the numerous literary allusions in his correspondence with Scott. His anonymous friend and biographer in the *New Monthly Magazine and Literary Journal* explained instances of similarity with present and past authors: "Whatever Maturin read, contributed something to his stock of acquirements, but nothing in a regular or useful order: all was accidental, occasional, scattered,—but from the vast mass of materials thus collected, he was able to produce works at once systematic and imaginative."[111] "Like Rousseau, who was in love with the last petticoat he saw until he had seen another, Maturin unconsciously adopted something of the last book he read until its recollection was obliterated by the next."[112] *Melmoth* was no exception to this composition method.

Maturin's seeming lack of originality is not surprising since his primary reason for writing was to make money to support his family, a motivation that he made known in the prefaces to his novels, in his correspondence, and more than likely in his conversation. Given his education, family background, and overall health, there were few options open for an educated gentleman to pursue at this time. Imitating the best-sellers of the day and having Sir Walter Scott as a mentor and friend were logical avenues to pursue, and Maturin enjoyed the work. "It must be admitted that other and less objectionable modes of literary exertion were open to him, but there were none so easy to access, and so quickly profitable, as that which he embraced ... he was obliged to be popular in the form and matter of his writings and it must be confessed, his own inclination never rebelled against that obligation."[113] Publishing under the pseudonym of Dennis Jasper Murphy was also prudent. Maturin really did not want conflict with church officials but was forced to reveal his identity or risk losing credit for his works.

Maturin's foray into the theater proved profitable with his first play, *Bertram* (1815), but not with the subsequent attempts of *Manuel* (1817) and *Fredolfo* (1819). The plays were a source of controversy in their content and authorship. His religious colleagues and conservative critics had a difficult time accepting that plays with questionable morality and ethics could—or should—be written by a clergyman. They further questioned the morals of a minister who associated with the likes found in the theater. It was acceptable to sermonize about the sinners, but not to directly socialize with them. In addition to these judgmental accusations, Maturin had to further contend with biased theatrical reviews. Samuel Taylor Coleridge wrote a scathing review of *Bertram* in 1817 which was influenced more by his own play being rejected in favor of Maturin's than any shortcomings of *Bertram*. Although Maturin was aware of Coleridge's review and wanted to return the favor in his preface to *Women*, Scott wisely advised against it, and Maturin listened.[114]

It was not Coleridge, though, who brought his brief theater career to an end. After the failure of *Fredolfo*, Maturin ceased writing plays and returned to novels for monetary reasons. By this time his family desperately needed money, so his novel-writing was spurred by the need to maintain his family rather than the leisurely pursuit of a gentleman. *Melmoth* was written out of necessity for Maturin; the advance he received for it through Scott's influence was needed to meet the basic necessities of his family. It is ironic that a novel written under such duress would become so influential. Even when *Melmoth* first appeared, it received extensive critical attention. Harris summarizes the flurry of criticism that followed its appearance:

> [T]he work was condemned when it was first published in 1820, mainly on the same ground that the author's works had been criticized: it was grotesque, yet frivolous; it was immoral, yet preachy; it was a mere copy of the German romances, yet too daringly original; it was stupidly simple, yet structurally overcomplicated. The fact that *Melmoth* appeared after the Gothic vogue had faded made it an immediate and almost inevitable target of those reviewers who confused momentary taste with enduring value.[115]

Some of his severest critics focused their objections on the immorality of the text, and the fear that it could inspire some of the more morally weak readers to "mischief."[116] Some of these areas that could be dangerous to the impressionable mind were "the propriety of venting vollies of infidelity without their accompanying antidotes of sound reasoning," "frequent use, or rather abuse, of sacred names and things,"[117] and blasphemy, brutality, and obscenity.[118] Others did not like the character of John Melmoth and what he specifically represented: "There are some subjects too sacred, and some too accursed, for familiarity. The name before which the world bends, and the name at which the world shudders, are not the legitimate topics of romance."[119] These critics overlooked the fact that Melmoth consistently fails in his efforts to tempt any of the characters. All hold steadfastly to their beliefs, even when it means they may die as a result. For all his scheming,

Melmoth is severely punished for his devil-dealings. Those who criticized the lack of a moral in *Melmoth* were so caught up in underscoring the offensive words, sentences, or passages that they not only missed Maturin's obvious message but also completely failed to see how the novel could serve as an extended parable reminiscent of the Book of Job.

To appreciate the instructive value of the story, one would have to look beyond some of the obvious elements that could prove problematic for the religiously inclined. *Melmoth the Wanderer* is a deeply disturbing novel in many places. It contains graphic scenes of physical and mental brutality; however, and perhaps what provoked the negative responses from the clergy and critics, the novel also presents a clear critique of many aspects of society that would have preferred to avoid scrutiny. *Melmoth* does not flatter family (particularly parents), Catholics, Jews, Protestants, the Irish, the English, the Spanish, or really just about anyone. This novel, which Maturin said began as an extension of one of his sermons, soon extended beyond its inspired origin as it twisted and turned its way toward completion and Melmoth's inevitable damnation.

Maturin prefaces his novel with the quotation from the sermon that provided the inspiration for the work. "At this moment is there one of us present, however we may have departed from the Lord, disobeyed his will, and disregarded his word—is there one of us who would, at this moment, accept all that man could bestow, or earth afford, to resign the hope of his salvation?—No, there is not one—not such a fool on earth, were the enemy of mankind to traverse it with the offer!"[120]

Coincidentally, this excerpt was taken from the sermon "Preached on the Sunday After the Death of the Princess Charlotte," in which Maturin addressed suicide. If those who so obsessively combed through *Melmoth* to document each word that offended their high moral sensibilities had taken the same care in reading his *Sermons*, they would have seen that the novel addressed various aspects of Maturin's collected sermons and served as a fictionalized presentation of serious topics of faith. The *Sermons* serve to frame the tales rather than just the brief excerpt Maturin chose to highlight in his preface.

From the moment his novel begins, Maturin contradicts his assertion from the pulpit. Yes, such a fool does exist—and he is none other than an Anglo-Irish landlord. John Melmoth did exactly what Maturin claimed no one would ever consider: he sold his soul and his salvation for 150 years of life on earth. Melmoth's only escape from this agreement is to convince someone else to take his place; at least, that is what Melmoth believes. In the time he has, the novel records his temptation of five people but all are repulsed by the offer. He leads them to misery on earth, but they die with their souls intact.

This brief summary of the novel demonstrates a surprising lack of success on Melmoth's part to corrupt anyone. It is the character's failure that was noted by Edgar Allan Poe, who analyzed Maturin's originality. Poe commented on Melmoth in his introductory "Letter to Mr.—" *Poems* (1831), which critiqued poetry both past and present. He talked about poets' claim to instruct their readers "with eternity in view"[121] yet their poetry is "professedly to be understood by the few, and it is the many who stand in need of salvation. In such case I should no doubt be tempted to think of the devil in Melmoth, who labors indefatigably, through three octovo volumes, to accomplish the destruction of one or two souls, while any common devil would have demolished one or two thousand."[122] Poe brings up a very interesting, though inaccurate, point. First, Melmoth is not any ordinary devil. He is still a man, and his humanity is his greatest obstacle. His passion for knowledge originally led him into his predicament, and that same passion keeps him from demolishing one or two thousand souls. Melmoth obsessively pursues one target at a time. He spends years studying his subjects before even making an appearance. He singles out those who are in the worst of circumstances, believing that they will be the most vulnerable to the bargain. When they refuse, he makes life even worse for them but, still, they do not waver, even as he becomes the driving force that leads to their destructions and sometimes even deaths. He is an unusually committed but not very successful minion of Satan.

The second point for the novel's defense in response to Poe's criticism is that, for all its morbid imagery and devilish dealings, the novel strikes an unexpected note of hope. No one would expect to encounter hope in a Gothic work written by a man who was experiencing terrible physical, professional, and financial hardships. But none of Melmoth's victims finds their situations so horrific that they give up on God.

> [Show] me a being crushed to the earth under all the accumulated evils of nature and fortune, one whom the rising sun wakens to the light up to suffer, and on whom it sets without bringing him the hope of rest, one whom the world has never regarded but with the averted eye of scorn or of hatred; and that being is blessed,—blessed above the lot of mankind,—if God is the stay of his heart, and the consoler of his sorrows.[123]

Like Job, the worse life becomes, the more tenaciously they grip their faith. Some of the characters even die rather than lose their souls. Actually, it seems that Poe made an error in his statement, since Melmoth fails to destroy any soul but his own. It is Melmoth's human failings, not God's failing, which leads to Melmoth's ultimate destruction. All Melmoth had to do was turn to God, as all his potential victims do, and he would have been saved.

Despite this spiritual message, there does not seem to be anything remarkable about a character who fails so miserably at his task appearing in a genre which was well past its prime when the novel was written. Maturin, however, managed to introduce several innovative ideas into a genre that was suffering from stock characters and predictable plots. There are few Gothic writers who stand out aside from Horace Walpole, Ann Radcliffe, and Matthew "Monk" Lewis, writers associated with the Gothic in the eighteenth century. All were English, and Maturin learned from them. In particular, Maturin learned from Radcliffe and Lewis, who published some of the most notable Gothic literature at the height of the genre's popularity. Radcliffe's *The Mysteries of Udolpho* (1794) and Lewis's *The Monk* (1796) exemplify what would later be identified as standard characteristics of the Gothic novel. David Punter highlights the contributions of each writer in *The Literature of Terror: the Gothic Tradition*. Radcliffe excelled in "character psychology, symbolic intensification, and an extraordinary use of suspense and doubt which constantly blurs the boundaries of reality and fantasy."[124] She pursued a single storyline from beginning to end that featured a "highly conventional eighteenth-century heroine" and "attractively cruel villain."[125] On the other hand, Lewis's novel is "two stories in one, and although there seems little narrative connection between them, their co-presence allows Lewis scope for the dramatic alterations which give the book a pace and energy quite foreign to the languorous, opiated mood of Radcliffe."[126] Lewis's story was classified as much more shocking than Radcliffe's. Despite these essential differences, Punter adds that both writers drew upon their extensive prior reading of literature for frequent allusion, inspiration, and inclusion.

Maturin shared in the literary background of Radcliffe and Lewis and included their works in his own vast repository of inspiration. Evidence of Radcliffe's use of the psychological, combined with Lewis's seemingly unrelated stories and shocking content, are readily and regularly apparent in *Melmoth*. In addition to their influences on *Melmoth*, a variety of others appear from an array of texts. As frequently noted by his contemporary and current critics, he borrowed from the literature at hand, but synthesized it in a way that made it his own, and he was consciously doing this as he explained in a letter to Scott early in 1813: "[The] tales of superstition were always my favorites, I have in fact been always more conversant with the visions of another world, than the realities of this, and in my Romance I have determined to display all by *diabolical* resources, out–Herod all the

Herods of the German school, and get the possession of the Magic lamp with all its slaves from the Conjurer [Matthew] *Lewis* himself."[127]

Although Maturin was not referring to *Melmoth* in this letter, he adhered to the same goals and methods while writing the novel, and although its contents were derived from a diverse array of famous characters, the final work emerged as an original. To achieve this, Maturin freely borrowed material from predecessors and contemporaries. He recycled the literary material of Radcliffe and Lewis as he "lifts names from *The Italian* and from Lewis's *Alfonso*, and throws off casual reference to vampires and the Black Mass."[128] He also mined older texts. Critics such as Muriel E. Hammond, Veronica M. S. Kennedy, Dale Kramer, David Punter, Richard Davenport-Hines, and Fred Botting have all discussed the Faust-Mephistopheles influence on Maturin's creation of Melmoth. Mephistopheles is the tempter, Satan's minion sent to lead Faust down the gently sloping path to damnation. As depicted not only by Marlowe but Goethe, Mephistopheles is quite devious in his purpose and achieves his goal. Faust desires all that Mephistopheles has to offer and does not seem too nervous that the price is his soul. However, Faust frequently dawdles and retreats on the path he claims to desire. This causes Mephistopheles to often retrace his steps, grab Faust by the collar, and drag him back onto the road to perdition. Melmoth, "a strange indefinable being—something between a Faustus and a Mephistopheles,"[129] fuses the qualities of both Mephistopheles and Faust. The combination does not make him a skilled tempter like Mephistopheles, since he retains the conscience of a man like Faust, but it is an original twist on two very familiar characters. This combination leads to conflict arising between his role as tempter and man and is most apparent in "The Tale of the Indians," where Melmoth tries to tempt Immalee/Isidora to take his place. He unfortunately falls in love with her, which complicates matters. He alternately tries to save and to seduce her, but, as Maturin himself declared in one of his sermons, "You cannot—no, you cannot point her with one hand to eternal life, and with the other drag her to perdition."[130] Melmoth succeeds in his seduction but, despite her love for him, she will not give up her salvation.

Faust and Mephistopheles are not the only earlier literary characters echoed in Maturin's work. Idman observes that Melmoth's death was inspired by John Polidori's *The Vampyre*,[131] which is further expanded upon by Dale Kramer.

While most of Melmoth's qualities derive from religious folklore, it appears that Maturin was directly energized in several of his tales by Polidori's *The Vampyre* which appeared in 1819. This story of a monster who sucks the blood of his victims to sustain his own perternatural immortality is an analogue to the Faust-Mephistopheles and Wandering Jew legends, though its basis is in East European folklore. Several of the vampire's adventures, covered in a sentence or two in the brief story by Polidori, are turned into motifs or short tales by Maturin.[132]

Maturin even utilized Polidori's tale for a physical description of Melmoth, as Veronica Kennedy explains: "The Wanderer has magnetic, blazing eyes … a fatal hypnotic power in the eyes is like that traditionally ascribed to the vampire; Polidori's Ruthven … has this quality."[133] Melmoth's predatory techniques also echo Ruthven. Both are outside observers who take time to stalk their victims to gather information and plan their destruction; however, Ruthven succeeds where Melmoth does not.

The list of Maturin's literary influences could go on for pages, since he was a voracious reader with diverse tastes. Everything from Irish folklore to Nordic myth has been identified as an influence on *Melmoth*. Kennedy provides a thorough list of the influences most often noted surrounding all the characters in the novel:

Melmoth the Wanderer himself includes touches of Zeus the Thunderer, Prometheus, the Satan of *Paradise Lost* and the Devil of folktales, of the German Faust of tradition as well as the Faustus of Marlowe and the Faust of Goethe, of the Wandering Jew, of the Biblical and the Byronic Cain, of the Byronic heroes—Lara, Manfred, and the Giaour—of Mephistopheles, of Vathek, of Ruthven, of the *Bonhomme Miser* of French folklore, of Celtic wizards, druids and demons, of the amourous and evil Genii of the *Arabian Nights*, of Don Juan and the Demon Lovers of ballad tradition as well as the hero-villains of such "Gothick" writers as Anne Radcliffe and M. G. Lewis. Similarly, Immalee-Isadora is at once the Noble Savage of Rousseau, Eve before the Fall, Goethe's Gretchen, Melmoth's Good Angel, the Great Mother goddess in her bridal aspect, and Ideal Beauty.[134]

Amy Elizabeth Smith further adds Denis Diderot's *La Religieuse* (1796) to this extensive list, explaining that the "Tale of the Spaniard" was essentially "borrowed" from this text.[135] Clearly, Maturin's ability to synthesize so many elements from such an array of literature is one reason *Melmoth the Wanderer* is more than a byproduct of the early nineteenth-century popular press. Its characters strike a chord of universality, as can be seen in Maturin's use of the "Wanderer" aspect of Melmoth's character. Bruce McClelland in his discussion of the vampire observes that: "the vampire is someone known in the community, even if not a resident ('wanderers' often being suspicious)."[136] The Wanderer is universally recognized, suspected, and feared; John Melmoth is not merely an Anglo-Irish landlord who sold his soul for a century and a half more of life. He has become part of the myths and archetypes from which he was created, the new mythology of the Irish vampire. Kennedy explains that Melmoth symbolizes the longing of man for knowledge, for power, for longevity—the longing to surpass the ordinary powers and status of man. He unites in one figure the Sage, the Tempter, the Lover, and the Magus. He is the Dark Hero but he is also a kind of superhuman being with Promethean qualities. He has some of the fatal interest of Lucifer, the charm of the damned and reckless soul, the fascination of the magnificently evil figure. He is truly the symbol of those larger aspirations of man that so often lead him to destruction, but might so easily lead him to glory ... child and adult, innocent and guilty, pursued and pursuer.[137]

Maturin's merging and subsequent reinterpretation of archetypes allowed him to revise the familiar Gothic themes and formulas to create a story and a character not previously seen in the genre, which supports the case for his originality and the Irish vampire. Despite the many faults recorded by his contemporary critics, they could not refrain from using words like "original," "genius," and "imaginative" when critiquing the novel. A reviewer from *Blackwood's Edinburgh Magazine* began his critique by saying that in *Melmoth* Maturin "has been contented with copying the worst faults of his predecessors and contemporaries in the commonest walks of fictitious writing" but two sentences later asks:

> And yet, where is the lover of imaginative excitement, that ever laid down one of his books unfinished—or the man of candour and discrimination, who ever denied, after reading through any one of them, that Maturin is gifted with a genius as fervently powerful as it is distinctly original—that there is ever and anon a truth of true poetry diffused over the thickest chaos of his absurdities—and that he walks almost without a rival, dead or living, in many of the darkest, but, at the same time, the most majestic circles of romance?[138]

Part of Maturin's originality was his ability to combine and rework existing myths; however, this may also seem to argue against another criterion: the use of Irish subjects. But Maturin does not disappoint. As Idman notes in his work, there are Irish subject connections:

> The works of Maturin demonstrate sufficiently that he was an ardent Irish nationalist who resented the Union; but he was, by temperament, nothing of a politician, and none of the family seem to have been involved in any political intrigues. There was, however, another side of nationalism—closely connected with the romantic movement in all countries—which he eagerly embraced. It expressed itself in an interest in the folklore, antiquities and early history of Ireland.[139]

By including a variety of archetypes, Maturin had purposely or inadvertently utilized elements of some very old Celtic folk beliefs and tales that formed a part of his interests.

One excellent example of this is pointed out by Jim Kelly when he talks about the depiction of Biddy Brannigan, a sort of Irish wise woman practitioner of folk arts, who is introduced at the beginning of *Melmoth*. After quoting her description and diverse resume, Kelly states: "It is the longest sustained description of folk superstitions that is given in Maturin's works."[140] He then adds that nearly the entire list is "a straightforward prose rendition of folk customs mentioned in Robert Burns' poem 'Halloween.'"[141] At first the further evidence of Maturin's plagiarizing proclivities do not seem to offer evidence of Irish subjects but when the *Melmoth*'s explanatory notes for those customs are reviewed, they not only credit Burns's poem but also say they "were commonly practiced among the peasantry of Scotland as well as of Ireland."[142]

Kelly presents additional evidence for Maturin's use of Irish subjects using Brannigan when he points out her role as a storyteller. "Brannigan provides the first and in some respects the most important account of Melmoth in which his relation to the Cromwellian plantation is sketched out, as well indicating his supernatural status."[143] While Kelly does not use this information in a discussion of Irish subjects, his observation assigns a place of distinction to Brannigan as an Irish storyteller:

> Story-telling has always been a favorite amusement of the Celtic race. In ancient times the professional story-tellers were classified, and were called, according to their rank, ollaves, shannachies, files, or bards. Their duty was to recite old tales, poems, and descriptions of historical events in prose or verse at the festive gatherings of the people. They were especially educated and trained for this profession, which was looked upon as a dignified and important one, and they were treated with consideration and amply rewarded wherever they went.[144]

Brannigan is the keeper and conveyor of oral tradition, giving her account of Melmoth more authority than the written and eyewitness stories that will appear later because her position carries the weight of centuries of tradition, inherent in the role of the Irish storyteller.

Among an Irish storyteller's repertoire of history and myth were stories of the powerful fairies and the wizards. One particular class of solitary fairies exhibits a connection to Melmoth's dilemma, the Leanhaun Shee: "This spirit seeks the love of men ... if they consent, they are hers, and can only escape by finding one to take their place ... [and death did not release them from the bargain; she] carried them away to other worlds, for death does not destroy her power."[145] Although Melmoth's motivation does not come from love for a beautiful woman, the solution to his problem is likewise to find a replacement for himself or he will also face being taken away to another world. Melmoth's motivation is similar to the stories of Irish wizards who possess power, knowledge, and immortality, which not only has direct parallels to Faust but also the vampire legend. According to Curran, the tale of the wizard/chieftain Abhartach has the distinction of being "the oldest recorded vampire [and the] story comes from Ireland."[146] Curran also provided stories of other vampiric characters in Irish folklore who share some interesting characteristics. The stories "are strongly linked to local Irish aristocracy."[147] Maturin's title character, John Melmoth, is from a local aristocratic family.

The folklore connections also overlap with the historical ones. Within the first chapter of *Melmoth*, the portrait of J. Melmoth (1646) appears with an ominous declaration from the current and dying owner of the estate. He says that the J. Melmoth who sat for that portrait in 1646 is still alive in 1816. The dying man's skeptical nephew is unnerved to glimpse "the living original of the portrait"[148] looking in on the room of the dying man. The young heir sends for Biddy Brannigan and an "odd story in the family"[149] soon comes to light.

> The first of the Melmoths ... who settled in Ireland was an officer in Cromwell's army, who obtained a grant of lands, the confiscated property of an Irish family attached to the royal cause. The elder brother of this man was one who had travelled abroad, and resided so long on the Continent, that his family had lost all recollection of him. Their memory was not stimulated by their affection, for there were strange reports concerning the traveller. He was said to be (like the "damned magician, great Glendower"), a gentleman profited in strange concealments.[150]

John Melmoth's family is directly connected to Cromwell, which, as far as Irish history is concerned, is equivalent to being in league with Satan himself. Given the association, it is not surprising to discover that the mysterious ancestor from the portrait was always seen in Ireland when a family member was on the verge of death, rather like the appearance of the banshee in Irish folklore to announce the death of a member of a prominent Irish family; Melmoth just accomplishes it with a lot less screaming. He is the man in the portrait who never aged, "was never heard to speak, seen to partake of food, or known to enter any dwelling but that of his family."[151] Such characteristics were also associated with the vampire myth. Accidentally or otherwise, Maturin synthesized Irish folklore into his work and effectively connected it to Gothic tradition.

Ironically, he furthered the Irish connection by continuing to work within the Gothic tradition, utilizing other standard Gothic devices but, again, achieving a different result. Two very recognizable Gothic motifs that Maturin extensively used are the Catholic Church and the theme of "sins of the father." Both are well-worn conventions of Gothic writing, but Maturin recasts them with originality. The story of the Moncada family is an excellent example of Maturin using these two themes. Alonzo Moncada is the oldest child of a Spanish, Catholic noble family. Usually, this is an enviable position, but not in Alonzo's case. He is not even twelve years old when his parents and their religious director earnestly try to convince him to join the monastery despite the fact that Alonzo has a younger brother for whom a religious vocation would be more suitable. Alonzo steadfastly resists the idea even after his father says, "Be reconciled, my child, to the will of Heaven and your parents, which you may insult, but cannot violate."[152] It is not until his mother reveals the shameful secret of his birth that Alonzo begins to understand his situation. He was conceived before his parents married. "[Y]ou are illegitimate,—your brother is not; and your intrusion into your father's house is not only its disgrace, but a perpetual monitor of that crime which it aggravates without solving,"[153] his mother states. Despite the facts that Alonzo's biological father is his present father, he is acknowledged by his paternal grandfather and accepted into the family home, and the specific date of his parents' marriage is not publicly known, his mother and father are convinced by the family's religious director that someone must pay for this abomination before the Lord. Alonzo's mother finally convinces her son by skillfully adding guilt to his shock:

> "Yes, my life; beyond the day that your inflexibility exposes me to infamy, I will not live. If you have resolution, I have resolution too; nor do I dread the result, for God will charge on your soul, not on mine, the crime an unnatural child has forced me to—and yet you will not yield—Well, then, the prostration of my body is nothing to that prostration of soul you have already driven me to."[154]

For an Anglican minister, Maturin exhibits a masterful understanding of Catholic guilt as can only be meted out by a devoted mother. Not surprisingly, Alonzo enters the monastery. His life takes the expected descent that only the forced monastic life among hypocritical clergy can take. Alonzo quickly realizes that "to enroll a son of the first house of Spain among their converts, or to imprison him as a madman, or to exorcise him as a demonic, was all the same to them."[155] Alonzo's tragedy culminates in his attempt to escape from the monastery through the aid of his brother, Juan. A bribed monk leads Alonzo out, but then murders Juan and returns Alonzo to the monastery.

The Catholic Church has few redeeming qualities, as portrayed in *Melmoth the Wanderer*. It is shown as superstitious in the novel's opening scenes with the Irish servants; malicious, greedy, and warped in Moncada's story of forced entry into monastic life; brutal in the Inquisition scenes; and comically absurd in the scenes with Donna Clara and Fr. Jose. Maturin closely knits the Catholic Church with the families his tales revolve around. The theme of "sins of the father" weighs heavily on the families, beginning with the Melmoths. The Melmoths' original sin was their association with Cromwell and participation in the destruction inflicted upon Ireland during his campaign. Even though the family is Protestant, guilt and penance are inescapable in Catholic Ireland. Melmoth haunts his family through the generations by appearing as they are on the verge of death and serving as a reminder of the family's guilt in Cromwell's campaign. He also torments and ultimately punishes himself because he cannot transfer his guilt to anyone else. The Catholic Church's solution for the guilt engendered by these sins is to exploit the wealth of the family; and, to be sure that the family's fortune is funneled into the Church coffers, the children are used to atone for the sin. As Diane D'Amico explains in her essay on Maturin's characters: "Maturin underscores his theme of inherited sin by depicting weak and ineffective parents whose children suffer as a consequence."[156] For Maturin, this portrayal has added significance given his previously discussed family history, his position as an Anglican minister, and his uncertain place in Irish society. Margot Gayle Backus explores this idea about *Melmoth* in *The Gothic Family Romance: Heterosexuality, Child Sacrifice, and the Anglo-Irish Colonial Order*: "In the novel's notoriously labyrinthe interior narratives, a series of children are sacrificed by their parents in the name of a variety of religious ideologies."[157] Backus goes on to list numerous instances in the novel where not only Catholic but Protestant and East Indian parents "sacrifice" their children to benefit some social or religious convention.

Interestingly enough, Maturin seems to address this idea in his sermon, "Necessity of Female Education": "Such is the fate of woman in countries where all the attention of man is given to their own indulgence—where woman, a dazzling victim, is arrayed and instructed in all that can dazzle the senses, and then led, a lovely, intoxicated victim, to the altar of sensuality, and sacrificed forever."[158] While the main point of this sermon is the importance of the religious education of girls because as women they are a vital part of nation, society, and the home, Maturin is stressing a Christian education and makes it a point to separate the benefits of a *Christian* education from a *Catholic* one: "Ay, and in such direct proportion to each other are the religion of the Gospel and the emancipation of the female sex, that their liberty is precisely varied according as the light of that religion is more or less obscure in the various countries of Europe. The women in the south of Europe are scarce better than their neighbors of the haram."[159] Maturin hardly needed to add Catholic Ireland to the list; it would have been readily understood by his audience. His depiction of Immalee/Isidora's return home to her Catholic family forcing her into an arranged marriage and then becoming a victim of the Inquisition vividly illustrates Maturin's feelings on the destructive force of Catholicism on women.

Catholicism is deeply embedded in the Irish identity. Closely tied to religion is the prominent political issue of Maturin's time, Irish independence. Born in 1780 as a Dubliner, Maturin witnessed history unfolding in the failed uprisings, the Act of Union, and the problems of absent landlords: "In his politics he was also a strong Nationalist, and in his writings expresses his regret at the existence of the Union."[160] Irish society and the Anglo-Irish in particular were experiencing tremendous political turmoil. The movement to reclaim Ireland from England was evident in several failed revolutionary attempts early in the nineteenth century. The Irish Catholics were gaining power while the English were exerting more pressure to maintain control. In the midst of this tense situation was the Anglo-Irish, attempting to come to terms with split loyalties and more than a little hereditary guilt. As Terry Eagleton aptly describes the dilemma in "Form and Ideology in the Anglo-Irish Novel":

> It is not hard to read Melmoth in Charles Maturin's magnificent novel as a type of the Anglo-Irish gentry, haunted by a primordial crime perpetrated in the seventeenth century which refuses to lie quiet in its grave but which stalks the centuries in search of expiation. The Faustian pacts Melmoth seeks to establish with the dispossessed are all about Irish class politics—about the ghastly bonds of hatred and affection between exploiter and exploited. In a bizarre paradox, the oppressor has put himself morally beyond the pale, and so has a kind of grotesque affinity to those he persecutes.[161]

This affinity and its resulting conflicts are seen clearly in "The Tale of the Indian." Isidora is a Spanish Catholic who was shipwrecked early in life on an island. Melmoth, the Anglo-Irish Protestant, finds Isidora on this island. Isidora was happily content before Melmoth came to her island and taught her his language and the ways of the outside world. Still, she welcomes him and falls in love with him. He initially teaches her in an attempt to gain her trust so he can seduce her and rid himself of his terrible burden. He unexpectedly falls in love with her, which complicates his original plan. It is beyond Melmoth's comprehension that he can wed Isidora and live happily with her while saving his own soul in the process. Instead, he opts to destroy her in an effort to save himself. He succeeds in his seduction but not in ridding himself of his burden. She refuses to sacrifice her soul and dies rather than trade places with him. Similarly, the English had set out to first conquer and then colonize Ireland for strategic purposes. The English colonists, rather than absorb the Irish populace, assimilated into the Irish culture, becoming the Anglo-Irish in the succeeding generations. Like Melmoth's situation with Isidora, the Anglo-Irish became confused about their national affiliations.

Given these colonial implications and uncertain national and personal identities, it is no surprise that Melmoth is such a conflicted character. He has much in common with the vampire, as characterized by McClelland: "Not only is the vampire effectively a mimetic double, he has no valid identity, no evident social position."[162] He has no home as a wanderer. He is clearly not welcomed at the place that could be considered home, but even if he were, the "home" in County Wicklow was seized from its original family and given to the Melmoths; Melmoth was not born there. He has no allegiance to any nation or even any religion. He does not remain with his family in Ireland to support the English claim, and any ties that he may have had with Christianity were severed when he made alternate arrangements for his soul. He does not even possess the ability to obtain a soul to replace his own in the bargain. Melmoth's inability to determine who or what he is leads to his destruction just as surely as his rejection of God.

Melmoth's situation partly parallels Maturin's own. As the grandson of the dean of St. Patrick's, the son of an influential government administrator, and a minister of the Anglican Church, Maturin was presumably a part of a privileged, ruling minority. However, as his biographers illustrate, he was often at odds with his superiors; to fit in, Maturin would have had to be someone he was not. He genuinely believed that Catholicism was preventing the Irish from gaining their freedom; one need look no further than his *Five Sermons on the Errors of the Roman Catholic Church* (1824) to see this. However, this strong belief was not enough to allow his superiors to overlook his other expressed beliefs which did not coincide with the Anglican Church. As Harris notes, "Maturin did not believe that adherence to any single sect was necessary to salvation; he believed Christians were to be found everywhere."[163] He stated these beliefs, which alienated him from the church and, in turn, did not make him an ideal servant of the Crown. Harris adds: "Ironically, Maturin's religious views not only kept him out of favor in the English Church but also kept him out of the mainstream of Irish nationalism. Whereas it was his deviation from accepted church doctrine which blocked his position in the Anglican Church, it was his adherence to the tenor of that church which modified his nationalist sentiments."[164] He was "an inside-outer in the Irish community."[165] Even in his writing career, Maturin did not quite fit in. Those writing in the genre were predominantly women[166] and those who were not did not have to endure prejudicial judgments made upon their character or their work because they were ministers. *Melmoth the Wanderer* reflects the identity crisis suffered not only by Maturin but by Anglo-Irish society at large, as pointed out by Morin: "[T]he problems of social and personal estrangement, alienation, and isolation so central to its [*Melmoth*] many tales are, the text implies, very much alive in present-day Ireland."[167] The novel's conclusion indicates that no compromise or solution is in sight. The reader could conclude that Melmoth is destroyed, and the young John Melmoth inherits an estate near ruin, reminiscent of Maria Edgeworth's Big House novels, allowing Melmoth the Wanderer the dubious distinction of being the ultimate absentee landlord. This is not a very flattering comparison or one that gives much hope to the young John Melmoth and the future of his estate. When one considers that the correspondence between Maturin and Constable indicated Maturin's desire to publish a sequel to *Melmoth*,[168] Melmoth's destruction at the novel's end becomes less certain and the future of the estate's new heir even less promising.

The novel is not completely dark, though. It is important to remember the section of the story where Melmoth meets Immalee. No matter how negative any of Maturin's contemporary critics were about *Melmoth*, something positive was almost always stated about this tale. After the horrific tales of Stanton in an insane asylum and Moncada's forced vocation at the hands of sadistic clergy and weak parents, the interlude of Melmoth and Immalee on the tropical island is a welcome respite, as noted by the *Blackwood's* critic: "[T]his tale of Immalee, or Isidora, which comes last in the series, has been judiciously selected by the Author to occupy that place of honour in his terrors."[169] Melmoth almost gives up his search for a replacement when he meets and falls in love with Immalee. The key word is "almost," however; he is tempted but cannot believe that there is any other hope for his salvation aside from drawing another in to take his place. When Melmoth focuses his energy on trying to damn Immalee, his soul and hope for an identity are lost. Melmoth has always possessed the free will to change his mind about his bargain with the devil. What prevents him from doing this is his consuming despair that cuts him off from God and hope. Melmoth seals his own fate when he suppresses the hope that begins to surface as a result of meeting Immalee. As D'Amico explains: "Melmoth need only believe in Immalee and her unselfish and constant love [like God's], love unshaken by suffering, to be free from the devil's bargain, for it is not Satan's offer which has doomed the wanderer as much as it is his own refusal to believe in the goodness of mankind."[170]

The women throughout Maturin's writing, not just in *Melmoth the Wanderer*, emphasize this theme repeatedly. D'Amico continues that "for Maturin, only when the individual finds a suitable partner, only when 'domestic felicity' is achieved, does the soul leave behind the hell within to find its own bit of paradise ... she must be an embodiment of both purity and passion, reconciling in herself all opposing qualities."[171] This concept is Celtic in its perception of women. Immalee mirrors Deirdre of the Sorrows and Cuchulain's wife, Emer, in her love, strength, and sacrifice as depicted in Lady Gregory's *Cuchulain of Muirtheme*. Deirdre is supposed to marry King Conchubar of the Ulster Red Branch. Instead, she runs away with Naoise, whom she loves, and lives in happy exile with him and his two brothers. Conchubar desires revenge on the three brothers for losing his bride and tricks them into returning to Ireland. Deirdre tries to persuade Naoise not to return, but he will not listen. He and his brothers walk into a trap and all three are killed. Rather than marry the king, Deirdre kills herself, sacrificing everything for her love. Emer, the wife of Cuchulain the famous hero of the Red Branch, likewise sacrifices herself for love. Unable to give Cuchulain a child, she frequently turns a blind eye to her husband's many relationships with other women, reputedly becoming jealous only once. When Cuchulain nears the inevitability of his death in battle, Emer tries to keep him from battle and then, when he is killed, dies from grief and is buried at his side. Both women of Celtic myth share similarities with Isidora. Isidora endures tremendous hardship because of her love for Melmoth. Like Deirdre, Isidora does not proceed with an arranged marriage because she loves Melmoth. Her choice leads to the death of her brother at the hands of Melmoth. They flee together, but Melmoth fails to protect her or heed her advice. She and her child die in the dungeons of the Inquisition because Isidora refuses to be "rescued" on Melmoth's terms. Like Emer, Isidora forgives her husband's failings and attempts to alter what she believes to be his fate because of love. When the women are unable to save the men whom they love, each dies broken-hearted.

The effects of women in the novel and in Irish myth are difficult to ignore. In his introduction to the 10-volume *Irish Literature* (1904), editor-in-chief Justin McCarthy stated: "The sentiment of nationality is also a pervading characteristic of Irish literature from prehistoric times down to the present day. The idea of Ireland is metaphorically embodied in the conception of a mythical goddess and queen, to whom all succeeding generations of Irishmen give a heartfelt, even when half unconscious, reverence."[172] Ireland has long been personified as a woman. According to C. L. Innes in *Woman and Nation in Irish Literature and Society, 1880–1935*, "Ireland has been represented by British imperialists as well as Irish nationalists and artists as female: she is Hibernia, Eire, Erin, Mother Ireland, the Poor Old Woman, the Shan Van Vocht, Cathleen ni Houlihan, the Dark Rosaleen."[173] The female personification would rise to even greater significance in Ireland during the latter years of Irish nationalism, a time period that saw women like Maud Gonne, Constance Markievicz, Lady Gregory,

Hannah Sheehy-Skeffington, Katharine Tynan, and Anna Parnell take active roles within the movement.[174] Therefore, it is not surprising that Maturin would depict women as the vehicles through which characters like Melmoth could be saved. What may be surprising is that Maturin would make this connection between women and nation sixty years before it became common; however, when one remembers that Maturin preferred the society of women in general and never lost the passion and admiration that he felt for his wife, his portrayal is less surprising. When Maturin elaborated on the invaluable virtues of women in one of his sermons, the reader could assume that he is not speaking in the abstract but from the experience of being the husband of Henrietta:

> In domestic life, it is women on whom we are dependent for the first years of existence, and for all its future felicity: it is she who tends us in sickness, who soothes us in care, who consoles us in calamity, to whom the heart instinctively turns in the hour of suffering, and never turns in vain. With all our boasted strength, we lean for support on one weaker than ourselves; and we find it is she who, in the hour of adversity, like the women of old, who gave up their ornaments for the exigencies of the state, gracefully converts those accomplishments, which distinguished her in happier hours, into the means of procuring that her protector fails to procure.[175]

Perhaps if Melmoth had the benefit of hearing one of Maturin's sermons, he would have appreciated what he had found in Immalee and listened to her. Instead, like Deirdre's beloved Naoise, he does not and therefore loses his identity and, soon, his life.

Melmoth's end does not bode well for Ireland or the creation of a distinctly Irish identity. The Irish would continue to wrestle with this issue and many others long after Maturin. Although Maturin may not have solved the problem of a national identity for his countrymen, he settled upon a solution for himself. In the preface of his first novel, he declares "I am an Irishman"[176] and makes the same declaration in the dedication to *The Wild Irish Boy*.[177] In the dedication to *The Milesian Chief* he writes: "I have chosen my own country for the scene, because I believe it the only country on earth, where, from the strange existing opposition of religion, politics, and manners, the extremes of refinement and barbarism are united and the most wild and incredible situations of romantic story are hourly passing before modern eyes."[178] In the preface to *Women* Maturin states: "In the Tale which I now offer to the public, perhaps there may be recognized some characters which experience will not disown. Some resemblance to common life may be traced in them."[179] Maturin sets this mirror of common life within a few years of Ireland's present. In *Melmoth* he again sets the story in Ireland and almost in the present, taking the time to note the inspiration of one of the most important Irish subjects to him in the entire story, his wife Henrietta: "The original from which the Wife of Walberg is imperfectly sketched is a living woman, and *long may she live.*"[180] Some may argue that the Irish setting in the frame tale is not enough to establish the Irish influence on the novel, but Morin counters this with: "Ireland and the problematic issue of Irish national identity represent such an important influence in Maturin's life that they vitally and consistently inform his writings, no matter how distant his fictional settings."[181] Maturin may not have found a defined place in Irish society, but it did not prevent him from identifying himself as an Irishman.

More important for Maturin were his personal relationships. Even though he was disappointed professionally, financially, and physically, often severely criticized for being a romance-writing minister, viewed as a failure (and in some circles insane), his friends and family never failed him. Scott, Byron, Lady Morgan, and other literary friends and publishers supported him, frequently financially. Still, Maturin felt the strain of poverty more often than not in his adult life; however, his peace and happiness (and his identity) were centered in his home. For a man who often wrote about the dark side of human nature, there were always some elements of hope and faith. These allowed Maturin to stand out among his Gothic contemporaries and predecessors; it is one of his claims to originality.

The argument of originality is thus furthered for Maturin through his exploration and reconciliation of the dark side that he believed existed in all humans. Maturin possessed a deep concern for individuals who repressed their dark side. His exploration into this concern resulted in some insightful depictions of human psychology. Maturin's innovations in the Gothic genre moved from the external "things-that-go-bump-in-the-night" to the internal workings of the human mind. For Maturin, one faces the greatest terror in confronting and conquering that part of the self that is inclined toward evil and, in the case of Melmoth, this evil would be giving in to despair. "Maturin reminds his readers that each man casts his own shadow."[182] He dealt daily with the shadows that threatened to impose despair upon his existence. He also saw a shadow of unrest descending upon his country in the form of armed rebellions which had to concern someone who felt so deeply for his family, parishioners, and Ireland. "[T]here is no doubt that *Melmoth* speaks of the ghosts haunting Maturin as he wrote, including contemporary Ireland and its violent past."[183]

According to Edward W. Wagenknecht, "The critics have never been fond of Maturin—did he not break all the rules?"[184] *Melmoth the Wanderer* is an excellent example of Maturin's penchant for rule-breaking. He wrote a novel that broke with the English Gothic tradition and thus demonstrated an originality that the leaders of the Irish Literary Renaissance would later encourage young Irish writers to pursue. Maturin's absorption of myth included Ireland's and also reflected the problems facing the country in his lifetime. He did not establish a definitive Irish identity, but he declared himself an Irishman and did contribute to the creation of a national identity and the Irish vampire by his own work. Even though Maturin was scarcely mentioned in *Irish Literature* (1904), he is now classified as an Irish writer as demonstrated in *The Field Day Anthology of Irish Writing*. "*Melmoth the Wanderer* begins and ends in Ireland, establishing a cultural and autobiographical frame that is far from trivial."[185] In retrospect, it is easy to see the abundant evidence that Maturin did more than pen just another Gothic novel. He was an innovator concerned with his country's plight as well as his own. Everything he wrote contained the fire and passion of a man with convictions who was not afraid to state them.

According to his many critics and biographers, Maturin influenced not only his Irish contemporaries like James Clarence Mangan (1803–1849) but future Irish authors and international ones, including Americans Edgar Allan Poe and Nathaniel Hawthorne (1804–1864),[186] Scots Robert Louis Stevenson and Sir Walter Scott, English Christina Rossetti (1830–94),[187] and Frenchmen Honore Balzac and Charles Baudelaire.[188] In Ireland, the Wanderer's portrait served as inspiration for his great-nephew Oscar Wilde's *Dorian Gray*.[189] "The whole shaping [of] an intricate verbal labyrinth … looks forward to such modern works of structural exorbitancy as *At Swim-Two-Birds* [Flann O'Brien] and *Ulysses* [James Joyce]."[190]

Two authors who are curiously absent from this list are works by an English and an Irish writer who were influenced by Maturin and contributed to the nineteenth-century vampire myth, but, like their mentor, have often been overlooked—James Malcolm Rymer (1814–84) and one of his penny dreadful successes, *Varney the Vampyre; or The Feast of Blood* (1845–47) and Dion Boucicault's (1820–90) drama, *The Vampire, A Phantasm* (1852).[191] While this work is about the Irish Gothic vampire and three of its primary shapers, a few paragraphs need to be devoted to Rymer's and Boucicault's works not only because of Maturin's influence on them but because they have rarely been noted.

Even the most superficial reading of *Varney* will result in abundant evidence of Rymer being influenced by *Melmoth*. The concept of a series of tales connected by the villain/hero who is an active part of the plot is obvious, though Rymer would have gained from having Maturin's editor and printer. There are also many other similarities to note, like the use of the portrait, the redemptive characterization of women, parents sacrificing their children, the monstrous behavior stemming from characters other than the supposed villain, the mob scenes, the fire, the protagonist trying to rid himself of his curse, and a Cromwell connection. Since an attempt to demonstrate all of these would be a serious digression from the stated point of the present work, only the portrait will be discussed.

Melmoth begins in Ireland with the young John Melmoth visiting his dying uncle. Not long after his arrival, he discovers a portrait:

> John's eyes were in a moment, and as if by magic, riveted on a portrait that hung on the wall…. It represented a man of middle age. There was nothing remarkable in the costume, or in the countenance, but *the eyes*, John felt, were such as one feels they wish they had never seen, and feels they can never forget….
>
> From an impulse equally resistless and painful, he approached the portrait, held the candle towards it, and could distinguish the words on the border of the painting,—Jno. Melmoth, anno 1646. John was neither timid by nature, or nervous by constitution, or superstitious from habit, yet he continued to gaze in stupid horror on this singular picture.[192]

Shortly after this, John sees "the living original of the portrait"[193] and then again, "beckoning and nodding to him, with a familiarity somewhat terrifying."[194] As John rises to chase it, his uncle causes a brief scene and dies.

Varney begins with much less subtle building of suspense—it is a dark and stormy night—but also features a portrait. After five paragraphs vividly describing the violent storm and then the interior of "an antique chamber in an ancient house,"[195] the focus shifts to a portrait: "There is but one portrait in that room, although the walls seem paneled for the express purpose of containing a series of pictures. That is of a young man, with a pale face, a stately brow, and a strange expression about the eyes, which no one cared to look on twice."[196] An intruder breaks into the chamber and attacks the young woman, Flora, who is sleeping there. Her brothers, Henry and George, burst into the room and rescue her. Later each notices the resemblance between the intruder and the portrait, especially the eyes.[197]

Like *Melmoth*, the story surrounding the portrait reveals a family connection from the past, an impossibly long life span, and a significant historical time period. Henry explains to a family friend that the portrait in Flora's room is "of Sir Runnagate Bannerworth, an ancestor of ours, who first, by his vices, gave the great blow to the family prosperity … [a]bout ninety years [ago],"[198] so the Bannerworths, like the Melmoths, live on an estate that is in decline.

The story of Runnagate, who will later inexplicably become Marmaduke in five chapters,[199] emerges as the evidence mounts to support the most unlikely but increasingly probable conclusion that Flora's attacker was the same person who appears in the old portrait. A torn piece of cloth from the incident matches the clothes in the portrait[200] and Henry says that an ancestor who reportedly committed suicide was buried in similar attire.[201] This prompts Henry, George, the family friend, and the village doctor to visit the Bannerworth family crypt and open Runnagate/Marmaduke's coffin, but they find it empty. On the coffin is "1640," the year of the ancestor's death. Since Runnagate/Marmaduke committed suicide ninety years ago, it would place the Bannerworth's current story in 1730; however, like Runnagate's name, the story's timeline also changes—to 1809.[202] This is close to *Melmoth*'s setting; however, in the interests of full disclosure to those who may not have read *Varney*, this is only one of several possible timelines given to Varney.

The 1640 death date on Marmaduke Bannerworth's coffin and the 1646 date on Melmoth's portrait place both characters' storylines at approximately the same time. Melmoth's date and story clearly connect his origins to Cromwell. Varney's personal account of himself before he became a vampire also ties him to this era, noting that this is again another timeline shift in *Varney*. Varney states that in life he "saw the head of a king held up in its gore at Whitehall"[203] and the resulting "dictatorship of Cromwell, made royalists in abundance,"[204] which allowed Varney to become "a thriving man from the large sums I received for aiding the escape of distinguished loyalists."[205] Cromwell's reign led both Varney and Melmoth on their paths to unnaturally long lives that are revealed to the present generation through a mysterious portrait with disturbing eyes.

Portraits and Cromwell are also prominently featured in Dion Boucicault's *The Vampire, A Phantasm* (1852). The drama opens in the summer of 1660 in Wales with the villagers of Raby Peveryl celebrating the death of Cromwell and the restoration of the monarchy. It is not a historically accurate setting since Cromwell died in 1658, but Boucicault was more attentive to the drama rather than the details of history or his plot,[206] and he provides abundant drama. Lucy Peveryl is on her way to meet her fiancé in the ruins of Raby Castle before he flees forever in exile because he fought against the royalists. Raby Castle has a dark history and the reputation of being cursed because fifteen years ago Alan Raby, the youngest member of the Raby family who was a Cromwell supporter, pursued his two royalist brothers back to the family castle, attacked, murdered his brothers, and took command of the castle. Alan's tenure was not long because royalists regained control, and "the murderer was hurled from a turret window down the precipice on the brink of which the castle stands."[207] The drama spans the next 200 years as Alan Raby wanders the Earth but returns every 100 years on the anniversary of his brothers' murders to take the life of a virginal female relative so that he may continue another 100 years.

The portraits that appear in the Second Drama [Act], which takes place in the restored Raby home on August 15, 1760, are all of Alan Raby's victims: his two brothers, Lucy Peveryl, and Lucy's fiancé Roland Peveryl, but there is a veiled portrait: "It is … the likeness of a stranger who was slain by accident on that very night we speak of [August 15, 1660]…. It is a superstition in our family that there is an evil influence in it, and whosoever looks upon it is sure to meet with some calamity."[208] Inevitably, another portrait of a young family member is added to the collection after Raby's visit on August 15, 1760.

Boucicault's play is a curious mixture of Polidori, Maturin, and Rymer with some original additions. Alan Raby is fatally shot but reanimates at the end of the First Drama, Scene III by being exposed to moonlight, just like Polidori's Ruthven. In the Second Drama, Raby ingratiates himself with Edgar Peveryl while traveling by saving his life, which costs Edgar a great deal by the end of the act—his sister Alice becomes Raby's next victim and Edgar goes mad in an effort to save her, much like what happens to Aubrey in *The Vampyre*. However, Maturin's influence is seen in the use of portraits, the Cromwell connections, Raby wandering and returning to his family home, and the pressing need to sacrifice someone else for his own benefit. Rymer's influence may be seen also in the Cromwellian connections, the atmospheric building of the dramatic tension through storms, the vampire using names other than his own, and the murder of a family member who caused the vampiric existence.

Boucicault does add a few original instances which should be noted. In the First Drama, Scene II, the character of Sir Guy Musgrave is a reluctant participant in the group going to the ruined castle as a storm threatens, but makes an interesting remark when one of the ladies comments that his wig is looking the worse for wear: "Yes. I caught an abominable bat in it. I dare say the creature mistook it for a tree, and I could not get him over the idea."[209] While there is no indication that Boucicault meant his audience to connect the bat to the vampire, it is an interesting detail.

It is in the Third Drama, set in August 15, 1860, with Ada Raby as the intended victim that is surprising. In Scene II, Ada demonstrates a connection to the vampire that anticipates Dracula's control over his victims forty-five years later. She refers to him as her "master" like Renfield does; and when she says, "When he is away and I can think—think freely—as I do now, I determine to resist his power. But he comes, his influence creeps like a shadow slowly over me and I am helpless"; "He comes! He comes!";

"You see him not; but I feel his presence,"[210] it is reminiscent of Mina Harker's awareness of her connection to Dracula which prompts her to convince Dr. Van Helsing to use it to their advantage.

Rymer also adds an element to the vampire myth that was not seen in *Melmoth*. One important difference between Varney and Melmoth is Varney's teeth, "projecting like those of some wild animal, hideously, glaringly white, and fang-like."[211] Herr points out in a footnote that "Varney is the first Vampire to have the distinguishing characteristic of fang-like canine teeth,"[212] which will be seen the following chapters. While Joseph Sheridan Le Fanu and Bram Stoker may have followed in Rymer's literary footsteps by giving Carmilla and Count Dracula their fangs, it was Maturin who had the greatest effect on their creations. It is his influence that directed the shaping of an Irish Gothic vampire that saw "its final nineteenth-century mythic embodiment in Bram Stoker's Dracula,"[213] and without Le Fanu, Stoker's count would have been much different.

4

Joseph Sheridan Le Fanu
Refining the Irish Vampire

"[Love] Beareth all things, believeth all things, hopeth all things, endureth all things ... [Love] never faileth.... For we know in part, and we prophesy in part.... For now we see *through a glass, darkly*; but then face to face: now I know in part; but then shall I know even as also I am known."
—1 Corinthians 13:7–9, 12. *King James Bible* (emphasis mine)

Joseph Sheridan Le Fanu's last collection of short stories, *In a Glass Darkly* (1872), appeared one year prior to his death. As the son of an Anglican minister, Le Fanu's slight alteration of a familiar Biblical passage on love for the title of his collection was no accident. By 1872, Le Fanu probably felt that he was "in a glass darkly." He had been a widower for almost fifteen years, his political aspirations had long been disappointed, and despite writing and publishing with unrelenting industry, he was still in debt. The situation in Ireland reflected his own personal turmoil. The results of these personal and national concerns emerged on the pages of his fiction and contributed to the further development of an Irish Gothic vampire as seen in the originality, Irish subject matter, personal and Irish identity, and passion evident in his work.

As pointed out in the prior chapter on Maturin, the biographical is an important element in writing and is an excellent place to begin with the case of Le Fanu and the Irish vampire. The biographical similarities between Charles Robert Maturin and Joseph Sheridan Le Fanu are plentiful. Both came from families of French-Huguenot descent. Both were born into the ruling Anglo-Irish social class, were educated at Trinity College in Dublin, and had an extensive familiarity with the Church of Ireland. Both resided in the Irish countryside but spent the majority of their lives in Dublin. Both struggled constantly to support their families and became the subjects of Dublin legends long before their deaths. Both wrote Gothic novels after it was fashionable and became key authors in the development of the Irish Gothic and the vampire.

Le Fanu, though, grew up in the generation following Maturin's, and the personal and public events that distinguished that time period also influenced Le Fanu's Irish Gothic fiction. His lifetime saw "the tithe war and the Repeal of the Union movement in the 1830s, the years of the famine and 'Young Ireland' (indeed, the European upheavals of 1848), to Gladstone's disestablishment of the Irish church (1868), in which his father had been a dean, and finally the beginnings of the land agitation."[1] Such occurrences would inevitably effect Le Fanu and the social class to which he belonged. Historian F. L. S. Lyons in his 1975 article "A Question of Identity: A Protestant View" stated: "If you look at the Protestant position in the long perspective of history, you can detect … four main phases … first of settlement, second of ascendancy, third of contraction and finally of siege." He further explained that the nineteenth century was "an age of contraction for Irish Protestantism" and it "ceased from around 1830 to be a badge of superiority."[2]

Maturin was part of the ascendancy period when the Anglo-Irish still had social standing and power. Maturin's life was too brief and his own personal concerns too numerous for him to see what the future might hold. Perhaps this is why his works, like his life, retain a feeling of hope, a tone not nearly as prevalent in Le Fanu's writings during the contraction phase. Le Fanu's contributions to Irish Gothic literature are also tied with the experiences of his life which were not, overall, terribly optimistic. This growing discontent with life's realities is one reason attributed as to why Le Fanu made the exceptional move from writing Irish historical novels to Irish Gothic ones. "He retreats from history rather than pursue it, and his retreat demonstrates the power of history in Ireland."[3] Although his later works were not historical as defined by Scott's influential works, Le Fanu did not so much retreat from history as shift the genre that he used as a vehicle to discuss it, which shows the inescapable power of history in Ireland. This history not only includes the public but also the private for Le Fanu. Unlike Maturin, who had enjoyed a privileged upbringing and early adulthood and found his solace in his faith and in his home during difficult times, Le Fanu's story contains more challenges with less comfort in either the domestic or spiritual realms.

Le Fanu was born in 1814,[4] the second child of Thomas and Emma (Dobbin) Le Fanu, who married in 1811. His mother was the niece of

Richard Brinsley Sheridan (1751–1816), the dramatist. Le Fanu had an older sister by one year, Catherine (1813–41), and a younger brother by two years, William (1816–94). They grew up in Phoenix Park in Dublin, where their father was the minister of the military school. William described their childhood in idyllic terms in *Seventy Years of Irish Life* (1893): "Here the first ten years of my life were spent in as happy a home as boy could have. Never can I forget our rambles through that lovely park, the delight we took in the military reviews, sham fights, and races held near the school, not to mention the intense interest and awe inspired by the duels occasionally fought there."[5]

According to W. J. McCormack's carefully researched *Sheridan Le Fanu*, in 1817 Thomas Le Fanu became rector of Ardnageehy Parish in County Cork, which had a small income, no residence, and few Protestant parishioners, so such an appointment was generally understood to be one that enhanced income but did not require a move to the parish.[6] In 1823, Thomas received another appointment as rector for Abington in Limerick, and although there was a parish residence and it was not as remote as the Cork appointment, the reverend did not move his family because recent unrest had made it "a place to avoid in 1823."[7] Once again, he became an absentee clergyman.

Then, in 1826, Le Fanu's father was appointed Dean of Emly,[8] which prompted him to move his family from Dublin to the glebe house in Abington, Limerick. The move would appear unremarkable to anyone unfamiliar with Irish history or, perhaps more specifically, the Tithe Wars. At the time, the countryside was populated predominantly by Irish Catholics who had their own church but had to pay tithes to absent Protestant ministers and rent to absentee English/Anglo-Irish landlords. The situation was hardly a new one, but the demonstrated discontent with it was. The Irish Catholic population had always outnumbered the Anglo-Irish one and rather regularly endeavored to unseat the ruling class through unsuccessful rebellions. The difference between the turn-of-the-nineteenth-century discontent and that in the 1820s was that the Irish Catholics were organizing into a political power backed by the Catholic Church and spoken for via a charismatic leader who was "one of them": Daniel O'Connell. The combination made the ascendancy very uneasy as to the solidity of their position in this changing society. It also made the Anglo-Irish rural clergy convenient targets for a great deal of verbal and physical abuse. Evidence of this dangerous situation was reported in "Irish Tranquility," an 1837 article in the *Dublin University Magazine*, then edited by Isaac Butts ("twenty-one cases, where Protestant clergymen were murdered or their lives attempted"),[9] which provides abundant and detailed descriptions of these incidents as well as the lack of action on the part of the government and police to protect the clergy and their families.

The Le Fanu family fortunately escaped murder but experienced other situations that were perfect examples of the Anglo-Irish dilemma for clergy. Le Fanu's father could not have chosen a worse time to relocate to the rural Abington parish. The family suffered financially, physically, and socially. Even though Dean Le Fanu's income at Abingdon was estimated to be £1,800, the reality was quite different.[10] As McCormack explains: "The rector's income derived almost entirely from tithes paid by all landholders in the parish, Catholic and Protestant alike."[11] But many of the local Catholic inhabitants refused to tithe to protest the law. This meant that the Le Fanu's income started low and dropped to virtually nothing. During the first year, the dean's income was reportedly £900,[12] half of what the rector should have expected to collect. By the time of his death nineteen years later, the estimated income had fallen to £650,[13] a third of what it had been and there was no guarantee that even this diminished amount could be collected. As already seen with Maturin's woefully insufficient curate's income, Dean Le Fanu's superiors did little to help alleviate the financial situation despite their perfect awareness of it. As a result, Dean Le Fanu often found himself either mortgaging or selling family properties to pay debt or generate enough income to meet the daily needs of his family.

The issue of tithes also made the Le Fanus targets of the discontented populace. "There was an intentional element in Irish violence which directed it, as the century rolled on, increasingly towards the class of which the Le Fanus were representative."[14] The family witnessed the violence between factions during their time in Abington and became unwitting targets of it. In 1832, when Catherine Le Fanu was just nineteen, the family personally encountered violence. "When Catherine with some girl cousins, visitors to the glebe, ventured out unprotected, they were pelted with mud and stones, and any excursion by the family was greeted with shouts and cursing."[15] A few years later, twenty-year-old William had a close brush with a protesting mob. In his memoir, William vividly retold the incident that resulted when he and a cousin attempted to distribute flyers about a reduction in the tithes. They were ambushed by an angry crowd and pelted with stones, but that was not the worst of it, as William recalled:

> One man only was on the road, and, as we got near him, I saw him settling his spade in his hand as if to be ready to strike a blow. I presented my pistol at him. "Don't shoot me," he called out; "I'm only working here." But just as I passed him he made a

tremendous blow at me; it missed me, but struck the horse just behind the saddle. The spade was broken by the violence of the blow. Down went the horse on his haunches, but was quickly up again, and on we went. Had he fallen, I should not have been alive many minutes; he brought me bravely home, but never recovered, and died soon afterwards.[16]

William's experience was even referenced in "Irish Tranquility": "In the same county [Limerick] the detection of the assailants of the lives of another clergyman's [The Dean of Emly] son and nephew"[17] was unsuccessful. The unpredictable and undeserved violence closely linked to money and status would serve as a recurring theme in Le Fanu's writing in addition to the isolation it caused. His protagonists, such as Maud Ruthyn in *Uncle Silas*, grow up in isolation due to her family's position and become the unwitting targets of violence because of wealth and status. They barely escape death, a fearful feeling shared by the Le Fanu children who were just entering their teens when their family moved.

These experiences and the isolation from society undoubtedly drew the family closer together. Even though Le Fanu and William were students at Trinity, financial constraints and family concerns resulted in their studies being done more in Abington than in Dublin. Catherine, her health always delicate, remained with her parents. William received his degree in engineering, and Le Fanu earned his in law but surprised both friends and family by pursuing newspaper ownership, editing, and writing. William echoed the thoughts of those close to him when he recalled that "this [newspaper purchase] was injurious to his future prospects, as it prevented his applying himself to a profession [law], for which his eloquence and ready wit fitted him, and of which his contemporaries had hoped to see him a distinguished member."[18]

As the brothers set out to establish themselves professionally in Dublin, another event that would greatly effect Le Fanu soon happened. By the late 1830s, Catherine's health was in serious decline. In March of 1841, Le Fanu and William received an urgent message in Dublin about Catherine's precarious condition and they hurried to Abington. "We were summoned from Dublin to her deathbed. Great was her joy at seeing us and having us with her. She had feared that we would not arrive in time to see her."[19] Catherine died soon afterward. The family was devastated by her loss, especially her father. For Le Fanu, it was his first experience with the death of someone very close to him, and he deeply felt the loss.

The family had lost Catherine but soon gained Susanna Bennett, whom Le Fanu married in 1843. She was the third youngest child of George Bennett, who "was the leading barrister on the Munster circuit."[20] Le Fanu and his new wife enjoyed an affectionate relationship. He was a prolific and published writer and a respected, well-liked public figure. Le Fanu "was remembered as a very pleasant, witty man, with a puckish sense of humor that manifested itself occasionally in practical jokes."[21] His brother William detailed many of Le Fanu's jokes in his reminiscences, illustrating his lively nature. He also "cut a fashionable figure"[22] in Dublin society and was active in politics, working to help regain Tory control and influence in Ireland. The sadness of his sister's death was eased by domestic contentment and public promise. Unfortunately, his happiness would soon be disrupted.

The year 1845 was a significant turning point in the national history of Ireland and the personal history of Le Fanu. The year began with the joy of the birth of Le Fanu's first child, Eleanor Frances, in February, but it turned to sadness with the death of his father in June, followed by a successful libel suit against Le Fanu's newspaper, the *Warder* for £500.[23] For the nation, 1845 marked the beginning of the Famine or Great Hunger, an event that would have broken Dean Le Fanu's heart if he had lived to witness it.[24] Dean Le Fanu had steadily declined since Catherine's death, and his final will bequeathed very little to his sons and nothing for the care of his wife. The years in Abington had taken their toll on the family's finances. Emma Le Fanu moved in with William and formed an even closer bond with her eldest son. Le Fanu's growing family and the settlement of his first libel suit strained his financial resources. "As far as his income was concerned, family inheritance did not provide adequate resources, and he and his wife depended on his commercial rather than professional earnings. The Bar had more or less failed him, and partly by choice he came to rely on his interests in journalism for his livelihood."[25] Personal grief and financial difficulties reflected the nation's public distress. Ireland faced a loss in the potato crop that swept the country in 1845.

> The peasants, except the few who had land enough to keep a cow, lived altogether on potatoes, with which on rare occasions they had a salt herring or two. Milk they could not get, for when—which was very seldom indeed—they could have afforded to buy it the farmers would not sell it, as they wanted it to feed their calves…. Meat they never tasted except on Christmas Day and Easter Sunday.[26]

The rural population's reliance on the potato for food proved catastrophic when the crop failed year after year. The results of the Great Hunger (1845–51) are well-documented. Ireland suffered a massive loss of lives in those five years from starvation, diseases related to malnutrition, and emigration. According to historians T. W. Moody and F. X. Martin, "In 1851 the population [of Ireland] was 6½ million, 2 million less than the estimated population of 1845. Something like a million had succeeded in getting away and another million perished."[27] In addition to the physical diminishment of the Irish population, there occurred an even greater psychological damage upon those who witnessed it, as D. George Boyce describes:

> Such a catastrophe might, in an earlier age, have been assigned to the judgment of God and regarded simply as divine punishment for some dreadful sin committed by the people. But the Great Famine was different, not only because of its scale, but because of its implications for the government of Ireland under the Union. The image of coffinless bodies consigned without dignity to famine pits, thirty or more at a time, has endured.[28]

As a newspaperman and aspiring politician, Le Fanu had to have been aware of the horrors of the national crisis, which would have left a lasting impression. At least one story from this time had a very personal connection because it was experienced by William and remained so vivid that it was the only story of those times that he told in his book fifty years later:

> [W]e passed near the old churchyard at Burnfort. Several dogs were fighting and howling there; my assistant ran down to see what they were about. He found them fighting over the bodies of some poor creatures who had died of famine, and had that morning been buried—if buried it can be called—without coffins, and so close to the surface that they were barely covered with earth. We had coffins made for them, and had them buried at a proper depth.[29]

This period of national loss saw the last of Le Fanu's Irish historical novels. As pointed out by Cahalan, *Torlogh O'Brien* (1847) "tells the story of how a Catholic hero proves himself in order to earn a place via marriage in the Ascendancy, portrayed as the proper place of any true Irishman, therein mythically merging the old Gaelic aristocracy and the post–Cromwellian Protestant Ascendancy."[30] The novel's publication also corresponded with the end of Le Fanu's political aspirations. According to McCormack, Le Fanu was "implicated on the fringes of the 1848 rebellion,"[31] something the conservative Tories would not forget a few years later when Le Fanu attempted to gain the Tory nomination in 1852; he did not win it. After that disappointment, McCormack states that "he withdrew into editorial work on the newspapers and into the tensions of a household increasingly affected by his wife's neurotic symptoms."[32]

By 1853, Le Fanu ceased writing fiction and did not pick up his pen again for nine years. Domestic tensions brought on by financial worries and Susanna's increasing "nervousness," the Le Fanus still maintained a busy social life and the appearance of domestic harmony. While Le Fanu continued a lively and apparently secret correspondence from Susanna with her sister Bessie, which sometimes included another sister-in-law (Mary) and his mother-in-law,[33] his brother William served as a great comfort to

Susanna as a religious confidant. William and Susanna engaged in discussions of faith that Le Fanu did not seem to share. "Joseph participated in the dinners, lunches, and sometimes even the walks, but apparently neglected his church attendance."[34]

Unfortunately, Susanna's professed faith could not sustain her when her father, George Bennett, died in 1856. It "brought about a major disruption of her emotional and spiritual life,"[35] one from which she never fully recovered. Rather than offer comfort and provide strength, Susanna's faith only seemed to further agitate her already unsettled mind. Her religious dilemma was strikingly reminiscent of one experienced by Le Fanu's sister Catherine just prior to her death. Her search for answers only caused further doubts: "It is not faith, but want of faith, that makes it necessary to fill our minds with any set of doctrines before we go to the Bible, as though that book would otherwise mislead us.... What is the use of reading, if we only find doubts and difficulties increase by study.... I find myself in an inextricable maze of doubt and uncertainty.... Why is doubt so painful to me?"[36]

After Catherine's death, Dean Le Fanu did not turn to his faith to deal with his grief. His sadness overwhelmed him and ultimately contributed to his own demise a few years later. It is not surprising that Le Fanu was unable to reassure Susanna after her own father's death since he did not share her depth of faith or concern for it. He had seen how religion had caused hate and division while growing up in Abington, and he later saw how faith failed to serve his sister and his father in their time of need. Now he saw his own young wife seize upon faith yet constantly question her worthiness to do so. Faith, and the conspicuous lack of it, would be a topic explored continually by Le Fanu in his Irish Gothic writings.

On April 26, 1858, Susanna had a hysterical attack and died two days later, not living to her 35th birthday. She left behind four children—Eleanor, 13; Emma, 12; Thomas, 11; and George, 4—and one devastated husband. The guilt and sense of failure that Le Fanu felt upon her death are evident in personal writing but would also be a recurring theme in his later Irish Gothic fiction. Le Fanu immediately wrote to his mother after Susanna's death: "I have prayed in agony to be delivered from this most frightful calamity. But into his wise and merciful hands I put all things ... she was always asking me—unworthy—to pray for her ... to me she was the light of my life & light in every day.... I adored her."[37] Le Fanu's sudden religious stirrings were brief and tormented. Instead of finding solace, Le Fanu expressed uncertainty and blamed God, the clergy, himself, and medical doctors for Susanna's death.

God be praised. I can rest upon this as upon a rock. I need trouble myself no more about Doctors, or their measures, or what might have been. It was the will of my heavenly Father that she should die exactly when & as she did, & in that certainty ends all speculation.

Yes. My adored redeemer has done it, and how—in love, or in wrath? Oh, blessed be God, in love.[38]

When Susanna's death was followed by the demise of Le Fanu's mother in 1861, his own life and his writing were dramatically altered. As Wayne Hall notes in *Dialogues in the Margin: A Study of the Dublin University Magazine*, "A close reading of his novels from the 1860s … reveals attitudes toward religion quite unlike the usual evangelistic fare in the *DUM*. Like every other potential human value in these works, religion fails to offer his characters any kind of certainty or comfort."[39]

Socially, Le Fanu became a less visible presence in Dublin after the death of his wife and mother, despite his purchase of the *Dublin University Magazine* in 1861.[40] In addition to his grief, another reason for Le Fanu's decreased public outings was that he was writing a lot and publishing his work in his newly acquired magazine. He still received visits from his closest friends and family—Mrs. Norton, Lady Gifford, Miss Rhoda Broughton, Percy Fitzgerald, Alfred P. Graves, Charles Lever,[41] Lord Dufferin, Nina Cole, William and Henrietta (Barrington) Le Fanu, and some of Henrietta's family.[42] He also saw to it that his children had regular opportunities to socialize. His daughters were introduced to society in 1864 and 1865, chaperoned by their Uncle William,[43] and he spent holidays with all of his children during the summers of 1864–66 at Beaumaris in Anglesey.

It was after he "gave up the editorship of the *Dublin University Magazine* in 1869, [that] he practically disappeared from mortal ken for the remaining four years of his life."[44] He was dubbed the "Invisible Prince" of the Dublin streets, and stories of his nocturnal forays among the booksellers' bins in search of books of the occult are legendary. Stories circulated that the author stayed up into the early hours of the morning writing his frightening tales by the light of a candle to avoid sleeping—to avoid recurring nightmares. As may be seen from what S. M. Ellis wrote of Le Fanu's writing habits, part of this seems to be true:

Le Fanu's method of work was rather peculiar. He wrote much at night, in bed, using bound books of copy-paper for his manuscripts. He always had two candles by his side on a small table; one of these would be left alight when he took a short sleep. Waking again about 2 a.m., he would brew himself some strong tea—which he drank habitually and frequently—and then write for another hour or two in the eerie period of the night when human vitality is at its lowest ebb and occult powers said to be in the ascendant…. But apart from drinking much strong tea, … he was a most abstemious man, and a non-smoker.[45]

Le Fanu's writing methods are not really that peculiar. With four children in the house and probably a few servants, the late night/early morning hours were quiet and less likely to be interrupted, especially if he stayed in bed where it was warm. If he got up to write in a library or study in the house, more than two candles would be needed to illuminate the way and give enough light to lay and light a fire in the cold room. The bedroom fire was already lit and tea could easily be made using it.

Whether the reasons for his writing habits were practical, atmospheric, eccentric, or a combination of all three, his methods elicited results; his writing production exploded at this time. He reworked the short stories he had previously published in Dublin magazines and newspapers into full-length novels with English settings. It was at this time that he wrote the novel *Uncle Silas* (1864) and the collection of short stories *In a Glass Darkly* (1872). These two publications show Le Fanu at his best and revealed the effect life had upon him, his losing battle to make sense of it, and the Irish Gothic nature of his fiction.

Among the many stories that persist about Le Fanu is a popular one allegedly surrounding his death, retold here by biographer Michael Begnal:

> Dreams played an important part in Le Fanu's writings, and it is said that at the end of his life he was plagued with recurring nightmares which he could not escape. By this time he had become a total recluse, refusing to see even his closest friends when they occasionally came to call. One such nocturnal phantasm involved an ancient and crumbling mansion on the point of toppling over while the dreamer was incapable of moving from the spot. On his death from a heart attack in February, 1873, his doctor is supposed to have commented that the house had claimed its victim at last.[46]

Like Maturin, though, the facts of Le Fanu's death became overshadowed by this legend. Brian Showers in his essay, "A Void Which Cannot Be Filled Up: Obituaries of J. S. Le Fanu," presents a much more likely account of Le Fanu's death as written by his daughter, Emma, in her letter to Lord Dufferin on 9 February 1873: "His [Le Fanu's] face looks so happy with a beautiful smile on it."[47] Showers continues with an interpretation of the significance of Emma's words: "Her use of the present tense, and the date of the letter being between Le Fanu's death and his burial, gives one the impression that she wrote these words in the presence of her father's corpse. Likewise, a plaster mask of Le Fanu, very possibly his death mask, is devoid of a tormented *rictus*; instead we see a face that would seem to be at peace."[48] Emma also shared in her letter what contributed to her father's death: "He had almost got over a bad attack of Bronchitis but his strength gave way & he sank very quickly & died in his sleep."[49] According to Showers's research from the *Mount Jerome Cemetery Register of Burials*, Le Fanu's cause of death was listed as a "Disease of the Heart."[50] For someone with a weak heart, a case of bronchitis could easily have led to death; much more probable than one nightmare too many of a falling house.

In a sense, though, the family home really did collapse for Le Fanu. When he died, his children had to leave their home at 18 Merrion Square.[51] His oldest daughter, Eleanor (Ellie), had been married two years, Emma was engaged, George away at school, and Thomas "displaying signs of irresponsibility and dissolution."[52] Le Fanu died in debt, owing his brother money, and even though Thomas was named as his father's executor, the burden fell upon William to settle his brother's affairs and see to his nieces and nephews. There was no money and no property, only bills and "paintings of the past, engraved silver, relics,"[53] a state many of Le Fanu's characters fell into and one definitely recognizable for Maturin's Melmoth. Only one of Le Fanu's children would remain in Dublin or even Ireland— Thomas died in 1879 and was buried with his parents. George left for England, and Eleanor and Emma moved away with their husbands. Yet it is Emma's words which serve as the best epitaph for her father when she writes to her fiancé after Le Fanu's death: "We [Thomas and Emma] were quite unprepared for the end ... [and] were so hopeful and happy about him even the day before he seemed to be so much better. But it comforts me to think he is in Heaven, for no one could have been better than he was. He lived only for us, and his life was a most troubled one."[54]

A distinct air of sadness pervades the life of Le Fanu, a feeling readily conveyed in his fiction. He continues the development of the Irish Gothic vampire, successfully building on a foundation left by Maturin and erecting the necessary framework for one of the most memorable and enduring Irish Gothic vampires, Bram Stoker's Dracula. However, this does not imply that Le Fanu did not write any enduring fiction in his own right. Le Fanu clearly proceeded to forge an Irish Gothic tradition in his lifetime of writing.

Critics have a great deal to say about Le Fanu. One reason is that he published profusely and with versatility—national ballads, poetry, historical romance, humor, short stories, novels, political commentary, reviews, mystery, and the supernatural. McCormack, in his thorough biography of Le Fanu, lists twenty novels and forty-two uncollected writings culled from the pages of the *Dublin University Magazine*.[55] McCormack further explains that the list is incomplete due to the number of anonymous pieces published in the magazine that could be attributed to Le Fanu.[56] Hall supports McCormack's findings of the tremendous volume of writing produced by Le Fanu at this time, stating that he serialized nine novels, a "handful of short stories, reviews, and political articles"[57] during his tenure as editor and owner of the *Dublin University Magazine*. Additionally, as reported by Stephen Colclough in "J. Sheridan Le Fanu and the 'Select Library of Fiction': Evidence from Four Previously Unpublished Letters," Le Fanu seized every opportunity to keep his work in print and receive remuneration for it, which sometimes meant that a work was published three times—serially, novel, and cheaper novel—and contained revisions to the work.[58] Unlike Maturin, who is usually discussed in reference to *Melmoth the Wanderer*, Le Fanu offers abundant choices for a discussion of the Irish Gothic vampire. Fortunately, the novel *Uncle Silas* (1864) and "Carmilla," in the collection of short stories *In a Glass Darkly* (1872), will serve as excellent examples of his work and Irish Gothic vampires. Each exhibits original style, Irish subject, personal/Irish identity, and passion.

A brief look at each work, though, also shows perhaps why the stories were not reprinted even in part in *Irish Literature* despite a brief biography indicating that Le Fanu's "chief power was in describing scenes of a mysterious or grotesque character, and the mystery in some of his stories is kept up with considerable skill to the end."[59] Originality is open to debate due to Le Fanu's penchant for revision and use of the convention of "narrator twice removed" as seen a generation earlier in *Melmoth*. *Uncle Silas* had its origins as a short story published in the *Dublin University Magazine* in 1838, "Passage in the Secret History of an Irish Countess." The formulaic use of the narrator is immediately evident in the story's subtitle, "Being the Fifth Extract from the Legacy of the Late Francis Purcell, P. P. of Drumcoolagh."[60] The Irish Countess who wrote the story is dead; Francis Purcell, who received the story from her, is dead. The story is presented by a third party, a nameless editor who prepared the story for publication. "Carmilla" is framed in a similar narrative format. The story, published eight years after *Uncle Silas*, first as a serial in *The Dark Blue* (Dec. 1871– March 1872)[61] and then in a collection of stories, *In A Glass Darkly* (1872), still follows the narrative frame seen in the 1838 publication of "Passage" and also contains more than one revised work adapted to fit within the framework. The collection is introduced as actual case files from the German physician, Dr. Martin Hesselius. Hesselius's unidentified assistant has compiled the notes for publication because the good doctor has since passed away and those cases being published are about people who have also long since died. A cursory view of the framing of the tales thus does not offer an encouraging argument for originality.

The case becomes even more precarious when the criteria of Irish subject and personal/Irish identity are considered. *Uncle Silas* began as a story set in Ireland, as the original title indicates. However, the novel transforms Irish countess Margaret into English heiress Maud Ruthyn. "Carmilla" sets young Laura's tale in an isolated schloss in Styria. Neither setting nor main character promotes an Irish national literature. Each plot features a young adolescent female protagonist as the first-person narrator. The young women hardly seem useful vehicles for a male Irish writer to "find all of himself" unless part of that "self" included getting in touch with his feminine side. To complete the case against Irish Gothic literature, both tales are excellent examples of traditional—in other words, English—Gothic writing.

Le Fanu spins out a classically Gothic story in "Passage in the Secret History of an Irish Countess," a tale that will form the basis of *Uncle Silas*. The Irish countess Margaret is the story's first-person narrator who relates a harrowing tale. She is the only child of a prestigious Anglo-Irish family. She never knew her mother, and although her father saw to his "duty" in raising his child, he never attempted any further parental relationship with her. He is a solitary figure due to a family scandal involving his brother, Sir Arthur, who reputedly murdered a houseguest over a gambling debt but was never formally accused due to a lack of evidence. Not surprisingly, Margaret's father dies when she is eighteen, leaving her the sole heir of a vast fortune and naming Sir Arthur as her guardian. Margaret explains her father's dangerous reasoning: "[H]e had placed me wholly in his [Sir Arthur's] power, to prove to the world, how great and unshaken was his confidence in his brother's innocence and honour, and also to afford him an opportunity of showing that this mark of confidence was not unworthily bestowed."[62] The stage for the classic Gothic tale has been set—the wealthy, young, orphaned, and naïve heroine is placed in the hands of the greedy uncle who not only possesses a suspicious past and an isolated manor but also stands to gain the most by his niece's death. The story progresses as even the most inexperienced Gothic reader would expect; Sir Arthur is *quite* unworthy of the trust placed in him by his brother regarding his innocence. First he tries to force Margaret to marry his loathsome son, Edward. She refuses. Sir Arthur then plans to murder her in the same manner by which he had dispatched his houseguest twenty years before. He almost succeeds but he mistakes his own daughter for Margaret and murders her by mistake while Margaret escapes. The Irish countess's tale remains the same in an 1851 republication of it as *The Murdered Cousin*, and, even in novel form, the essential Gothic elements of the imperiled heiress are retained.

Le Fanu's "Carmilla" operates similarly within the Gothic tradition while also making an obvious contribution to the myth of the vampire. Again, the main character and first-person narrator of the story is a young woman relating the story in retrospect. Nineteen-year-old Laura lives with her widowed father in a remote schloss in Styria. Her English father has retired from the Austrian service and her mother, a Styrian aristocrat, died when she was an infant. Again, the expected story seems to unfold. A mysterious young woman is welcomed into the household, becomes immediate and intimate friends with Laura, and soon young girls in the neighborhood fall ill with an odd sickness that drains them of energy and, usually within a week, of life itself. Eventually young Laura's health is mysteriously compromised, and she begins having strange dreams at night from which she awakens with "the same lassitude, and a languor weighed upon me all day. I felt myself a changed girl. A strange melancholy was stealing over me ... [and] Carmilla became more devoted to me than ever."[63] Although not apparent to Laura, she has begun a transformation into a vampire. Before the change can be completed, a friend of Laura's father arrives. They hunt down the vampire, stake her through the heart, cut off her head, and save the day. As a Gothic tale, "Carmilla" is Le Fanu at his riveting best. However, the use of the vampire was not new nor was it considered in literary circles as very "Irish." The English Romantic poets Lord Byron (1788–1824), Samuel Tayor Coleridge (1772–1834), and John Keats (1795–1821) popularized the literary use of the vampire that had long existed in folklore.[64] John Polidori's "The Vampyre" (1819), James Malcolm Rymer's 1840s installments of *Varney the Vampire; or, the Feast of Blood*, Dion Boucicault's *The Vampire, A Phantasm* (1852), and countless poems featuring vampiric characters were well-established when Le Fanu's "Carmilla" saw publication in the early 1870s. The writing was considered definitely English in tradition and the subject of the vampire was internationally well-established.

Le Fanu's tales are clearly Gothic, which means they possess the requisite amount of passion. However, originality, Irish subject, and personal/Irish identity are not in evidence. As described above, both Laura and Maud are presented as traditionally Gothic heroines, with Maud representing "one of the Gothic novel's most ubiquitous characters, the orphan."[65] Another obstacle to both originality and Irish subject are the novels' settings. The publishers with whom Le Fanu contracted "advised that novels with Irish loci did not sell,"[66] and in "1863 he signed a contract with the English publisher Richard Bentley, which prohibited Irish settings."[67] As a result, *Uncle Silas* dispensed with Irish ties early on in its evolution and no connection was made in "Carmilla"; thus, Irish subject let alone Irish identity would be difficult elements to locate. Personal identity appears absolutely impossible in stories that feature young English heiresses in their late teens as their first-person narrators. Given this information, which was readily seen by the editors of *Irish Literature*, it is no surprise that they chose to include Le Fanu's more Irish early poems in their volumes because his "English" popular novels appear to have no claim as a part of a serious national literature.

Yet appearances, as any seasoned Gothic reader knows, can be quite deceiving. Originality abounds in Le Fanu's fiction. *Uncle Silas* evolved from Le Fanu's "Passage in the Secret History of an Irish Countess," which Patrick Diskin of University College Galway compared to Poe's "Murders in the Rue Morgue" (1841) in his essay, "Poe, Le Fanu and the Sealed Room Mystery." Diskin explains that the "parallels between the stories are, in fact, sufficiently close and sufficiently numerous to allow us to conclude without hesitation that Poe was unconsciously indebted to Le Fanu for the idea."[68] In other words, Poe should be sharing credit for the locked room mystery with Le Fanu since "Passage" preceded "Murders in the Rue Morgue" by three years. Peter Penzoldt pointed out another impressive literary credit that Le Fanu could claim from his creation of Dr. Hesselius. "Even if Balzac's Dr. Desplein was the ancestor of the long line of 'psychic doctors,' which include Dr. Reymond, John Silence, and perhaps even that great lay scientist, Sherlock Holmes, it was certainly Le Fanu who introduced the prototype into English fiction."[69]

Additionally, the development of "Passage" into *Uncle Silas* with the main character of Maud Ruthyn strengthens the argument for originality. Maud is not a typical Gothic heroine—naïve, friendless, in constant peril (real or imagined), and in need of a timely rescue. First, she retains loyal family and friends. After her father's death, her cousin Lady Monica Knollys, her father's friend Dr. Bryerly, devoted maid Mary Quince, cousin Milly, the miller's daughter Meg Hawkes, Meg's admirer Tom Brice, and the attractive Lord Ilbury all work to keep Maud safe. Even with such support, Maud is not a passive recipient of the plot unfolding about her. She is a strong young woman of character, an excellent example of an observation made by Begnal in his analysis of Le Fanu: "It is this sensitivity and perception which separates them [Le Fanu's female characters] from the usual run of Victorian heroines and makes of them characters who seem more at home in the twentieth than the nineteenth century."[70]

Maud may lack worldly experience, but she is not stupid or deficient in courage. Early in the novel, Maud is initially impressed with Lady Knollys's nephew, Captain Charles Oakley, but even before Lady Knollys puts a stop to Charles's attentions and tells Maud exactly why, Maud is not completely taken in by his charm: "I was shy, but not a giggling country miss. I knew I was an heiress; I knew I was somebody. I was not the least bit in the world conceited, but I think this knowledge helped to give me a certain sense of security and self-possession, which might have been mistaken for dignity or simplicity."[71] *I knew I was somebody.* With this statement, Le Fanu gives his heroine power and a sense of identity. It is something that sets her apart from other Gothic heroines and, as Wayne E. Hall states, defines "the novel's main center of energy as a female one."[72] The difference manifests itself in a variety of ways as the story progresses. Though a loving, quiet, and obedient child, Maud is not docile. When her father employs Frenchwoman Madame de la Rougierre as Maud's governess, a battle begins. Madame quickly reveals her ulterior motives in regard to Maud, and they are not for the welfare of her young charge. Madame enjoys trying to bully Maud in private while in public exhibiting such exemplary behavior as to have Maud's father completely fooled. Madame's successful deceit of Mr. Ruthyn allows her to engineer an introduction of Maud to a strange young man on one of their walks to a distant church. It also nearly results with Maud's abduction on another walk. Both times, Madame's plans fail due to Maud's active resistance. She stands up to Madame and finally succeeds in securing the plotting governess's dismissal, though at the cost of nearly being kidnapped.

Maud further shows her spirit when dealing with the unwelcome advances of her cousin Dudley Ruthyn and, later, Captain Oakley. Dudley attempts to kiss Maud and discovers it is a mistake. Rather than submit out of duty or even fear, Maud resists. "I think I was perfectly right to resist, with all the vehemence of which I was capable, this attempt to assume an intimacy which, notwithstanding my uncle's opinion to the contrary, seemed to me like an outrage. Milly found me alone—not frightened, but very angry."[73] Like the Gothic heroines before her, Maud has been orphaned and placed in a precarious situation; however, she is far from allowing herself to be victimized by it.

The audacious Captain Oakley does not fare any better than Cousin Dudley. Oakley attempts to see Maud in secret because he is aware that Lady Knollys does not approve of his interest in her young, wealthy cousin. Maud's fortune is worth the risk, and discovery of the rendezvous is minimal due to Maud's attraction to him and her inexperience with men. However, he underestimates the "simple" heiress. She is neither impressed by his lack of manners nor his obvious disregard for social convention and her reputation when she considers his written plan.

Were I to answer this handsome and cunning fool [Captain Oakley] according to his folly, in what position should I find myself? No doubt my reply would induce a rejoinder, and that compel another note from me, and that invite yet another from him; and however his might improve in warmth, they were sure not to abate. Was it his impertinent plan, with this show of respect and ceremony, to drag me into a clandestine correspondence? Inexperienced girl as I was, I fired at the idea of becoming his dupe, and fancying, perhaps, that there was more in merely answering his note than it would have amounted to.[74]

She wisely turns the sticky matter over to her Uncle Silas, who happily discourages the unwanted suitor. Despite her guardian's refusal to allow a visit, Captain Oakley appears the next day on the grounds of the estate and quite "unexpectedly" meets Maud and Milly on their daily walk. The captain is charming and glibly dismisses Silas's terse note. Maud reveals the nature of a typical adolescent female as she considers forgiving the captain using a convenient rationale: "I really can't see the advantage of being the weaker sex if we are always to be as strong as our masculine neighbors."[75] Oakley is forgiven but interrupted in his clandestine courting by Cousin Dudley. A fight quickly ensues and the captain, who is used to fighting by the rules, receives the worst of it from the pub-brawling Dudley. Maud is appalled by the barbaric behavior of both "suitors" and quickly flees the scene with Milly, changing her mind once again about the captain while reinforcing her loathing of Dudley.

Such scenes show Maud as a dynamic character who develops throughout the novel. This is an unusual element in a Gothic novel, in which the success of the story does not rely on the evolution of the heroine but on the action occurring around her. Furthermore, she takes an active role in keeping herself out of harm's way rather than wait to be saved by the hero. Maud's emerging romantic interest in Lord Ilbury naturally casts him as the hero, yet he does not come to her rescue when it becomes obvious to Maud that she will meet the same fate as her uncle's gambling companion of twenty years ago.

She has been locked in the room where her uncle's gambling guest had inexplicably died two decades ago. The entire household has been emptied save for Silas, Dudley (allegedly in France), the estate's miller, Dickon Hawkes, and Madame de la Rougierre, who is supposedly chaperoning Maud to France to meet with Milly. Madame has not been briefed on the true plan and drinks the drugged claret meant for Maud. Madame falls asleep on Maud's bed, so Maud is locked in the dark room by herself. She hears muffled noises as her murderers cautiously approach. "I knew that I was in a state of siege! The crisis was come, and, strange to say, I felt myself grow all at once resolute and self-possessed. It was not a subsidence, however, of the dreadful excitement, but a sudden screwing up of my nerves to a pitch such as I cannot describe."[76] Maud blends into the shadows as Dudley enters her room from a cleverly hinged window. He does not see who is on the bed and, following the commands of his father, throws a blanket over the drugged figure, and proceeds to bludgeon Madame to death. Silas enters after the act is done. They move to the window in preparation for dropping the body down into the courtyard and then into a shallow grave already dug in one of its remote corners. As they move, so does Maud. "Coolness was given me in that dreadful moment; and I knew that all depended on my being prompt and resolute. I stood up swiftly. I often thought if I had happened to wear silk instead of the cachmere [sic] I had on that night, its rustle would have betrayed me."[77] Maud nearly runs into Hawkes as she makes her escape from the house and into the front drive. She fears she has been caught when she is grabbed by Tom Brice only to discover that he is carrying out Meg's orders and will take Maud to Lady Knollys. It is a race to the estate, where Maud meets her anxious cousin at the door. She collapses into the motherly arms of Lady Knollys, not those of Lord Ilbury.

Another original twist on character appears in "Carmilla." While the novella utilizes the popular vampire myth, its originality lies in the character of a female vampire who focuses her attention upon the female protagonist, Laura. It is an unusual combination since most previous literary vampires were males who would befriend the male protagonist but feed on females. As Nina Auerbach plainly states in *Our Vampires, Ourselves*: "no male vampire of her [Carmilla's] century confronts the desire within his friendship."[78] The relationship between Carmilla and Laura not only confronts this desire, it clearly depicts it. In fact, their relationship is such an original addition to the existing vampire myth of the time period that it illustrates the other elements of Irish literary criteria—Irish subject, passion, and Irish and personal identity.

The relationship between Carmilla and Laura introduces elements of Irish subjects into Le Fanu's story. Though not physically set in Ireland, Margot Gayle Backus notes distinct Irish parallels: "Laura's girlhood in Styria closely resembles the enclosed and isolated childhood of an Anglo-Irish girl. Her family resembles an Anglo-Irish family in its internal dynamics, its ambivalent relationship to the culture that surrounds it, and its economic raison d'etre."[79] The same observation can also apply to Maud's situation even though her story is set in England. All that Le Fanu needed to do was recall the situation of his teenage years at Abington, where he "found life physically isolated and uncertain at best, violent and potentially apocalyptic at worse times,"[80] to convey the special challenges faced by Anglo-Irish families in remote areas.

Another distinctly Irish subject was Le Fanu's consistent use of the symbol of the Big House. "Politically and psychologically, the House is an emblem of the decadence and certain demise of the Ascendancy in Ireland as well as of Le Fanu himself."[81] Maturin began and ended *Melmoth* with the Irish Big House in literal decline. Le Fanu gives it further significance in *Uncle Silas* and "Carmilla" by completely removing the families from the House and Ireland. "Laura's [and Maud's] situation, in its geographic isolation, the constriction of her family unit, and its cultural insularity, represents a reductio ad absurdum of the Anglo-Irish settler colonial family."[82] When Maud's father dies, she leaves her home to live with her uncle, becoming an absentee landlord. Carmilla's absenteeism is an extreme case of poor tenant and land management; those who did not become her victims fled, leaving the town in ruins and the land untended.[83]

Paul E. Davis further develops the Irish subject of the Land Question for Anglo-Irish writers of the nineteenth century who addressed it in the Agrarian novel. "Once Anglo-Irish writers had accepted that the land problem in Ireland was probably insoluble, the novels moved from the superficially social-realist ... to the overtly surreal. The crucial change was that the problem of Ireland was seen to be eternal and as such it could not 'die.' We are approaching the world of the undead. The process culminates in vampirism, in *Dracula*."[84] Davis traces the use of the Agrarian novel as it merges with the Gothic and Sensational novel forms to their natural end, *Dracula*, but he begins with Maturin's *Melmoth* and Thomas Moore's *Memoirs of Captain Rock* before building his case using *Uncle Silas* and "Carmilla."

"Carmilla" continues to address the issue of Irish subjects by distinctly drawing a connection between Carmilla and Laura as relatives through the maternal line. Biological mothers are absent from both Maud's and Laura's lives, but each story provides them with a selection of possible maternal equivalents. Maud must choose between the deceptive and dangerous influence of Madame de la Rougierre and the protective and sincere one of Lady Knollys. Maud easily chooses her cousin. Laura faces a similar choice. She describes Madame Perrodon as "a good-natured governess, who had been with me from, I might almost say, my infancy. I could not remember the time when her fat, benignant face was not a familiar picture in my memory"[85] and Mademoiselle de Lafontaine, "a finishing governess."[86] But it is the "stranger" Carmilla whom Laura is drawn to even though her first instinct is that of horror stemming from the "dream" of her childhood where she was attacked by a beautiful woman who looked exactly like Carmilla. Carmilla quickly eases Laura's fears by fabricating a dream from her childhood where Laura appeared as the beautiful young woman, concluding that "it does seem as if we were destined, from our earliest childhood, to be friends. I wonder whether you feel as strangely drawn towards me as I do to you."[87] Laura admits that she does, selecting Carmilla over both of her governesses. In doing this, Laura not only displays her preference for a friend but also a family heritage. Auerbach explains this connection: "Carmilla and Laura not only share dreams or visions; they share a life.... Both have lost their mothers and their countries; each suffuses the image of the other's absent mother."[88] Laura feels this inexplicable kinship for Carmilla long before it is confirmed by the restored 1698 portrait of Mircalla Karnstein, an ancestor of Laura's mother. The matrilineal line of descent was a cultural feature of Celtic society. Celtic myth possesses many memorably strong and individual female characters (like the fiercely independent warrior queen, Maeve of Connaught), so for Le Fanu to depict startlingly singular women is certainly in keeping with Irish traditions.

Another Irish aspect strongly represented in the stories is the use of the vampire, a familiar figure both in the folklore of Ireland's past and in the politics of Le Fanu's present. As explained by Jarlath Killeen in "An Irish *Carmilla*?": "That vampires could be used to speak about Ireland initially might appear unlikely, but for a nineteenth-century British reader, vampirism and Ireland were related and analogous sites of infection and terror. In *The Tomahawk*, August 7, 1869, an illustration entitled *The Irish Vampire! Brought to Life by the Moonbeam* directly associated Irish Catholic nationalist agrarian insurgency with vampirism."[89]

These findings are further supported by Renee Fox in "*Carmilla* and the Politics of Indistinguishability," noting that "political cartoons at the end of the century represented *both* the native Irish *and* the Protestant landlords as vampires—the figure of the vampire in nineteenth-century Irish culture represents neither the land-stealing former nor the monstrous latter, but rather the production of each class by the other."[90] With each side feeling victimized by the other, it is no surprise that the vampire was utilized by both to illustrate the other. Both were familiar with the vampire from earlier fiction like Polidori's and Rymer's. In addition to fictional accounts, the vampire outbreak in Hungary in 1732 that allegedly originated with Arnold Paul[91] was reported in English news, and when French Benedictine Abbot Dom Augustin Calmet's (1672–1757) *Dissertations Upon the Apparitions of Angels, Daemons, and Ghosts and Concerning the Vampires of Hungary, Bohemia, Moravia, and Silesia* was translated from its original

French into English in 1769, it was thoroughly reviewed by the English press.

Before the vampire reports in the English press or even the serious studies completed by Benedictine abbots, the vampire had long been a figure in the myths and legends associated with Ireland. As noted in the first chapter, Geoffrey (Jeoffry) Keating wrote about the undead in Irish in *Foras Feasa ar*[92]*Eirinn (History of Ireland)* (1629–31) when telling the story of the Tuath de Danans. Patrick Weston Joyce further supported the case for Irish vampires with his tale of the wizard Abhartach in *The Origin and History of Irish Names of Places* (1870). Yeats's description of the Leanhaun Sidhe as energy-draining muses also show vampire tendencies, and Bob Curran offers several examples of Irish vampire stories in his article, "Was Dracula an Irishman?" which makes a connection between Irish vampires and the aristocracy.[93] Laura is a direct descendant through the female line of the aristocratic and vampiric Carmilla.

Montague Summers describes the creatures in such stories as *deargdul*, saying: "In ancient Ireland the Vampire was generally known as *Deargdul*, 'red blood sucker,' and his ravages were universally feared."[94] Wright includes in his collection a brief account of a female vampire: "At Waterford, in Ireland, there is a little graveyard under a ruined church near Strongbow's Tower. Legend has it that underneath the ground at this spot there lies a beautiful female vampire still ready to kill those she can lure thither by her beauty."[95] Although Summers's investigation into this story revealed that there was no such place in Ireland called Strongbow's Tower, and the legend was probably confused with a non-vampiric one involving Reginald's Tower and a frog.[96] An old and favored tale is often very difficult to uproot, even with facts. The lovely vampire of the nonexistent Strongbow's Tower is reminiscent of Carmilla.

It is difficult to prove whether Le Fanu was familiar with these stories, so it is hard to say for certain that he was definitely influenced by them. However, it is well-established that Le Fanu had a long-standing interest in Irish legends, myths, superstitions, and antiquities. S. M. Ellis, who knew Le Fanu's son George Brinsley well and thus heard many stories from him about his father, relays the following in his book *Wilkie Collins, Le Fanu, and Others*: "Le Fanu had naturally, being an imaginative boy, from his earliest youth found an equal pleasure in the wild legends, the superstitions, and ghost stories of his native land. As he said, 'In my youth I heard a great many Irish traditions.'"[97] Ellis continues by stating that Le Fanu "became an authority on the superstitions and archaeology of Ireland."[98] His interest did not seem to diminish as he grew older, especially when one considers the regular appearance of articles published in the *Dublin University Magazine* during his tenure as editor and owner, including "Legendary Fictions of the Irish Celts" (Jan. 1867), "Glimpses of Celtic and Anglo-Saxon Literature" (Sept. 1864), "Draoideachta: The Magic of the Ancient Irish" (Feb. 1864), and "Fairy Mythology of Ireland" (Jun. 1864). No authorship is attributed to these articles so it is unknown if Le Fanu wrote them; however, as editor/owner, he most assuredly read them. He had a great amount of Irish subject material at his disposal, and it is interesting to note that "Draoideachta: The Magic of the Ancient Irish" included a version of Keating's undead soldiers who had to be staked.[99]

The presence of a vampire in a story almost guarantees the element of passion; in "Carmilla," such scenes abound between Laura and Carmilla:

> Sometime after an hour of apathy my strange and beautiful companion [Carmilla] would take my hand and hold it with a fond pressure, renewed again and again; blushing softly, gazing in my face with languid and burning eyes, and breathing so fast that her dress rose and fell with the tumultuous respiration. It was like the ardour of a lover; it embarrassed me; it was hateful and yet overpowering; and with gloating eyes she drew me to her, and her hot lips travelled along my cheek in kisses; and she would whisper, almost in sobs, You are mine, you *shall* be mine, and you and I are one for ever." Then she has thrown herself back in her chair, with her small hands over her eyes, leaving me trembling.[100]

This is merely one scene of many between the young women, which certainly fulfills the criteria of passion. Maud also has passionate experiences. She is courted by Dudley, the Captain, and Lord Ilbury. Dudley repulses her but serves as the typical arranged marriage that the Gothic heroine desires to escape. The captain is the charming cad of romances, a fortune-hunting "bad boy" who has nothing to recommend in him beyond his good looks, smooth talk, and easy manners. Lord Ilbury is the "hero" of the tale. Though he does not save Maud from her uncle's plan, he is part of the happy conclusion by marrying the heroine.

Romance, love, and sex are not the only forms of passion found in the stories. Another form is evident in the characters' obsessive dedication to an idea, belief, and even an addiction. Austin Ruthyn, Maud's father, maintains the innocence of his brother Silas in the murder he is suspected of committing. Austin holds to this belief even at the expense of his own reputation. It is only toward the end of his life that he begins to entertain thoughts that *perhaps* Silas had killed his friend, but Austin does not live long enough to transfer these changing beliefs into a new will.

Both Austin and Silas exhibit a passion for their belief in Swedenborgianism, though Austin's pursuit of it is more purely motivated than Silas's. Silas has a stronger commitment to laudanum, the tincture of opium.

Maud is unaware of the cause of her uncle's fragile health, but she is very observant of the effects. During one of her rare visits to her uncle's rooms, she witnesses the "tic—neuralgia, or something,"[101] as Silas calls it, and desires to call a doctor. The servant explains that Silas has had these "fits" for over twelve years and the doctor knows all about them. Ironically, it is Silas's passion for laudanum combined with his passion for Maud's inheritance that ultimately leads to his death. Likewise, Carmilla's own passion for Laura leads to her destruction at the hands of General Spielsdorf, who is motivated by a different passion, revenge for his ward Bertha's death.

The passions of the characters play a significant role in the formation of their Irish identities, or, as is the case with both main characters, the multiple conflicts each faces as she tries to forge her own sense of self. Maud asserts early in her story: "I knew I was somebody."[102] She was an heiress and that gave her the freedom to make more choices than other women of her age. However, as Maud's increasingly limited freedom on her uncle's estate illustrates, she does not have the ability to exercise her identity because she is still operating within the confines of societal expectations. In Victorian society, a wealthy young heiress was obligated to make an advantageous match with the son of an equally prestigious and financially secure family. At the conclusion of *Uncle Silas*, Maud establishes her individual identity through connecting it with others while her family's name is literally erased. At the end of the novel, Maud states: "I am Lady Ilbury, happy in the affection of a beloved and noble-hearted husband. The shy, useless girl you have known is now a mother."[103] Silas does not survive his failure to murder Maud. He is found dead that very night, his death "caused by an excessive dose of laudanum, accidentally administered by himself."[104] Dudley escapes to Australia and changes his name to avoid prosecution; his sister Milly marries a clergyman which changes her name; Maud's marriage to Lord Ilbury changes her name; and Silas's estate collapses with his death. The family name of Ruthyn will not continue. Maud's personal story may have ended happily, but the disappearance of her family name and the unification of her estate with her husband's indicate a constriction in society, an all too common feature in Anglo-Irish circles. Richard Davenport-Hines in *Gothic: Four Hundred Years of Excess, Horror, Evil, and Ruin* describes this shrinking of the Anglo-Irish in relation to "Carmilla," but it can easily be applied to *Uncle Silas*, too.

> Their [Laura and her father's] isolated cultural self-consciousness resembles that of besieged Anglo-Irish gentry living in the hermetic world of the great house. The analogy, however, is more extensive even than this…. This abandoned village suggests the gross depopulation of the Irish countryside after the great famine of 1845–47; but the

extinction of the Karnsteins [or Ruthyns], which is reiterated in the story, had a special Irish significance. Since the Act of Union of 1800, which absorbed Ireland into the newly created United Kingdom, the Irish peerage was both declining in numbers and only able to regenerate by a sort of legal vampirism. Under the 1800 legislation, no new Irish peerages could be created without the extinction of three old ones.[105]

With the eight years that elapsed between the publication of *Uncle Silas* and "Carmilla," Le Fanu must have seen the further decline of the Anglo-Irish for he moved from Maud, who not only declares that she knows who she is but whose story ends with the anticipated closure of marriage and motherhood, to Laura, who is often in a state of confusion and who does not seem to find any resolution at her story's conclusion. Backus identifies the central relationship between Laura and Carmilla as the illustration of this identity crisis on several levels. "Carmilla's relationship to Laura is also shot through with anxiety concerning the Anglo-Irish child's national identity."[106] In Laura's case, the typical teenager's quest for identity is greatly complicated by issues of colonialism, nationalism, lesbianism, incest, and parental failure to protect. Laura's father is English but married to a Styrian woman with aristocratic ties and remained in Styria after her death because he could live more economically there than he could in England. As a result, Laura has never seen England though her father insists upon speaking English and practicing English customs in an environment far removed from his homeland.

Despite his efforts to raise an English child with French governesses in a remote area of Styria, Laura's father is not successful in shaping his daughter's identity or meeting his parental obligations. In England, a young woman of Laura's age would have been presented in society and attended the necessary gatherings that would allow her to meet young men who would be suitable husbands. Instead, Laura is isolated, stating "there were two or three young lady friends besides, pretty nearly of my own age, who were occasional visitors for longer or shorter terms; and these visits I sometimes returned.... My life was, notwithstanding, rather a solitary one, I can assure you."[107] Rather than send her to London with her two French governesses for a season, the text hints that Laura's father may have come to some sort of an agreement with General Speilsdorf for Laura's hand in marriage that included her father marrying Bertha in exchange.[108] If such plans existed, they were destroyed when the general allowed Millarca to befriend his niece and when Laura's father invited Carmilla into their home. Instead of facilitating Laura's transition from daughter to wife, her father unwittingly exposes her to unimagined influences on her forming identity that do not remotely include Victorian wife.

The greatest influences are Laura's suspicion, then discovery that she and Carmilla are related, and Carmilla's intent to turn her into a vampire like herself. Both events significantly influence Laura's identity. Even though Carmilla does not seem to succeed in turning Laura into a vampire, her attempt results in experiences that would complicate Laura's already difficult task of personal identity formation. Carmilla befriends and seduces Laura, who is open but yet uneasy about intimacy. From their very first meeting, Laura reports feelings of attraction and repulsion, with attraction usually prevailing.[109] It is a source of conflict for Laura. Le Fanu adds to her dilemma by showing the direct familial connection between Laura and Carmilla which would suggest incest. While the homosexual nature of their relationship is often commented upon, it is important to note that same-sex female relationships were viewed quite differently from male ones. As Renee Fox explains:

> [A]lthough today we quickly use the term *lesbianism* to define the relationship between Carmilla and Laura, studies of relationships between women in nineteenth-century Britain have pointed out that "the lesbian was not a distinct social type during the years 1830 to 1880, although male sodomy was a public and private obsession" (Marcus 2007, 7). Intimate, even passionate friendships between women pepper the most canonical Victorian texts ... the intimacy—both emotional and physical—of Laura and Carmilla's friendship would have had a very different resonance in the nineteenth century than a similarly erotic male friendship.
>
> Carmilla's vampirism makes her dangerous, but her interest in women does not definitively mark her as perverse, unnatural, or different.[110]

When information about the Victorian beliefs surrounding the matrilineal connection between the characters is also considered, an interesting picture emerges. According to Jarlath Killeen, "the maternal blood link between Laura and Carmilla is a significant one, partly because it goes some way to explain the intensity of the relationship between them" because Laura's feeling of being drawn to Carmilla "may be due not only to a (repressed) sexual desire for her guest ... but to their familial connection."[111] Victorian doctors believed that "mother's hereditary disorders were likely to be passed on to their daughters and on down the female line,"[112] so the blood of the Karnsteins, that "bad family" with their "blood-stained annals" and "atrocious lusts,"[113] not only ran through Carmilla's veins but Laura's, too—even before Carmilla attacked her.

Carmilla, though, is the one perceived as a threat that must be removed because she undermines the male authority in the text. If Bertha and Laura were part of a marriage arrangement made by the general and Laura's father, then Carmilla's power over them means that "they lose [their] masculine power over [the girls]."[114] Therefore, the males in the form of Laura's father,

Dr. Spielsberg, General Spielsdorf, and Baron Vordenburg must reassert their control by killing Carmilla and whisking Laura off to Italy for a year. However, the story's end seems to indicate that the male victory was more appearance than reality. Years later, as Laura writes about the experience, Carmilla remains a strong presence. She is so strong that Laura's story lacks the expected Gothic ending that even Maud's has: marriage to a suitable man and a child. Of course, her childless and spouseless status may result from further male control since the Victorian doctors also "warned mothers with a background of family illness (whether physical or mental) to refrain from reproduction if at all possible as the threat of 'infection' was particularly high. Insanity was a condition believed to be passed from mother to daughter with terrifying ease."[115] The bad blood of the Karnsteins passed to Laura through her mother, compounded by the traumatic vampire attack of a female Karnstein, could easily have rendered Laura ineligible for marriage and motherhood. She is still troubled by what happened, still thinks about Carmilla, and still hears her step in the hall. When this is added to the fact that she was seeing Dr. Hesselius in his professional capacity, it would not be surprising if those near her thought she was insane.[116] She was certainly trying to understand her experiences and determine how they fit into her own identity. As Robert Smart points out, "if anything, her [Laura's] willingness to submit to the urgings of Martin Hesselius reveals that for the remainder of her life she worried about who she was, who or what she had become, and perhaps most important for a woman who represents the end of her family line, what the future held for her."[117] Laura's identity is far less certain than Maud's, who is Maud Ruthyn as her story begins and Lady Ilbury when it ends. Laura does not even have a last name, eerily recalling what McClelland stated about vampires and their identities: "[They have] no valid identity, no evident social position."[118]

The final question of identity that remains to be answered is how Le Fanu finds his own via his writing. In his biography, Begnal offers one possible connection:

> LeFanu cannot help becoming one of his own protagonists. A tortured man like…. Silas Ruthyn, he seems to utilize his art as a stabilizing force upon his own personal life. For him, the novels and their creation function as both purgation and catharsis, allowing him both the objectivity and involvement without which he cannot live…. It is a tribute to the strength of his inherent beliefs that he was able to hold out so long against futility and despair.[119]

It is an interesting observation. There are biographical elements of Le Fanu in his characters. For example, Maud records several observations about her father that bear a striking resemblance to Le Fanu's own life. She talks about her father's "failure in public life" of politics[120] and the fact that he "was a man of generous nature and powerful intellect, but given up to the oddities of a shyness which grew with years and indulgences, and became inflexible with his disappointments and affliction."[121] As shown by Ellis's reference to T. P. Le Fanu's *Memoir of the Le Fanu Family,* Le Fanu's nephew lists the similarities between Austin Ruthyn and his uncle: "It was peculiar figure, strongly made, thick-set, with a face large, and very stern; he wore a loose, black velvet coat and waistcoat ... he married, and his beautiful young wife died ... he had left the Church of England for some odd sect ... and ultimately became a Swedenborgian."[122]

Perhaps most telling, though, are the similarities Le Fanu shares with his female narrators. Like Maturin, Le Fanu was a member of Anglo-Irish Dublin society but became increasingly separated from that social class as he aged. He was an Anglo-Irishman but fell out of favor with his party, could not even bring himself to put on the façade of Anglican piety, and ultimately retired from society altogether. What better protagonists were there than young women who were at the mercy of others to decide their fates to convey the isolation, loneliness, and helplessness that must have been felt by the Anglo-Irish minority? The impossible situation was even more pronounced for the Anglo-Irish in Le Fanu's time. As explained by Joe Spence in "Nationality and Irish Toryism: The Case of *The Dublin University Magazine*, 1833–52," the "English ... refused to recognise the Irish Protestants as different from the Catholics [due to their Irish birth]; the Roman Catholics Irish [refused similar recognition of the Irish Protestants] because they regarded the Protestants as divorced from their ancient heritage, spiritual and cultural."[123]

Le Fanu identifies with his female characters on a more personal level too. Le Fanu "seems to have been very close to his daughters, and the combination of the memories of Susan Le Fanu's death and the task of bringing up these young women seems to give him a new closeness to all things female."[124] When one further considers that Le Fanu's oldest daughter, Eleanor, published her serialized fiction in the *Dublin University Magazine* along with his niece, Rhoda Broughton, and two other young female writers (Nina Cole and Annie Robertson), it is no surprise that during his mentoring of these novice writers that he learned a great deal about how young women think and act. In fact, McCormack comments that the magazine was associated "in the public mind with a distinctly feminine imagination; during his editorship Le Fanu was the only male contributor of fiction of ability—if we discount Mortimer Collins."[125] According to McCormack, Le Fanu was quite adept at writing in a feminine style, saying:

Even in *Guy Deverell*, which follows immediately on *Uncle Silas*, there is evidence of a curiously effeminate sentimentalism, and by the end of the decade Rhoda Broughton's heroines were a good deal more robust than her uncle's heroes. Eleanor Frances Le Fanu did not so much imitate her father's style, as stimulate his tendency to mimic the attitudes of others, drawing him close to her own immaturity. Apart from the characteristically hyperstatic use of portrait-imagery, and the themes of revenant and suicide, *The Tenants of Malory* is all but indistinguishable from the work of the author's twenty-two year old daughter.[126]

While this is not the most flattering analysis of Le Fanu's writing, it does indicate that he was heavily influenced by the young women living and writing around him and that he was such a careful observer of human nature and such a skilled writer that he could replicate any style and any character on the page.

Le Fanu could also draw upon the deeply emotional moments from his own life and readily use them to describe his characters' feelings during similar times of experience. When her father dies, Maud writes:

I do not know how those awful days, and more awful nights, passed over. The remembrance is repulsive. I hate to think of them. I was soon draped in the conventional black, with its heavy folds of crape. Lady Knollys came, and was very kind. She undertook the direction of all those details which were to me so inexpressibly dreadful…. I have often thought since with admiration and gratitude of the tact with which she managed my grief.

There is no dealing with great sorrow as if it were under the control of our wills. It is a terrible phenomenon, whose laws we must study, and to whose conditions we must submit, if we would mitigate it.[127]

Le Fanu knew sorrow, and it was his brother William who saw to Susanna's funeral arrangements and supported the family in their grief.[128] While Victorian social conventions addressed the outward appearance such as black apparel, draping mirrors, funeral processions, and mourning periods, there was little recourse for the person who continued to mourn internally unless he could place his trust in his faith. Le Fanu could not find solace in religion; he saw what it did to his sister, his father, and his wife. The title of the short story collection published near the end of his life supports this. *In a Glass Darkly* is a slight alteration of 1 Corinthians 13:12: "For now we see *through* a glass, darkly; but then face to face: now I know in part; but then shall I know even as also I am known." Le Fanu, professional writer and minister's son, knew the significance of changing one word in the passage. "Through" supplies a few interpretations, among them that the present is temporary and fleeting—a comforting thought to someone suffering physical or emotional pain. Life on Earth always offers the hope of tomorrow and, if that fails, there is the promising hope of eternity. Yet, Le Fanu replaced "through" with "in." "In" gives the impression of permanence or being trapped; there is no point in looking optimistically to tomorrow because it will be the same. It is an even more bleak substitution when one considers that 1 Corinthians 13 is one of the Bible's famous passages about love. For Le Fanu, who deeply felt the absence of the people he loved and desperately sought to understand why they died, love could not "endure all things" and the promise "to know" eluded him and offered little comfort. He decided to find solace via the most natural avenue available to him— writing, and from it emerged a remarkable female vampire one year before his death. As Auerbach astutely observes in her discussion of "Carmilla," "For Le Fanu, the strangeness of vampirism is its kinship to the commonplace ... his vampire invokes rather the horror inherent in the Victorian dream of domestic coziness, the restoration of lost intimacy and comfort."[129] Le Fanu certainly experienced the horror of that dream. To the outsider, his domestic life appeared to encompass this ideal of Victorian domesticity yet his biographers paint the reality of his situation, which included debt, a home which was not his own, and a wife who was mentally unstable.

Mental instability is also a claim made for Le Fanu as well. Peter Penzoldt states that "towards the end of his life, Le Fanu, who had always been extremely sensitive, and was probably a neurotic, became definitely abnormal"[130] and explores this idea using psychoanalytic criticism to reveal "four very important facts":

> [F]irst ... being a neurotic, he was prone to neurotic fears which are reflected in his work....
>
> Secondly, his self-identification with weak, feminine, child-heroines shows that in the face of neurotic terrors he reacted as a helpless child....
>
> Thirdly, as we have already mentioned, Le Fanu's neurosis kindled his interest in psychological problems....
>
> Fourthly, the creation of Dr. Hesselius was an attempt to fight his own problems.[131]

Penzoldt continues his analysis and makes several interesting statements, including, "Le Fanu's great gift for psychology is also evident in his stories of guilty conscience. Conscious in fact was one of his favourite themes"[132]; "Le Fanu's stories impress by their terrible air of authenticity, their visionary quality"[133]; "This astonishingly accurate psychiatry marks Le Fanu as one of the earliest masters of the psychological ghost story"[134]; "His general attitude to the supernatural was also new in his day.... He believed that men were constantly surrounded by preternatural powers"[135]; and "Le Fanu was an ardent Swedenborgian, but he always remained hostile to spiritualism, which he despised for its ineffectual messages and mild manifestations."[136] Since I am not an experienced psychoanalytic critic, I cannot engage Penzoldt using the expertise of his field; however, I can offer another way to interpret some of his conclusions presented above using a significant event of Le Fanu's life as the basis. Rather than attributing the above conclusions as stemming from Le Fanu's proposed neurosis or abnormal state, they could have their origins in the experiences surrounding Le Fanu's marriage to Susanna, which could be argued as having a tremendous influence on his writing and his life, continuing even after her death.

All biographical accounts of Le Fanu indicate that he adored Susanna but also note that she increasingly experienced some "nervous" behavior throughout their marriage. The exact nature of her condition is never named, but most sources also allude to "tension" in the household. Carol A. Senf even states in her essay, "Women and Power in 'Carmilla'," that "whatever the reason for their marital unhappiness, Le Fanu apparently felt like the victimized party."[137] This is a logical conclusion considering his position. He witnessed Susanna's steady mental decline and felt frustrated and powerless; he could not help her, nor could doctors or faith. If he loved her as much as he professed, when she suffered, he suffered, too. Penzoldt theorized that Le Fanu's ability to show the varying aspects of the psychological condition, including neurotic behavior, was because Le Fanu was neurotic. Perhaps he was; however, another possibility could be that after fifteen years of observing Susanna's struggles, he possessed intimate and detailed knowledge of how someone suffering psychologically would behave. He drew upon this experience when describing the psychology of his characters.

It is not surprising that these characters were often haunted by guilt when one considers the possibility that Le Fanu may have spent much of his life trying to come to terms with his guilt about Susanna's death at such a young age. First, Le Fanu reportedly had a well-developed sense of humor, which his family and friends all recalled specific instances of. One of these examples is seen in the secret correspondence that he maintained with his sister-in-law, Bessie. While there are no indications that Le Fanu and Bessie were having an affair, McCormack makes an interesting observation on the correspondence: "The tone of his comments ... suggests that he instinctively absorbed attitudes and mannerisms from the individual with whom he was in immediate contact. Thus, with Bessie Bennett, he was casual, witty, and even *risqué*."[138] The light, easy banter in his letters to Bessie was probably not reflected in the tone of his relationship with Susanna, whose increasing religious intensity and doubts of his affections must have weighed heavily upon him. For someone fond of humor, there did not seem to be much in his home, and the fact that he could not make Susanna happy must have made him feel very guilty.

An even greater source of guilt is evidenced in his behavior surrounding her death. McCormack's transcription of Le Fanu's 1858 notebook contains a stream of thoughts about Susanna yet there seems to be some self-censoring, as if there was something weighing heavily upon his mind but he was stopping short of writing about; he suspected Susanna committed suicide.[139] According to Le Fanu's notebook, Susanna was preoccupied with death:

> The idea of death was constantly present to her mind, & it's (*sic*) gloom & horror most beautifully softened, while its chastening influence was always present. Her conversation & her correspondence were full of this great subject & her hopes & longings for eternity—and all this had been brought about gradually within little more than a year & most remarkably & in the greater part during the last winter.[140]

So, after Susanna's father died on May 26, 1856, she experienced "a major disruption of her emotional and spiritual life,"[141] which developed into an obsessive interest in death. Prior to her death, Susanna reported being visited by her father, who told her that "there is room in the vault" for her.[142] Then, on April 26, 1858, "Susanna was taken dangerously ill with an hysterical attack" and died two days later.[143] In his notebook, Le Fanu wrote: "I will not trouble myself with the faithless thought that the errors of art or the misapprehensions of the beloved patient hastened her death."[144] He obviously is troubled by how she died even though he uses a fair amount of ink writing about God's great forgiveness and planning: "It was the will of my heavenly Father that she should die exactly when & how she did, & in that certainty ends all speculation."[145] Speculation of what? How she died? In his research on the Bennett family burial place, Showers observed: "Curiously, a man by the name of James Nichols gave his Signature of Attestation [for Susanna] in the *Register of Burials*, not Joseph. Susanna Le Fanu died the 28 April 1858. Her exact cause of death is not given."[146]

If Le Fanu even had a suspicion that Susanna had hastened her own death, it would have caused him a great deal of guilt. McCormack, in his biography of Le Fanu, mentions a cousin of the family who had threatened suicide in the summer of 1838 and explains the Victorian perspective on mental illness and suicide:

> [T]he family who had a child or relative in an asylum was never immune to the fear of discovery. Fundamental anxieties about religion, parental authority, and sexual drives lay at the root of at least some mental disorders, and these implications intensified the family guilt, forcing the secret into deeper areas of neurosis. If Victorian enlightenment knew enough to admit that the mad were not morally bad, there was still a residual fear that they might be *metaphysically* bad. Suicide, the ultimate blasphemy to the Christian, became closely identified with insane behavior.[147]

Given the previous discussion of the Victorian belief that mothers were more likely to pass on mental illness to their daughters than their sons, Le Fanu had a vested interest in keeping the details of Susanna's condition and the circumstances surrounding her death secret if he suspected suicide. He had two daughters who were just entering their teens and would soon be entering society to meet eligible young men in the hopes of making a good match. No respectable family would want their son to marry a young woman who had a mother about whom there was even the rumor of suicide. Le Fanu could no longer do anything to help his wife, but he could still do something to protect his girls. Such thoughts, though, could very well wear away at a person's mental state; however, Le Fanu was fortunate in that he had an outlet for dealing with his concerns. He wrote about them.

Although not identified as one of Le Fanu's short stories, "A Glimpse of the Supernatural in the Nineteenth Century" appeared in the *Dublin University Magazine*'s November 1861 issue and certainly exhibited some of the hallmarks of a classic Le Fanu ghost story. It is about the haunting guilt of young George Seymour, who secretly marries a farmer's niece and has a child, suddenly becomes heir to his family's fortune when both of his older brothers die, regrets his secret, falls in love with an heiress and plans a wedding, and murders both his secret wife and child in a moment of anger when he shoves them over the side of a bridge and into the river (because she will not give him their marriage license in exchange for money). A week before George's wedding to the heiress, his secret wife's ghost appears and beckons him into the water, where she pulls him under with her. "The body of George Seymour was never found, nor did the mysterious apparition ever again appear on the bank of the river."[148]

This story is mentioned because Le Fanu not only had a great interest in ghost stories,[149] but because it specifically addresses guilt suffered from an action that is deeply regretted but cannot be fixed: "Is it not, indeed, the most terrible of all the agonies which human nature can endure, to bear about the consciousness of a deadly crime, once committed, and never, never, in all the eternal ages, to be recalled?"[150] George had several reasons for his guilt, the greatest being responsible for throwing his wife and child into the river and then doing nothing to try and save them when he did. If Susanna committed suicide, Le Fanu may very well have tormented himself with the guilt of not having somehow prevented it. His guilt became an essential part of his identity.

Le Fanu's personal identity was tied to Irish identity and appeared as the underlying theme of his writing. He pursued writing to support his family, but he also wrote for personal reasons that caused this fiction to evolve from historical romance to Irish Gothic, a conclusion supported by E. F. Bleiler.

> LeFanu started his writing career as a follower of Lever, Carleton, and other Irish regionalists; he ended as an independent writer, with a position of his own. His techniques and purposes, too, changed with the years, and if the powerful later work occasionally makes the earlier look crude and unsubtle, the earlier work nevertheless retains the breath of horror and strangeness that was LeFanu's own personality.[151]

Le Fanu's contribution to Irish Gothic influenced future Irish writers. As Begnal concludes, Le Fanu's "attention to more general and ethical problems may certainly be seen as something of a link to the work of George Moore and James Joyce. Though Le Fanu produced nothing so outwardly Irish as *Esther Waters* or *Dubliners*, he does show his contemporaries that literature emanating from Dublin need not carry with it a collection of stage Irishmen or peasant folklore."[152] Other critics note that his work influenced Charlotte Bronte's *Jane Eyre*,[153] Stevenson's *The Strange Case of Dr. Jekyll and Mr. Hyde* (1886), Wilde's *The Picture of Dorian Gray* (1891), Henry James's *The Turn of the Screw* (1898),[154] and Dorothy L. Sayers.[155] One of his greatest influences was on Bram Stoker's *Dracula*, but perhaps his most surprising is the effect he had on Yeats. In his introduction to *Uncle Silas*, W. J. McCormack directly connects the novel to Yeats's play *Purgatory*, "with its homicidal and misbegotten heir killing his bastard son to finish 'all that consequence,' and its structural use of Swedenborgian phantasmagoria or 'dreaming-back.'"[156] Another Le Fanu–Yeats connection comes from the "much-quoted phrase, 'A terrible beauty is born' … that Yeats owed the expression to a poem by Joseph Sheridan Le Fanu."[157] A final Yeats connection was noted by David Annwn in his essay, "Dazzling Ghostland: Sheridan Le Fanu's Phantasmagoria": "W.B. Yeats was seven when Le Fanu died. It has been mooted that Yeats' poem 'The Stolen Child' owes much to the older writer's *Laura Silver Bell* (1872)."[158] Ironically, it was Yeats's contemporary Bram Stoker who would write an Irish novel that would define the modern vampire: *Dracula*.

5

Bram Stoker
The Realization of the Irish Vampire

"The story is one long nightmare, full of mad-house imaginings, vampires, and everything that is likely to keep nervous people from sleep at night. It is a curious compound of realism and sensationalism, but though it does not belong to a school that I admire, it is written at times with considerable power....

The middle part of the book, where the scene is mainly in England, strikes me as less good. Vampires need a Transylvanian background to be convincing."[1]—Book review of *Dracula*, June 12, 1897

"The plot is ingenious, and the more interesting as it is laid chiefly in England at the present day."[2]—Book review of *Dracula*, July 4, 1897

"Nervous persons, young children and sufferers from delirium tremens, will do well not to look within its [*Dracula*] covers."[3]—Book review of *Dracula*, July 3, 1897

Bram Stoker's *Dracula* (1897) enjoyed positive reviews in which he was often compared to Wilkie Collins and Anne Radcliffe. They usually said that he had surpassed them with his vampire. Interestingly enough, it was his mother, Charlotte Stoker, in a letter to her son after reading the novel, who was the most prophetic:

My dear it is splendid, a thousand miles beyond anything you have written before, and I feel certain will place you very high in the writers of the day.... No book since Mrs. Shelley's "Frankenstein" or indeed any other at all has come near yours in originality, or terror—Poe is nowhere. I have read much but I have never met a book like it at all. In its terrible excitement it should make a widespread reputation and much money for you.[4]

While *Dracula* did not make Stoker any great fortune during his lifetime, it has earned him a place with Mary Shelley in the literary annals, and it would surpass even the goals of an Irish national literature to achieve the status of an international myth. *Dracula* is an entertaining novel whose existence was due, in part, to the Irish and English Gothic works that preceded it, since they provided Stoker with an expansive literature to imitate. He borrowed extensively from Maturin and Le Fanu, but he still managed to write an original novel that utilized the necessary features of Irish subject, Irish and personal identity, and passion.

Before a discussion of these elements, a biographical account of Stoker is necessary. Stoker is probably the best known of the three authors and has also been most frequently the subject of biography, so, unlike Le Fanu and most definitely unlike Maturin's biographical sections, Stoker's will be brief.

Abraham Stoker was born on November 8, 1847, in Clontarf, Ireland. His birth occurred in the midst of the historically devastating famine for Ireland, and 1847 was a particularly traumatic year. But the Stokers, living near Dublin and not relying on the potato crop for their survival, fared better during the famine years than those in the countryside. In fact, the family thrived. Stoker was the third child of Abraham (civil servant) and Charlotte (Thornley) Stoker who was twenty years younger than her husband. Stoker's brother, William Thornley, and sister, Matilda, preceded him in birth and siblings Thomas, Richard, Margaret, and George followed him. Although the Stokers did not suffer from the famine, they were concerned about the health of their third child. For the first seven years of his life, Stoker suffered from an unnamed illness, as he mentions in *Personal Reminiscences of Henry Irving*: "It is true that I had known weakness. In my babyhood I used, I understand, to be often at the point of death. Certainly till I was about seven years old I never knew what it was to stand upright.... This early weakness, however, passed away in time and I grew into a strong boy and in time enlarged to the biggest member of my family."[5]

The mysterious illness that just "passed away" has been a source of speculation for many Stoker scholars. One interesting idea proposed by Dick Collins in his essay "The Devil and Daniel Farson: How Did Bram Stoker Die?" determined that Stoker suffered from spina bifida occulta, an internal condition that affects the nerves rather than the spinal vertebrae.[6] Collins explained:

> The enormous majority of sufferers do not suffer at all—the deformity can predispose them more easily to slipping a disk, but mostly it is harmless and so unsuspected, and usually only found by chance if there is a post-mortem that invades the lower back. But around 2% of sufferers can have a far worse time of it: and as children they can suffer a range of symptoms that include bedwetting, a difference in the length of the legs,

sensory loss to the legs and feet, and problems walking—yes, including a long delay in learning to walk. All these things can be overcome, and apparently eradicated, with time and patience. Poor health or a bout of illness can allow it to resurface.[7]

Collins's theory appears to be a viable one when Stoker's overall health record is reviewed. Stoker did overcome his childhood illness and grew up healthy and very athletic. At Trinity College he was on the rugby team, an oarsman, a long-distance walker, weight-lifter, and University Athlete in 1867.[8] He completed his studies but, as biographer Barbara Belford describes, "extracurricular activities came first," including the Philosophical Society and Historical Society.[9]

In 1865, Stoker's father retired from the civil service. Abraham, Sr., Charlotte, and Matilda and Margaret left Ireland in 1872 to live abroad, where his pension would allow them to have a more comfortable lifestyle than in Ireland.[10] Abraham had made certain that all his sons were educated, and they had done well. Thornley became a well-known surgeon who was later knighted; Richard went into medicine in India; George also became a doctor who served in the Balkans and became "Stafford House Commissioner (the Stafford House Committee was a forerunner of the British Red Cross…)"[11]; and Thomas retired from the foreign service "as secretary to the Governor of the North West Provinces."[12]

Stoker was as educated and industrious as his brothers. He earned two degrees from Trinity, worked at Dublin Castle during the day, wrote theater reviews at night, and found time to begin his first book, the meticulously detailed *The Duties of Clerks of Petty Sessions in Ireland* (1879). After Stoker's father died in October 1876, he met the legendary actor Henry Irving, and the meeting itself has been recounted so often that it has become common knowledge, with Stoker's emotional response to Irving's dramatic recitation as the story's climax. In the three years that followed the meeting, much would happen. In 1878, Stoker married the beautiful Florence Balcombe, moved to London almost immediately, and became business manager for Irving's Lyceum Theatre. A year later Stoker had his only child, Irving Noel Thornley, and published his first book, *The Duties of Clerks of Petty Sessions in Ireland*.

As Irving's manager, Stoker was busy with the day-to-day business of the theater and awake late into the night as Irving held court at his famous dinner gatherings after performances. It was a time-consuming schedule yet somehow Stoker found time to study law and write. In 1890, he was called to the bar and also published his first novel, *The Snake's Pass*. In the same year he began planning[13] what would be published as *Dracula* in 1897, one of eighteen books that he would write in his lifetime. While modern readers know him as the author of *Dracula*, Stoker was known during his lifetime as Irving's theater manager and for *Personal Reminiscences*. Stoker managed everything for Irving, including eight American tours, but Irving's penchant for lavish entertainment made it difficult to balance the books, especially after the theatre fire in 1898 followed by Irving's illness. These two events prompted Irving to agree to syndication of the theatre for "a cash settlement of £26,000, plus shares in the company" without consulting Stoker.[14] As Paul Murray explains in *From the Shadow of Dracula: A Life of Bram Stoker*: "In fact, he [Stoker] was on the Atlantic or in the United States when the parent company or syndicate was formed. When he returned he found the Lyceum Theatre Company was a *fait accompli*."[15] Both the Lyceum and Irving began their decline with this business deal. Financial difficulties increased for the Lyceum Theatre syndication for the next few years until, on July 19, 1902, Irving held the final performance on its stage.[16]

Following the closing of the Lyceum, Irving performed on provincial stages, and although their relationship was challenged by Irving's ill-advised business decisions,[17] Stoker remained loyal to him. However, loyalty did not pay the bills, and Stoker had to now rely on other means to support himself and Florence. He published articles and essays in addition to managing to write and publish almost one book a year. Irving's health declined, but Stoker would manage him when he did perform. On Friday, October 13, 1905, after his performance in *Becket* at the Theatre Royal Bradford, Stoker and Irving parted with a handshake; "They never parted with this gesture," and Irving got into a waiting cab with his long-time dresser, Walter Collinson, went back to the hotel, stumbled in the lobby, was assisted to a chair, lost consciousness, and died.[18] Upon receiving word that Irving was ill, Stoker rushed to the hotel "to find that Irving was already dead.... Stoker closed his master's eyes."[19]

Irving's funeral was large and public, attended by the Prince and Princess of Wales, but "Stoker's name was conspicuous by its absence from the funeral arrangements."[20] Despite twenty-seven years of friendship, loyalty, and service, Stoker, like Collinson and H. J. Loveday, Irving's stage manager, was not even left tokens of remembrance from Irving's estate, which totaled £20,527.[21] Irving's death marked the beginning of Stoker's financial and physical decline. Within a few months of Irving's death, Stoker had a stroke.[22] "He was unconscious for twenty-four hours; his walk and eyesight were permanently impaired; he could talk but needed the aid of a magnifying glass to write."[23] Yet he managed to write the *Personal Reminiscences* and have it published in 1906.[24] He recovered and, in addition to writing, put his speech skills to work. Stoker was an excellent and engaging speaker who "was active on the lecture and after-dinner speaking circuit, putting his extroverted personality and public speaking abilities to good use."[25] Despite his continued industry, Stoker could not afford to maintain the lifestyle that he and Florence shared when the Lyceum was thriving and moved to a smaller residence in 1907.[26] In 1910, Stoker suffered a second stroke but seemed more concerned about finances and their effects on Florence than his declining health: "It is harder on poor Florence (who has been an angel) than on me.... She had to do all the bookkeeping and find the money to live on—God only knows how she managed."[27] Florence, however, expressed her concerns for Stoker in a 1910 letter to his brother, Thornley: "Poor old Bram is no worse, this wet weather stiffens him up so, it makes it so hard for him to get about. He is an Angel of patience, & never complains, & it is so hard for him being so helpless."[28]

By the beginning of 1911, it seems that Stoker's health and Florence's ability to maintain the household expenses were experiencing serious challenges. Stoker wrote an application to the Royal Literary Fund on February 22, 1911, and followed it up with a letter that contained a more detailed resume of his work history and an account of his recent health problems that prompted him to write:

[At] Sir Henry Irving's death I devoted myself to literature entirely.
So the beginning of 1906 I had a paralytic stroke. Fortunately the stroke was not a bad one and in a few months I resumed my work. Just a year ago I had another breakdown from overwork which has incapacitated me ever since. The result of such a misfortune shows[29] at its worst in the case of one who has to depend on his brain and his hands. For a whole year already I have been unable to do any work with the exception of completing a book begun some time before and the preparatory study for which had been largely done. This book "Famous Imposters" has been just published but I shall not divine[30] any substantial benefit from it for about a year. At present I do not know whether I can in the future do much, or any, literary work, and I am emboldened to look to my fellow craftsmen in my difficulty. I may say that I have already written fifteen books besides many articles for magazines and newspapers and a number of short stories as well as doing a fair share of ordinary journalism.[31]

Included in the record of Stoker's application and letter are three letters of support from Anne Ritchie, Henry F. Dickens, and W. S. Gilbert, a receipt that Stoker received £100 from the fund on 9 March 1911, and a thank-you note from Stoker to the committee expressing his tremendous gratitude.

Sadly, as fate would have it, Stoker did not have much longer to worry about finances. On April 20, 1912, he died at the age of sixty-four at his home, 26 St. George's Square, Pimlico.[32] Like his birth, his death occurred during a historically significant time; during the early morning hours of

April 15, the *Titanic* sank to the bottom of the Atlantic Ocean, taking over 1,500 lives. Finding her resting place and determining the actual cause of the sinking has occupied many over the last century and prompted as much fact as fiction. Stoker's cause of death has likewise provoked much speculation, most likely prompted by Daniel Farson's postscript in his biography that his great-uncle died of tertiary syphilis.[33] Belford does not give this cause of death much credence. Her consultation with a respected neurologist ascribed Stoker's lack of coordination to the two strokes that he suffered.[34] Murray explores the possibility that Stoker had syphilis and likewise consults medical experts.[35] One expert concluded that "Stoker died of uraemia from chronic nephritis; the balance of probability is that he was also suffering from syphilis but this was not the direct cause of death."[36] Collins's theory of spina bifida occulta from Stoker's childhood could also explain the author's difficulty in movement toward the end of his life: "No other condition covers all these points ... so well. I recommend it as the clearest explanation. Similarly, the reading of the death certificate that Dr. Browne intended to convey is that Stoker died of heart failure, a consequence of long-term hypertension, secondary to renal disease. The most straightforward explanation often is to be preferred."[37]

Unlike Maturin and Le Fanu, who died leaving financial difficulties for their families, Stoker left everything to Florence in his will—£4723 5s 11d[38]—which was speedily probated on May 15.[39] When Stoker's brother Thornley died two months later, Florence also received the bequest of £1,000 that her brother-in-law had left for her husband.[40] A little over a year later, Florence auctioned off her husband's books and manuscripts. The *Times* stated that the sale earned the widow £400 12s,[41] but the *Athenaeum* reported a significantly larger amount of 5,367*l* 17s.[42] It is unclear whether this larger amount is the total for the entire auction or for just Stoker's library. What is clear is that Belford's description of the widow indicates that she no longer experienced financial distress:

> Florence stayed on for two years at St. George's Square before moving to a better address, 4 Kinnerton Studios.... Her life as an attractive widow was far from boring. She went on Hellenic cruises, to Foyles book lunches; took refuge in Catholic ritual at the nearby Brompton Oratory; and visited Seaview on the Isle of Wight, where Noel and his family summered.[43]

Florence also seems to have astutely managed Stoker's literary estate, which certainly contributed to her ability to live well, especially when she sold the film rights to *Dracula* in 1929 for $40,000.[44] When she died in 1937, she left an estate of £6913 to Noel,[45] but "the gross value of her estate came to over £20,000, a large sum indeed for the time."[46]

Stoker's estate and his widow's show that the fortunes for writers shifted in the little over a century from when Maturin wrote to support his family to Le Fanu's equally industrious endeavors for the same purpose to Stoker, who found time for a writing career with his management of a popular theater. The connections among the writers' lives are interesting to note, but the most significant for Stoker are the parallels and innovations where Maturin and Le Fanu are concerned. Stoker was very familiar with Le Fanu's work, as explained by Susan Parlour in "Vixens and Virgins in the Nineteenth Century Anglo-Irish Novel: Representations of the Feminine in Bram Stoker's *Dracula*": "Delivering his maiden speech entitled 'Sensationalism in Fiction and Society' as a member of Trinity College's Philosophical Society served to clarify Stoker's interest in Irish writing of the supernatural. By focusing on the literary endeavors of a fellow Dubliner, J. S. Le Fanu, Stoker not only qualified his admiration for Le Fanu's work, but also established a close literary affinity with him."[47]

His interest in Le Fanu's writing may have been one reason why Stoker offered his free services as theater reviewer to Le Fanu's *Evening Mail*[48] and frequented gatherings at Sir William and Lady Wilde's Merrion Square home, near Le Fanu's.[49] He was also obviously familiar with *In a Glass Darkly*. When Dracula says to Mina, "You know now, and they know in part already, and will know in full before long,"[50] he echoes 1 Corinthians 13:12: "For now we see through a glass, darkly; but then face to face: now I know in part; but then shall I know even as also I am known." This is the same Biblical line that inspired the title of Le Fanu's short story collection. In that collection is "Carmilla," which clearly inspired Stoker as evidenced in "Dracula's Guest" and early notes written for *Dracula*, which gave Styria as the count's initial home[51] before it changed to Transylvania.[52] Stoker was known for reciting Le Fanu's "Shamus O'Brien" for the theater company.[53] Stoker was also familiar with Maturin's work, as Belford notes in her biography: "*Melmoth* fascinated Stoker."[54]

It is no surprise that Maturin's and Le Fanu's literary influences appear in the pages of *Dracula*. Stoker's novel mirrored the narrative structure, non–Irish settings, and similar plot features of his Irish Gothic predecessors' works. His narrative structure is reminiscent of Maturin's *Melmoth the Wanderer*, which relies on multiple points of view told in the first-person via written or oral accounts. Stoker updates the delivery of these accounts but retains the immediacy and layering of the multiple first-person points of view. In addition to narrative framework, Stoker was influenced by Maturin's multiple settings. Where Maturin's novel moves from England to Spain to a tropical island to Ireland, Stoker forgoes even a marginal Irish setting in preference of England, the high seas, and Eastern Europe.

Within his Eastern European setting, Stoker pays the first of many tributes to Le Fanu's "Carmilla." Originally the second chapter of *Dracula*,[55] *Dracula's Guest* (1914) was published as the title piece in a short story collection two years after Stoker's death. It refers to a Styrian countess, an abandoned village, and the crypt of a suicide. The countess does not appear in the final version of Stoker's novel because, according to Paul E. Davis in his essay "Dracula Anticipated: The 'Undead' in Anglo-Irish Literature," it appears that, as a result of a dispute between Stoker and the Estate of J. S. Le Fanu, the chapter was removed from Stoker's novel shortly before publication because it was "too close" to Le Fanu's "Carmilla"[56]; however, the abandoned village surrounding the castle and the grave of the suicide where Lucy is first attacked both do. Another similarity to Le Fanu is the character of Dr. Abraham Van Helsing. Although Stoker had stated in an interview for the *British Weekly* shortly after the novel was published that Van Helsing was "founded on a real character,"[57] the inspiration supplied by Dr. Martin Hesselius is difficult to ignore. Other striking parallels include the scenes of seduction by Carmilla of Laura and the trio of vampire women seducing Jonathan Harker, and Carmilla's staking and that of Lucy Westenra.

Stoker further demonstrates his familiarity with and admiration for Le Fanu by clearly being inspired by *Uncle Silas*. Like John Melmoth and Silas Ruthyn, the title characters of their novels, the title character Dracula is likewise conspicuously absent from a great deal of the story. There are also great similarities between the physical appearances of Silas Ruthyn and Count Dracula. When Maud first meets her uncle, she notes "A face like marble ... vivid strange eyes ... venerable, bloodless, fiery-eyed, with its singular look of power.... [He] welcomed me with a courtly grace which belonged to another age."[58] This appearance is repeated by Jonathan Harker's description of his host, the count whose courtly manners,[59] "extraordinary pallor,"[60] and strength[61] are all recorded. Davis further notes similarities between the two characters, stating that "both are associated with foul weather and wolves" and "can enter and leave sealed rooms."[62]

In addition to their title characters, both novels present parallel experiences for the characters who visit them. Both Maud and Harker journey along steeply, zigzagging roads that ascend to the homes of their hosts. The journeys involve the setting sun, encamped gypsies, barking dogs, and decrepit ancestral homes in remote locations. Granted, evening arrivals to neglected and isolated homes of the aristocracy surrounded by gypsies are rather standard fare for most Gothic tales as Fred Botting, in his study entitled *Gothic*, aptly notes,

> In the setting of *Dracula* stock features of the Gothic novel make a magnificent reappearance: the castle is mysterious and forbidding, its secret terrors and splendid isolation in a wild and mountainous region form as sublime a prison as any.... Throughout the novel ruins, graveyards and vaults—all the macabre and gloomy objects of morbid fascination and melancholy—signal the awful presence of the Gothic past.[63]

After their arrivals, this final destination almost literally becomes that as each character is skillfully imprisoned by his/her expertly manipulative captors. Each tries to send a surreptitious letter for help but it is intercepted. Each is threatened by vampire women; Harker literally so and Maud in the form of Madame de la Rougierre who "like the Brides of Dracula, is herself implicitly vampiric in her apparent ability to lie with the dead before rising again."[64] Each develops a risky but ultimately successful plan of escape, and it is here where the similarities end. Maud's story ends with her escape; Harker's only begins with it. Stoker demonstrates the first in many instances of originality as he transforms what appears to be straightforward borrowing from his Irish Gothic predecessors and revises it in a new and very effective manner.

For example, Stoker undeniably used the multiple points of view of Maturin's *Melmoth the Wanderer*, but rather than frame tales within tales that crisscross a span of 150 years, Stoker selected the necessary perspectives to tell a story in chronological order that played out in the immediate present of its Victorian readers. The reader is not buffered by a safe distance of several years when the story occurred; the threat of Dracula is a present danger that cannot be easily dismissed as the delusions of an unreliable narrator or the fancy of a bygone era. Dracula's threat is further enhanced by his goal for this present time period. Unlike Melmoth, who seeks one victim, Dracula is planning an invasion with the purpose of conquering. Using multiple credible first-person narrators heightens this feeling of being threatened by unwittingly contributing evidence to the existence of something that logically just cannot exist. The evidence is presented by a young solicitor, an aristocratic young woman, a schoolmistress, a respected doctor, and an aged European expert.[65] With the exception of Van Helsing, all the main characters contributing text to the assembled story are solid representatives of English society. If an *Englishman* can conclude that vampires exist, then they must. Their acknowledgment adds an uncomfortably disturbing dimension of reality to the tale.

To add further weight to the uneasy feeling of realism, Stoker includes every modern marvel familiar and, in some cases, quite new to his late

Victorian audience. There are trains and train schedules, shorthand, type-writers, phonographs, telegraphs, newspapers, cameras, and blood transfu-sions. Stoker even includes references to the New Woman, a source of controversy to conservative Victorians. These innovations heighten the overall effect of fear in the novel. As Malcolm Smith explains in "Dracula and the Victorian Frame of Mind," "Stoker recontextualised the threat of the vampire. Dracula was presented not simply as an ancient, foreign and long-vanished threat, but as a real figure in a recognizable social land-scape."[66] Stoker's use of modern technology also resulted in an original contribution to the Irish Gothic of Maturin and Le Fanu, described by Carol A. Senf in *Science and Social Science in Bram Stoker's Fiction* as a "syn-thesis of science and the Gothic."[67] This phrase could also be applied to Mary Shelley's *Frankenstein* (1818), which is often considered one of the first science fiction works, and Senf presents a thoughtful argument for not only Stoker's *Dracula* as a work of science fiction but also five of his other novels: *The Snake's Pass* (1890), *The Jewel of Seven Stars* (1903), *The Lady of the Shroud* (1909), and *The Lair of the White Worm* (1911).[68]

Another modern element of originality is the novel's adaptability to stage and film production. While Maturin had experience with stage pro-duction, several sources note that playwriting was the one genre Le Fanu specifically avoided. For Stoker, adapting *Dracula* for the stage was a natural decision, and he wisely secured the copyright in his reading of a play version on May 18, 1897.[69] David Skal describes that "Stoker himself had a strong sense of the book's theatrical possibilities. By the time of *Dracula*'s publi-cation he had served as the acting manager of the Lyceum Theatre for sev-enteen years."[70] Given his fascination with new technology, Stoker was undoubtedly aware of the novel's excellent potential for the cinema, too. Leonard Wolf remarks that "Stoker's mosaic plot structure gives it a sin-gularly filmic quality,"[71] which was destined to be utilized repeatedly in twentieth- and twenty-first century cinema.

Stoker continues his revision of the existing Irish and English Gothic with the vampire. As a vampire, Count Dracula is not a new creature; vam-pires in folk tales and literature were well-established characters by Stoker's time, and he was well-aware of fellow Irishman Dion Boucicault's *The Vampire: A Phantasm Related in Three Dramas* (1852)[72] and Le Fanu's "Carmilla." However, the count strays from the expected characterization. As Stephen Arata explains: "Unlike Polidori and Le Fanu … who depict their vampires as wan and enervated, Stoker makes Dracula vigorous and energetic…. Dracula represents the nobleman as warrior."[73] Carmilla is "very languid,"[74] and Silas Ruthyn, though described in vampiric terms, would never be mistaken as "vigorous and energetic." He is too weak even to carry out the murder of his niece and must force his son Dudley to perform the actual killing to gain the needed inheritance. As the novel develops, it also becomes apparent that Silas's unnerving gaze is most likely the result of his addiction to laudanum.

Dracula, on the other hand, does not require pharmaceutical assistance to achieve any alarming effects. He is a true warrior and is not content with the aspirations of the preceding Irish Gothic vampires or English Gothic villains. He does not need a bloodstained inheritance nor does he desire merely one innocent young heroine. "My revenge is just begun! I spread it over centuries, and time is on my side. Your girls that you all love are mine already; and through them you and others shall yet be mine—my creatures, to do my bidding and to be my jackals when I want to feed."[75] Dracula plans to conquer England, making him the most ambitious villain in Irish or English Gothic literature and, from the English perspective, the most frightening.

Dracula is not a superstition that can be explained away with the light of day or a mad criminal to be easily tracked and imprisoned. He is a greater threat than either because he can pass as "one of them." As Arata points out:

> Dracula is the most "Western" character in the novel. No one is more rational, more intelligent, more organized, or even more punctual than the Count. No one plans more carefully or researches more thoroughly. No one is more learned within his own spheres of expertise or more receptive to new knowledge.[76]

Botting agrees:

> Dracula is more than a Gothic villain ... more than the mercenary and mundane bandit that they too often turn out to be. As the sublime synthesis of the human and supernatural terrors of Gothic writing, he is both villain and ghostly diabolical agent whose magic and power cannot be reduced to mere tricks or effects of overindulgent, superstitious imagination: more than rational, he serves to elicit rather than dispel superstitious beliefs, demanding, not a return to reason and morality, but a reawakening of spiritual energies and sacred awe.[77]

Dracula is a dangerous new force who cannot be explained away or ignored. His existence must be acknowledged and thoroughly understood before he can be defeated.

Stoker's original additions to the existing Irish Gothic tradition only begin with the character of Dracula. The novel's other primary characters illustrate an awareness of the Irish and English Gothic formulas while simultaneously displaying innovations to them. The characteristic "child sacrifice" by parents,[78] as described in previous chapters in the works of

Maturin and Le Fanu, runs rampant throughout *Dracula*, oddly manifesting itself by both the failure of the parent to protect as well as the entire extended family represented in the band of characters.

Aside from Van Helsing, the parental figures in *Dracula* are either dead or die during the story. Harker and Mina are both orphaned so young that neither remember their biological parents, so they are grieved by a second "orphaning" in the loss of their father figure, Mr. Peter Hawkins. Although Hawkins allows Harker to rise to the prestigious position of partner, it was Hawkins who originally sent Harker to Dracula's castle in his place and thus unwittingly imperiled the sanity and life of the young man he thought of as a son. By accepting Dracula as a client, Hawkins also endangers Mina since the business transaction he sends Harker to conduct allows the count to buy property in England adjacent to the asylum where he first attacks Mina.

Lucy Westenra's mother is no more effective in protecting her daughter. She is a very sick woman who is anxious to see that her daughter will be "taken care of" after she is gone. For a young woman of Lucy's social position, this means an advantageous marriage to Arthur Holmwood (later Lord Godalming). Mrs. Westenra even alters her will after Lucy's engagement so that Arthur, not Lucy, is her sole beneficiary. She never considers that Lucy would follow her so closely in death even after she inadvertently assists Dracula in gaining access to her. Mrs. Westenra removes all the garlic wreaths from Lucy's room after Van Helsing specifically states that their presence is important to her daughter's recovery. The act permits a nearly fatal attack on Lucy. Mrs. Westenra then seals Lucy's fate with her dying act of ripping the protective garlic away from Lucy's neck.

Finally, Arthur is forced to leave the bedside of Lucy, rendering her unprotected, to attend to his own father (who inevitably dies). Even Van Helsing, mentor to Seward and father figure for the entire group, is not exempt from the charge of endangering those he should protect. He is aware of the danger threatening Lucy yet leaves her at the most critical times. Likewise, he makes the decision of removing Mina from the hunt for the count, which gives Dracula the opportunity to attack her. Furthermore, Van Helsing's inability to recognize that Mina has become the count's next victim, despite the fact that she is exhibiting the same symptoms that he treated Lucy for, ultimately provides Dracula with the opportunities that culminate in the blood exchange, hastening Mina's transition into a vampire.

One of Stoker's greatest moments of originality comes when he completely inverts the entire concept of the Gothic heroine while simultaneously using elements of the Irish Gothic, as already seen in the prior comparison between Jonathan Harker and Maud Ruthyn. As Botting observes of Castle Dracula and its occupants, it is "as sublime a prison as any building in which a Gothic heroine was incarcerated. *The place of the heroine, however, is taken by the naïve young lawyer Harker*" (emphasis mine).[79] Botting is correct; Stoker completely revises the Gothic heroine in the initial chapters of his novel by using a male character. Apart from being male, Jonathan Harker is the perfect Gothic heroine. He is unsuspectingly lured to the castle and lulled into a false sense of confidence with the count's unfailing hospitality. He is wonderfully naïve—it is not until the very end of Chapter 2 that Harker finally realizes what the reader has known for pages: "The castle is a veritable prison, and I am a prisoner!"[80] Harker demonstrates the requisite hysteria when he confesses, "I think I must have been mad for a time, for I behaved much as a rat does in a trap."[81] Harker continues to serve as the model Gothic heroine in every respect—short of wandering around in a white nightgown. He dutifully writes the letters to his employer and Mina requested by the count, not forgetting to date them in advance as asked. He is then explicitly told not to go wandering about the castle and, especially, not to sleep in any other room but his own. Naturally, Harker does exactly the opposite when he is sure the count has left the castle. Harker discovers a room that causes him to romantically muse "at a little oak table where in old times possibly some fair lady sat to pen, with much thought and many blushes, her ill-spelt love-letter."[82] Of course, he falls asleep in this room.

It is here that Harker encounters the most unspeakable of all threats to the Gothic heroine: the "fate worse than death" or seduction of the helpless, frightened ingénue by her lustful and unprincipled captor. Stoker adds a few unexpected twists to the familiar scene. Harker's "virtue" is not threatened by just one seducer, but three. Stoker also shows the first instance of recasting the vampire: "[H]e gentrified female vampires, who, for the first time, are monogamously heterosexual."[83] This lovely young trio is quite determined to seduce Harker, not each other, and he is not adverse to the idea of being "the victim": "I felt in my heart a wicked, burning desire that they would kiss me with those red lips."[84] Unlike any typical Gothic heroine before him, Harker does nothing to discourage the three women's advances but excitedly awaits them: "I lay quiet, looking out under my eyelashes in an agony of delightful anticipation."[85] The scene that follows has little in common with any Gothic heroine fighting for her virtue. Even Laura, who is unable to reject Carmilla's advances, speaks of confusing feelings throughout the story when Carmilla is being seductive: "In these mysterious moods

I did not like her. I experienced a strange tumultuous excitement that was pleasurable, ever and anon mingled with a vague sense of fear and disgust."[86] When Carmilla finally does attack Laura, she is in the guise of a large cat rather than herself, and Laura recalls terror and pain, not sexual arousal: "I could not cry out, although, as you may suppose, I was terrified…. I felt it spring lightly on the bed. The two broad eyes approached my face, and I felt a stinging pain as if two large needles darted, an inch or two apart, deep into my breast. I waked with a scream."[87] Harker has only one fleeting moment of "repulsion" but does not indicate any further fear of the three vampire women.

> I was afraid to raise my eyelids, but looked out and saw perfectly under the lashes. The fair girl went on her knees and bent over me, fairly gloating. There was a deliberate voluptuousness which was both thrilling and repulsive, and as she arched her neck she actually licked her lips like an animal, till I could see in the moonlight the moisture shining on the scarlet lips and on the red tongue as it lapped the white sharp teeth. Lower and lower went her head as the lips went below the range of my mouth and chin and seemed about to fasten on my throat…. [I] could feel the hot breath on my neck. Then the skin of my throat began to tingle as one's flesh does when the hand that is to tickle it approaches nearer—nearer. I could feel the soft, shivering touch of the lips on the supersensitive skin of my throat, and the hard dents of two sharp teeth, just touching and pausing there. I closed my eyes in a languorous ecstasy and waited— waited with beating heart.[88]

The engaged barrister seems to have forgotten his fiancée awaiting his return in England. Harker is just seconds away from what would have been a sizzling addition to the original passages of passion in Irish Gothic literature. However, Harker is "saved" from ravishment. His unlikely champion is the count, and Dracula's motivation for the timely rescue had never been so explicitly stated in either Irish or Gothic literature prior to *Dracula*. After the count throws the blonde vampire off Harker by grabbing her by the neck and hurling her across the room, he rages at the three women:

> "How dare you touch him, any of you? How dare you cast eyes on him when I had forbidden it? Back, I tell you all! This man belongs to me! Beware how you meddle with him, or you'll have to deal with me." The fair girl, with a laugh of ribald coquetry, turned to answer him:—
> "You yourself never loved; you never love!" On this the other women joined, and such a mirthless, hard, soulless laughter rang through the room that it almost made me faint to hear; it seemed like the pleasure of fiends. Then the Count turned, after looking at my face attentively, and said in a soft whisper:—
> "Yes, I too can love; you yourselves can tell it from the past. Is it not so? Well, now I promise you that when I am done with him, you shall kiss him at your will."[89]

Dracula's uncontested claim of Harker followed so closely by an "attentive" gaze and a statement that he, too, can love implies a definite "fate worse than death" as far as the Victorian male was concerned. As Auerbach clearly explains: "The Labouchere Amendment of 1885 ... criminalized homosexuality among men.... The [Oscar] Wilde trials of 1895 put a judicial seal on the category the Labouchere Amendment had fostered. As a result of the trials, affinity between men lost its fluidity. Its tainted embodiment, the homosexual, was imprisoned in a fixed nature."[90] Wilde was tried, convicted, and imprisoned in 1895; he was released in 1897, the same year that *Dracula* was published. Dracula's assertive statement—"This man belongs to me!"—may recall to his readers the Wilde trial and all its attendant scandal; the readers know what must be racing through Harker's mind. Dracula's claim of him proves to be too much for Harker. He faints—as any respectable Gothic heroine would at this point. This scene and its resulting assumptions are ironic when Auerbach's assessment of Stoker's notes is considered: "[T]he heart of *Dracula* was not blood, but an assertion of ownership."[91] Dracula considers Harker a vital employee—not a love interest or a friend. Dracula needs Harker to achieve his goal of traveling to England and that is why he is angry with the vampire women. If the women fed on Harker too soon and killed him, then Dracula would be unable to complete the required paperwork to purchase his English properties.

Of course, Harker does not know this. The harrowing incident prompts Harker to escape the castle, somehow arrive in Buda-Pesth, collapse of brain fever, and be slowly nursed back to health in a hospital run by Catholic nuns. His fiancée Mina races to his rescue the moment the nuns contact her. When Harker has regained sufficient strength, he and Mina marry, which would be the usual happy conclusion of any Gothic tale. Again, Stoker demonstrates originality with Irish and English Gothic traditions, since the novel is far from over with the marriage of Mina and Jonathan.

If Harker is the non-traditional heroine, then Stoker would quite naturally have a different perspective of the hero in the novel. The "heroes" are abundant but dismally unsuccessful when it comes to saving Lucy, which is not in keeping with the Gothic tradition. Arthur Holmwood, Dr. Jack Seward, Quincey Morris, and Professor Van Helsing are a very active and frequently inept quartet for the first half of the novel. Holmwood, Lucy's fiancé, is absent throughout most of Lucy's terrifying ordeal. Seward is completely baffled by her condition and calls upon his former mentor, Van Helsing. The professor immediately suspects the cause of Lucy's infirmity after their first meeting but does not commit to any active course to rescue the patient but rather uses it as a long, drawn-out teaching opportunity for his former student, Seward. The series of mistakes made by the heroes result in frequent blood transfusions for Lucy and, ultimately, her death.

It is throughout these scenes of heroic ineptness to save Lucy that another original addition to the Irish Gothic appears, which also shows a use of an Irish subject. Upon hearing that Mrs. Westenra threw all the flowers away, Van Helsing breaks down: "He raised his hands over his head in a sort of mute despair, and then beat his palms together in a helpless way; finally he sat down on a chair, and putting his hands before his face, began to sob, with loud, dry sobs that seemed to come from the very racking of his heart."[92] This is one of a series of scenes that demonstrate an unprecedented amount of male hysteria in the novel. Men who continually give sway to their emotions do not reflect the typical behavior associated with the Gothic hero. However, these scenes do support an observation made by Declan Kiberd in "Undead in the Nineties: Bram Stoker and *Dracula*." Kiberd explains that there was a "crisis of masculinity in the 1890s."[93] The Victorian male faced problems of identity brought on by the New Woman. "Such an active womanhood presupposes a passivity in the New Man. The 1890s male had in consequence a choice: if he repressed his own more sensitive aspect for the sake of manliness, he ran the risk that the repressed might erupt, reducing him to a blubbering baby or laughing hysteric. Stoker was attracted by older, Celtic codes of heroic manliness, but he knew that they were no longer negotiable."[94]

Kiberd notes that this situation "had become an especially acute problem in Ireland, whose men had been typecast throughout the nineteenth century as effeminate and unstable."[95] Kiberd's insights support Stoker's inclusion of Irish subjects since the sheer number of emotionally excessive scenes among the male characters in the first half of the novel is extremely hard to ignore or correlate with the behavior anticipated from a traditionally heroic male. Every male in the novel—with the sole exception of Dracula—gives vent to his emotions, sometimes repeatedly. In the sole presence of Mina, both Seward and Morris have a brief but nonetheless emotional moment. Seward confesses that, "of late I have had cause for tears, God knows! But relief of them was denied me; and now the sight of those sweet eyes [of Mina], brightened with recent tears, went straight to my heart."[96] Mina provokes a similar response from Morris when she offers to comfort him: "He saw that I was in earnest, and stooping, took my hand, and raising it to his lips, kissed it. It seemed but poor comfort to so brave and unselfish a soul, and impulsively I bent over and kissed him. The tears rose in his eyes, and there was a momentary choking in his throat."[97] Harker's, Van Helsing's, and Holmwood's emotional responses are even more pronounced.

Harker records several instances in his journal while at Dracula's castle where he loses control or fears that he is mad, and he ultimately succumbs to a brain fever after his experiences at the castle. He confides in Mina what this means: "You know I have had brain fever, and that is to be mad."[98] Madness was considered weakness, a condition attributed to the "weaker" sex. When Harker later sees a much younger Count in London, he swoons:

> The poor dear was evidently terrified at something—very greatly terrified; I [Mina] do believe that if he had not had me to lean on and to support him, he would have sunk down.... I drew him away quietly, and he, holding my arm, came easily ... [later that day] Jonathan still pale and dizzy under a slight relapse of his malady.[99]

Van Helsing sobs when Lucy's mother unknowingly exposes her to danger, and, after Lucy's funeral, he "gave way to a regular fit of hysterics.... He laughed till he cried and I [Seward] had to draw down the blinds lest anyone should see us and misjudge; and then he cried till he laughed again; and laughed and cried together, just as a woman does. I tried to be stern with him, as one is to a woman under the circumstances; but it had no effect."[100] The most dramatic male hysteria is Holmwood's. When Lucy dies, he "sat down, and covered his face with his hands sobbing in a way that nearly broke me [Seward] down to see."[101] He loses his composure again the next day, and falls weeping into the arms of Seward.[102] Van Helsing's desire to drive a stake through Lucy nearly unhinges Holmwood, but he resolutely performs the task. Afterward, the "hammer fell from Arthur's hand. He reeled and would have fallen had we not caught him. Great drops of sweat sprang out on his forehead, and his breath came in broken gasps. It had indeed been an awful strain on him."[103] Then "[Arthur] put his hands on the Professor's shoulder, and laying his head on his breast, cried for a while silently, whilst we stood unmoving."[104]

It is probably no coincidence that Stoker assigned the greatest scenes of hysteria to an English aristocrat or that it is Mina *Murray* Harker, a character with Irish connections,[105] who ultimately consoles him. In Lord Godalming's first conversation with Mina, he no sooner utters Lucy's name then he cannot speak further.

> In an instant the poor dear fellow was overwhelmed with grief.... He grew quite hysterical, and raising his open hands, beat his palms together in a perfect agony of grief. He stood up and then sat down again, and the tears rained down his cheeks. I felt an infinite pity for him, and opened my arms unthinkingly. With a sob he laid his head on my shoulder, and cried like a wearied child, whilst he shook with emotion.[106]

During the second half of the novel, the men band together and rise to the challenge of tracking and defeating the threat of Dracula. The emotional excesses of the men within the first part of the novel evolve into demonstrations of exemplary manly men in the second part. Kiberd notes that with this shifting manner of characterization, Stoker readily showed his agreement for Wilde's and Shaw's "celebrations of androgyny in the ideal male" and the dispelling of "the either/or binaries of the imperial mindset."[107] Stoker directly supports Kiberd's conclusion in an entry dated August 5, 1871, in *The Lost Journal*, where he writes: "Will men ever believe that a strong man can have a woman's heart."[108] Harker could be described this way. He exhibits many elements of "a women's heart" where he shows several characteristics of a Gothic heroine, but in the second half of the book he is a man of action as well as intelligence as he tracks Dracula's legal trail and delivers one of the decisive blows to the count that causes him to crumble to dust and saves his wife, who also dispels a few either/or binaries of her own.

Kiberd adds that nowhere in the novel is Stoker's support for this new outlook more apparent than in his "integrated, balanced and wholly androgynous figure of Mina Harker who takes control of his narrative in the end."[109] As a result, she is also "largely responsible for the capture and ultimate destruction of Dracula."[110] She is a vampire slayer, and as a woman, female vampire slayers in folklore are rare.[111]

The character of Mina Murray Harker adds a new dimension to the Irish Gothic and provides further evidence for Irish subject and Irish national identity. As Van Helsing succinctly describes her: "Ah, that wonderful Madam Mina! She has man's brain—a brain that a man should have were he much gifted—and woman's heart."[112] These two elements form the basis for the "integrated, balanced and wholly androgynous figure"[113] that Mina becomes, which not only illustrates the validity of Kiberd's claim but also serves to build upon Le Fanu's female-centered, Irish Gothic writings that feature Maud Ruthyn and the unforgettable Carmilla.

Mina's woman's heart allows her to exhibit many of the traditional characteristics of the proper Victorian lady. She is modest and very concerned with the prevailing social conventions. She gives her slippers to Lucy and fastens her shawl about her as she guides her in the middle of the night away from the suicide's seat and back home. She is relieved to see no one around "for I wanted no witness of poor Lucy's condition."[114] She also takes a moment to cover her feet in mud just "in case we should meet anyone, should notice my bare feet,"[115] but "we got home without meeting a soul."[116] Mina "was filled with anxiety about Lucy, not only for her health, lest she should suffer from exposure, but for her reputation in case the story should get wind,"[117] and they agree not to tell anyone what happened. Mina's Victorian awareness of etiquette and appearances is repeatedly demonstrated throughout the novel. As a wife, it is her duty not to question her husband, so she seals his diary that recorded the events in Dracula's castle rather than intrude upon his privacy and read it. She is later self-conscious of her husband holding her arm in public. "I felt it very improper, for you can't go on for some years teaching etiquette and decorum to other girls without the pedantry of it biting into yourself a bit."[118] When she is consoling the distraught Godalming, Mina takes his hand and thinks, "I hope he didn't think it forward of me."[119] Given her awareness of manners, it is no surprise to find that Mina is not an advocate of the New Woman as her pointed remarks about eating habits and marriage proposals show.[120]

Her woman's heart is further shown in her reactions to terrible news. She is deeply distressed by Lucy's death and her own husband's condition. She cries after hearing the account of Lucy's demise, yet her grief is never the hysteria of Lord Godalming's, despite the closer and longer relationship shared between Lucy and Mina. Likewise, she gracefully bears the silent weight of Jonathan's illness until her concern overwhelms her: "The pity for Jonathan, the horror which he experienced, the whole fearful mystery of his diary, and the fear that has been brooding over me ever since, all came in a tumult. I suppose I was hysterical, for I threw myself on my knees and held up my hands to him [Van Helsing], and implored him to make my husband well again."[121] As a wife, her first thoughts are for her husband's well-being and feelings rather than her own. She nurses him through his illness and helps him discover the truth of its cause, yet she hides her own developing "illness" from him:

> I wonder what has come over me to-day. I must hide it from Jonathan, for if he knew that I had been crying twice in one morning—I who never cried on my own account, and whom he has never caused to shed a tear—the dear fellow would fret his heart out. I shall put a bold face on, and if I do feel weepy, he shall never see it. I suppose it is one of the lessons that we poor women have to learn.[122]

As Carol A. Senf notes, Stoker does not completely restrict Mina to the role of a Victorian woman. "By emphasizing Mina's intelligence, her ability to function on her own, and her economic independence before marriage, Stoker stresses certain aspects of the New Woman."[123] She has been an assistant schoolmistress teaching young ladies the rules of propriety, an acceptable and respectable occupation given her status and social situation: Mina is an orphan. Since she does not have any family to support her and provide opportunities for education and matrimony, she realized early in her life that she would need to support herself. There were few occupations available for a respectable woman at the time, and one of these was teaching. However, Mina does not limit herself to the life of a teacher (who, again, is awaiting a spouse so she can retire from the classroom and to the home). She masters the new technology of the time. She can type, and she both writes and transcribes notes in shorthand. She learns these skills so she can help Jonathan in his work, apparently planning to continue working even after she marries.

The initiative that this new Irish Gothic heroine demonstrates professionally is also reflected personally. When Mina discovers that Lucy's sleepwalking has caused her to wander from the house in the middle of the night, Mina does not hysterically awaken the entire house and send the servants out to find her. She sets out alone to find Lucy and bring her back. When Jonathan needs care, Mina takes the long journey alone to Buda-Pesth to nurse him. When they return to England, she again serves as tremendous support for his fragile body and mind. Her strength and courage are later shown when she opens Harker's diary, taking the risk of learning that he is insane. She transcribes and types a copy of the account and gives it to Van Helsing. This act of assembling the text is significant because Mina becomes its "author."[124] Her persistent initiative serves to restore Harker's sanity, strength, and manhood, ultimately saving him from his fear of madness: "She [Mina] showed me in the doctor's letter that all I wrote down was true. It seems to have made a new man of me. It was the doubt as to the reality of the whole thing that knocked me over. I felt impotent, and in the dark, and distrustful. But now that I know, I am not afraid, even of the Count."[125]

Mina is also Lucy's only effective guardian. She rescues her friend from Dracula at the suicide's seat, and her continued presence with Lucy each night interferes with the count's plans of further victimization. Mina locks doors and windows to keep Lucy safely inside at night. She sleeps by her side and is immediately roused when Lucy tries to leave. It is not until Mina is called away to attend to Jonathan that Dracula can successfully prey upon Lucy. Mina unknowingly protects Lucy from a threat that several men—even those who know the cause of her illness—cannot.

It is also Mina who provides the essential coordination and distribution of the evidence at hand to inform, unify, and motivate the group to hunt Dracula. Mina takes the papers, transcribes the recorded journals, researches the newspapers, and includes the reporter's copy of the captain's log book from the *Demeter*. She organizes all the information chronologically and makes multiple copies of it. It provides a compelling documentation of what is seemingly impossible. Van Helsing, Seward, Harker, Morris, and Godalming meet—with Mina "as secretary."[126] Mina's work is shared with the group, the men plan to search the neighboring abbey, and Mina is dismissed by Van Helsing on behalf of the men:

> "And now for you, Madam Mina, this night is the end until all be well. You are too precious to us to have such risk. When we part to-night, you no more must question. We shall tell you all in good time. We are men, and are able to bear; but you must be our star and our hope, and we shall act all the more free that you are not in the danger, such as we are."[127]

Mina accepts their decision because she is clearly outnumbered, not because she agrees.

> All the men ... seemed relieved; but it did not seem to me good that they should brave danger ... through care of me; but their minds were made up, and, though it was a bitter pill for me to swallow, I could say nothing, save to accept their chivalrous care of me....
>   Manlike, they have told me to go to bed and sleep.[128]

Ironically, it is their decision to leave Mina behind in safety that exposes her, unguarded like Lucy, to the direct threat of Dracula. Mina becomes pale and fatigued. The men who notice her condition attribute it to the stress she has endured and use it to confirm their decision of keeping her uninformed. It is the dying words of the mad Renfield that warn Seward and Van Helsing too late of Mina's danger. The group break into the Harkers' bedroom and find Jonathan is "in a stupor," leaving Mina alone to fight the count.

> With his [the count's] left hand he held both Mrs. Harker's hands, keeping them away with her arms at full tension; his right hand gripped her by the back of the neck, forcing her face down on his bosom. Her white nightdress was smeared with blood, and a thin stream trickled down the man's bare breast, which was shown by his torn-open dress. The attitude of the two had a terrible resemblance to a child forcing a kitten's nose into a saucer of milk to compel it to drink.[129]

Despite Dracula's superior strength, she is not a compliant victim. The count must restrain her arms and force her to drink his blood. For such a "sweet-faced, dainty-looking girl,"[130] Mina is giving Dracula some trouble.

   Still, she is ashamed at her unsuccessful resistance and she sobs hysterically after the attack, but soon regains her composure. She recounts the attack, pausing only once to calm herself. She asserts: "There must be no more concealment ... we have had too much already. And besides there is nothing in all the world that can give me more pain than I have already endured—than I suffer now! Whatever may happen, it must be of new hope or of new courage to me!"[131] Unlike Lucy, Mina cannot and will not be shielded from the consequences of the attack. She faces it with great courage, and while the men engage in the physical pursuit of the count,

Mina engages in a mental battle with Dracula. She knows what he is think-ing, and though this knowledge facilitates the men's tracking and destruc-tion of Dracula, it also gives Mina a sympathetic understanding of the count. Kiberd states that Dracula is the only character who "is largely silent in the novel once he has told his life's tale to Harker. Lacking a confidant, thereafter he has no person to narrate."[132] Mina is the closest Dracula has to a confidant after the opening scenes of the novel. As "author," she con-trols the story, and as Dracula's victim, she possess a connection to him that allows her to provide the only empathy for the count: "[B]ut it is not a work of hate. That poor soul who has wrought all this misery is the saddest case of all. Just think what will be his joy when he too is destroyed in his worser part that his better part may have spiritual immortality. You must be pitiful to him too."[133] Mina's connection is further supported by McClelland's findings in folklore: "An examination of early Balkan folklore reveals that the vampire slayer ... is the vampire's true mirror image. The slayer is the heroic and opposing reflection that is curiously, but necessarily, generated by the presence of evil, and he is as closely bound to evil as a reflection is to its original."[134]

The original aspects of Stoker's characters are only the start of *Drac-ula*'s Irish literary characteristics; Irish subjects also abound in the novel. The vampire story, as presented in prior chapters, does not originate in Eastern Europe with Count Dracula nor, in the case of Stoker's count, does the fictional vampire share any characteristics with the historical figure of Vlad the Impaler beyond the name Dracula. In his thorough examination of "The Historical Dracula: the Theme of His Legend in the Western and in the Eastern Literature of Europe," Grigore Nandris traces the history and folklore of the famous Vlad V "The Impaler," Prince of Walachia. Nan-dris confirms Vlad V's place in history as a heroic warrior who viciously but effectively stopped the Turkish invasion of Europe. Vlad V is an esteemed hero in Romania, not a feared monster. "There is no association in Rumanian folklore between the Dracula story and the vampire mythol-ogy.... The Dracula story did not penetrate into the Rumanian vampire tradition. It was Bram Stoker who transformed Dracula into a vampire."[135]

This is further supported in Stoker's notes where he references the name "Dracula" once from typed notes made from William Wilkinson's *An Account of the Principalities of Wallachia and Moldavia* (1820), as editors Robert Eighteen-Bisang and Elizabeth Miller carefully explain in a foot-note: "This excerpt from Wilkinson[136] contains the only references to the historical Dracula in Stoker's Notes. Nor is there any other information about him in any of the sources that we know Stoker consulted. The role of the historical Dracula (Vlad the Impaler) in Stoker's conception of *Dracula* has been grossly overstated."[137]

Although Stoker's notes only indicate that he used the name of an Eastern European aristocratic warrior as the title character of his story, the other sources that he lists in his notes indicate that he was familiar with the vampire folklore and stories that abounded in many regions. His notes indicate that he consulted a range of sources, including Emily Gerard's "Transylvanian Superstitions," considered "one of Stoker's most important sources of information about folklore,"[138] while A. F. Crosse's *Round About the Carpathians* (1878) "is one of Stoker's most important sources of information about Transylvania."[139] He also wrote notes from Sabine Baring-Gould's *The Book of Were-Wolves* (1865)[140] and had an extensive article from the February 2, 1896, issue of the *New York World* entitled "Vampires in New England."[141] In all, Eighteen-Bisang and Miller list twelve sources that Stoker made notes from and another twenty complete entries of listed sources throughout his notes.[142] Not all the sources listed by Stoker dealt with folklore, vampires, or superstitions; however, Eighteen-Bisang's and Miller's careful notes that connect Stoker's notes for *Dracula* to the published novel show that Stoker utilized his research while writing the text. Therefore, it is no surprise that a great variety of folklore appears in *Dracula*. Patrick Johnson in his essay, "Count Dracula and the Folkloric Vampire: Thirteen Comparisons," sifts through a variety of sources to separate folklore from fiction. Johnson examines the following vampire attributes: blood-drinking, victims becoming vampires, drinking the blood of a vampire, shapeshifting, weather control, destruction of a vampire, garlic repulsion, "inability to cross running water,"[143] daylight, mirror reflection, high intelligence and sophistication, noble birth, and "vampire cadet school."[144] He concludes: "No single vampire in folklore has all of the attributes of Stoker's Count Dracula. Yet the Count's attributes can be considered to be a collection drawn from many of these folkloric vampires. The one exception is Dracula's inability to cast a reflection. Known folklore regarding vampires is mute on that point."[145]

Although Johnson does not specifically focus on Irish folklore, he does mention when discussing the vampire's inability to cross running water, "It is not known how Stoker arrived at this notion … there are precedents for this in folk beliefs [in Greece and China]…. There are also precedents in the British Isles, albeit these apply to other supernatural creatures."[146] Stoker would have been aware of these stories of "other supernatural creatures" through tales his mother told to him during his childhood illness,[147] his friendship with the Wildes,[148] and the increasingly energetic movement during the nineteenth century to collect and preserve Irish folktales from the Irish speaking areas of the country. Lady Wilde published *Ancient Legends, Mystic Charms, and Superstitions of Ireland* (1887) in two volumes. The second volume includes information about the usefulness of running water: "If pursued at night by an evil spirit, or the ghost of one dead, and you hear footsteps behind you, try and reach a stream of running water, for if you can cross it, no devil or ghost will be able to follow you."[149] Since the vampire is connected with evil, the devil, and the dead, it would not have been a great leap of logic for Stoker to appropriate this for one of the many weaknesses of the count.

This is not the only connection that may be made to the count. The collection mentions garlic as an ingredient in a remedy for the bite of a mad dog.[150] It also provides abundant evidence of shapeshifting, particularly noting: "Transformation into wolves is a favourite subject of Irish legend."[151] The Sidhe, the Irish fairy folk, are noted for their ability to shapeshift: "they [the Sidhe] live a life of joy and beauty, never knowing disease or death.... They can assume any form...."[152] As evidenced in the first chapter, the Sidhe are also associated with sickness, deaths, storms, and vicious beatings.[153] Yeats classifies the Irish fairies in *Fairy and Folk Tales of Ireland* (1888, 1892) and describes the Leanhaun Sidhe in vampiric terms:

> This spirit seeks the love of men. If they refuse she is their slave; if they consent, they are hers, and can only escape by finding one to take their place. Her lovers waste away, for she lives on their life. Most Gaelic poets, down to quite recent times, have had a Leanhaun Shee [Sidhe], for she gives inspiration to her slaves and is indeed the Gaelic muse—this malignant fairy. Her lovers, the Gaelic poets, died young. She grew restless, and carried them away to other worlds, for death does not destroy her power.[154]

Lady Wilde seems to be describing the Leanhaun Sidhe when she explains how the Sidhe came to interact with humanity.

> The Sidhe race were once angels in heaven, but were cast out as a punishment for their pride. Some fell to earth, others were cast into the sea, while many were seized by demons and carried down to hell, whence they issue as evil spirits, to tempt men to destruction under various disguises; chiefly, however, as beautiful young maidens, endowed with the power of song and gifted with the most enchanting wiles.[155]

Stoker's trio of vampire women and Lucy could easily have been inspired by the ill-fated Sidhe described above. Another Irish folkloric aspect that connects to Lucy is Maeve of Cruachan, Queen of Connaught. She is a warrior who not only commands her army of soldiers and whose hand was sought by many suitors, but part of her marriage agreement required that her husband not be jealous: "And it would not be fitting for me to be with a husband that would be jealous, for I was never without one man being with me in the shadow of another."[156] Unlike Victorian Lucy, who must choose only one suitor rather than "marry three men, or as many as want her,"[157] Maeve chooses to marry Ailell because he agrees to her terms, one requirement being that she may take to her bed any man she desires to favor with her company—and she does.

While the myths and folktales collected and published by Stoker's contemporaries provide intriguing possibilities as to Irish influences on the creation of the Transylvanian count, as presented in prior chapters, folklorist Bob Curran offers a case for Dracula's Irish heritage beginning with the story Irish chieftain, Abhartach. The essential vampiric characteristics are there—Dracula and Abhartach are aristocratic, fed on the blood of their subjects, feared by their people who require outside assistance in ridding them of the vampire, and only eliminated through complicated rituals. There are several more stories of the undead in Ireland that Curran adds to support his claim. A very intriguing one is the recollection that "during a lecture in 1961, the Registrar of the National Folklore Commission, Sean O Suilleabhain ... mentioned a site which he called Dun Dreach-Fhoula (pronounced droc'ola) or Castle of the Blood Visage."[158] If Stoker was unaware of the story of Dun Dreach-Fhoula, then the coincidental naming of his title character is quite astounding.

With so many direct links between *Dracula* and Irish folklore, it would be natural to expect similarly identifiable instances of Irish identity. By the end of the nineteenth century, the issue of Irish identity had increased in complexity. Where Le Fanu's work demonstrates the challenges of expressing Irish subjects, Stoker's illustrates the difficult task surrounding the definition of Irish identity and, ultimately, Stoker's own identity. A major factor in arriving at a definition of Irish identity lies in Ireland's necessary acknowledgment of its English influences while, at the same time, understanding that crediting an influence does not mean that the Irish were English. Stoker was well aware of the unique position of the Irish in relation to the English and sought to convey some of the problems that arose through subtle details found in his characters and setting. In his study of Irish identity, *Dracula's Crypt: Bram Stoker, Irishness, and the Question of Blood*, Joseph Valente explains several connections between the fictional and actual history. Using Van Helsing and Mina, Valente draws attention to an important figure in both English and Irish history:

> [T]here is an understated inversion of the single most pivotal event in Anglo/Irish history. Instead of a Protestant Dutchman, William III, being called across the water to save England from the perils of Catholicism and, by the time of the Boyne, from its Irish exponents, Stoker gives us a Catholic Dutchman called across the water to save

England, and William's namesake, with the sacred objects of Catholicism and, by extension, the sectarian markers of Irishness.[159]

Valente is referring to William of Orange, who became William III of England (1689–1702). When Henry VIII (1509–1547) broke with the Catholic Church in Rome and died leaving a young, inexperienced, and unhealthy son to inherit the throne (Edward VI 1547–53), England experienced a period of great instability. The religion of the reigning monarch became an intensely important issue when vying for power in the court. Catholicism and Protestantism battled for the privilege of being the national religion, and both fell in and out of favor depending on who was on the throne: Catholic Mary I (1553–58), Protestant Elizabeth I (1558–1603), Catholic James I (1603–1625), Catholic Charles I (1625–49, beheaded), Puritan Oliver Cromwell (1649–58), Protestant/Catholic Charles II (1660–85), and Catholic James II (1685–88). Fearing a recurrence of the civil war from Charles I's time, the English Parliament deposed the insistently Catholic James II, who fled to Ireland to gather Catholic support and an army. Parliament called upon the Protestant son-in-law of James II, William of Orange, in the Netherlands to assume the English crown with his wife Mary and defend England from the Catholic threat posed by James II. William of Orange won the Battle of the Boyne in 1690 (due in part to James II's hasty retreat). It was a symbolic turning point in the conflict for the English forces and the event is still celebrated with great controversy by the Orangemen in Northern Ireland.

Valente connects William of Orange to Van Helsing (the Catholic Dutchman) and Mina (William III's namesake). Mina's full name is mentioned once in the novel: Wilhelmina, the female derivative of William. Valente's connection suggests a great deal, yet William of Orange is not the only William of significance in English history. Six hundred years prior to William III, another important William redirected the course of English history.

William the Conqueror [1066–1087] planned and executed the invasion of England [in 1066] on a grand scale; recruits flocked to his banner from France, Germany, and other parts of Europe. He had some claim to the English throne, and his fleet sailed from Normandy with the blessing of Pope Alexander II. His conquest of England was systematic, ruthless, and complete.[160]

Protestant William saved England from the Catholic threat and a possible civil war; Catholic William literally conquered England and subjugated the native Anglo-Saxons with the pope's blessing. It is unclear if either William served as Stoker's inspiration for the unusual first name of his heroine, Wilhelmina, since her character is specifically described as being an orphan, her own personal history is as unclear as the historical inspiration for her name. However, the lack of her family history coupled with the unclear historical reference serve to emphasize the difficulty faced by the Irish to define an identity, given their complicated history with the English and the personal history that emerged from it.

Stoker further underscores this complex relationship in Mina's maiden name, as explained by Valente: "In a coincidence too pointed to discount, her.... Irish birth name filiates her with native Celts of the name O'Muireadhaigh,[161] which was anglicized to Murray sometime during the colonial occupation."[162] According to Seamus Deane,

> The naming or renaming of a place, the naming or renaming of a race, a region, a person is, like all acts of primordial nomination, an act of possession.... All the various names for Ireland and for the Irish connection with Great Britain are themselves indications of the uncertainty, the failure of self-possession, which has characterized the various relationships and conditions to which the names refer.[163]

Mina's name is symbolic of the unclear relationship between the Irish and English. She is descended from an ancient Irish family as is indicated by O'Muireadhaigh. Her ancestors were then colonized by the English, resulting in the family being Anglicized to "Murray." Murray is still recognized as Irish, but the act of renaming serves to distance Mina from her Celtic background and affiliate her with the English conquerors. Stoker is not satisfied with the short distance between Mina and her family heritage, though. To fully illustrate the effect of English colonization on the Irish, Mina lives in England, a circumstance not uncommon for the Irish (especially after the widespread famine of the 1840s). She is also an orphan, a circumstance that further separates her from her Irish heritage. Her occupation is a schoolmistress who serves young aristocratic ladies like Lucy Westenra by teaching them, ironically, how to be English ladies whose ultimate goal is to be proper English aristocratic wives. Mina possesses the knowledge to groom the elite young women of English society, but she herself could never aspire to be such a young lady because she belongs to the Irish middle class. The very best that Mina can do to elevate her status is also a final result of colonialism; she marries Englishman Jonathan Harker and takes his name, relinquishing the last fragment of connection to her Irish identity.[164]

The theme of the relationship between the colonizer and the colonized manifests itself in another way through the character of Mina. She is the only character with any Irish affiliations who survives to the end of the novel[165]—a significant point to note since she is a woman, which is traditionally symbolic of Ireland. She was Erin, Hibernia, or Cathleen Ni Houlihan; England was as decidedly masculine as John Bull. The characterization of Ireland as a female was in keeping with how Victorians viewed men, women, the English, and all "others" which McNally explains:

> The British overlords, many infected with social Darwinism, claimed that Englishmen were manly and adult in behavior, whereas the Irish were childish and feminine, and notoriously disloyal, like most women of their day, much in the same way that the British depicted the Hindus of India whom they had to dominate as part of The White Man's oh-so-reluctant Burden. As Declan Kiberd put it, "at the root of many an Englishmen's suspicion of the Irish was an unease at the woman or child who lurked within himself."[166]

Dracula's victimization of Mina can thus be construed as "an assault on the feminine persona of Ireland, Erin."[167] As the politics of Home Rule escalated in the late nineteenth century, Smith explains that these familiar symbols were joined with the vampire myth in the daily newspapers prior to the publication of *Dracula*: "The vampire myth did in fact lend itself easily to political propaganda as, for example, in Teniel's cartoon in Punch in 1885, at the beginning of the crisis over the Irish demand for Home Rule, which featured the vampire of the National League preying on the swooned virginal figure of Hibernia."[168] Murray notes that there was a reply to this cartoon in the *Irish Pilot*'s November 7, 1885, issue which features *"British Rule"* in the form of a large bat and Ireland depicted as a female warrior with a sword and shield that reads "National League."[169] The vampire symbolism becomes even more politically volatile when the reader remembers that even though she is attacked, the Irish Mina ultimately survives the ordeal. Lucy Westenra, the English aristocrat, does not fare as well as her friend.

The threat of Dracula continues to develop in complexity and menace when his home and character are examined. Dracula comes from the foreign and therefore "uncivilized" east—Transylvania. The Victorian reader knew about the exotic cultures and people of the East. Eastern natives were different from the Western English, so their inferiority to the English was felt to be a natural conclusion. Harker's own observations show an attitude of superiority of the English over others not like them by commenting on the superstitions, unreliable train schedules, and appearance of the locals: "The women looked pretty, except when you got near them.... The strangest figures ... were the Slovaks, who are more barbarian than the rest.... They are very picturesque, but do not look prepossessing. On the stage they would be set down at once as some old Oriental band of brigands."[170]

By Harker's account, Transylvania appears to possess more similarities between it and Laura's isolated schloss in Styria than any Western country.

However, as already seen in previous chapters with the declining estates of the John Melmoth and Silas Ruthyn, there are parallels between Dracula's Castle in Transylvania and the Big Houses of Ireland. "Dracula resides in his decaying Big House with its battered battlements. Dracula embodies the kind of isolated 'garrison mentality' common to the English landowning class in Ireland."[171] Furthermore, Valente explains that "*Transylvania*, 'Beyond the forest,' irresistibly suggests 'beyond the Pale,' which historically refers to the broad expanse of Ireland that remained outside and resistant to British military and political control for most of the colonial epoch."[172] His interpretation is supported by McNally who says:

> Transylvania is at a minimum a metaphor for Ireland, as both Transylvania and Ireland are frontier territories on the fringes of the empire, fought over often by foreigners.... The common people are as superstitious and as "wild" as Irish peasants were thought to be. The dominant class to which Dracula belongs is alien to the common people.... Similarly to both vampires and werewolves the Transylvanian landowning aristocracy fed on their subjects.[173]

If Transylvania and Count Dracula possess Irish characteristics, then the late Victorian fear of reverse colonization is impossible to ignore in *Dracula*. This unease with the "invasion" of the "foreign" Irish existed decades earlier in English society, as illustrated in the July 1828 article "Immigration of Irish Authors" in the *New Monthly Magazine and Literary Journal* by M. While the article seems to strive for a satirical tone when describing the problem of Irish immigrants who have insinuated themselves in all aspects of English life, including authorship, racist stereotypes frequently erupt into the language and reveal that the writer may be expressing his actual feelings of the Irish. The writer attempts a light tone as the article begins:

> Well! God be thanked, we have got a Tory Ministry once more, to our heart's content; and Ireland, it is to be hoped, will at last be reduced to some Christian rule. There's no pleasing those Irish, strike where we may;—whichever way we turn, we are met by them. Irish poverty, Irish turbulence, Irish popery, and Heaven knows how many other Irish abuses, are ringing in our ears from morning till night.[174]

By the second page, M's tone takes a decided turn when talking about the Irish influence on politics: "Not contented with breaking up three successive ministries … they [the Irish] are now determined to ruin Old England out and out, by overrunning the land with their papistical, poteen-bibbing, potatovorous population of paupers, (there's a magnificent alliteration!)."[175] M continues to reinforce Irish stereotypes by next addressing the dangers of the increasing number of Irish births: "To this complexion we must come at last, if we suffer the Irish rebels to multiply like the Antediluvians, and spread their spawn unrebuked over England"[176] and "One-half of Ireland is actually in a state of combination with the other to over-populate the empire; and the accursed *officina gentium* is making papists by millions."[177] M also expresses great concern about the Irish immigrants coming to England and taking English jobs.

> Of what use will it be for an honest Englishmen … to rear a promising youth, and to give him the best of educations, at the university, or at a penny-a-week auxiliary supplementary Bible school, if, when he is ready to be bound apprentice,—no matter whether it be to a Secretary of State or a pin-maker,—a tall, lanky, hungry-visaged, two-handed fellow, shall be suffered to stalk over from Ireland, with his fist in one hand, and a shillelagh in the other, and a short pipe stuck in his hat, and offer to do the young gentleman's business at half-price?[178]

After three pages of "reporting" on the extent of the Irish threat, M finally presents the subject which was indicated in the article's title, the Irish author immigrant.

> Forty years ago, the whole parliamentary branch of literature was carried on by Scotchmen; and half Grub-street spoke the language of Allan Ramsay. But at present that business has fallen altogether into the hands of the Irish.... Truly, I would have you look to your Editor's chair. It is familiarly known in Ireland that delicate-faced youths can make a livelihood in London, as well as the stoutest chairmen; and that there is a decent provision for them all, if not as porters, as reporters. Literature, or, as they more commonly call it, *litherature*, is the very element of an Irishman. It is the only trade to which he takes naturally, except turf-cutting and fighting; for it is the only one which requires no capital.[179]

M continues the article in the same vein, shifting to the Irish invading playwriting thanks to Shiel's and Maturin's success,[180] Banim ruining the novel writing trade,[181] the proliferation of Irish reviewers,[182] Irish poets,[183] and Irish Catholic question pamphleteers.[184] The only respite the reader receives from the anti–Irish diatribe is when M shifts to the most destructive trend in the literary profession, "the new passion for writing which has sprung up among peers and ladies of *haut ton*."[185] M still manages a dig against the Irish while complaining about the aristocracy: "Why the devil don't they write in Irish? They would be just as intelligible; or some professional writer might live by their translation."[186]

M's article has a decidedly modern ring to it even though it was written almost 200 years ago in 1828. The author expresses the fear of immigrants coming to his city, of bringing poverty, of a religion different from his own, of competition for jobs, of their seemingly higher birthrate leading to their majority rather than minority, and of their inclination for violence. While the country of origin changes over time, the reasons for fearing new immigrants seem to remain the same. M concludes the article with a recommendation to the new government:

I would press upon Mr. Wilmot Horton, since he will take the bull by the horns, to begin with this the least unmanageable branch of the subject. If he can reduce the literary population of Ireland, it will encourage him to proceed with the rest of the peasantry. It would only require to engage Murray or Colburn to settle in America, and the authors would follow instinctively, like flies after the honey.[187]

While M follows up with a joint-stock company to encourage "literature in the back-settlements" to move the aspiring Irish writers elsewhere, acknowledging that such companies are "out of fashion, but the case is desperate. Over-population is the master-vice of the nineteenth century; and Hippocrates writes that extreme diseases require extreme remedies."[188] One cannot help but think of the Irish Famine that would begin in less than twenty years, depopulating Ireland through disease, death, and immigration. Perhaps M lived to see it and regret his thoughtless words. Regardless of the author's personal feelings, the article shows that almost seventy years before Stoker published *Dracula*, some members of the English population already felt threatened by the Irish presence and feared the prospect of reverse colonization.

Patrick Brantlinger in *Rule of Darkness: British Literature and Imperialism, 1830–1914* connects Stoker's novel with a "popular literary form, invasion-scare stories, in which the outward movement of imperialist adventure is reversed."[189] Arata elaborates: "*Dracula* enacts the period's most important and pervasive narrative of decline, the narrative of reverse colonization ... this narrative expresses both fear and guilt. The fear is that what has been represented as the 'civilized' world is on the point of being colonized by 'primitive' forces.'"[190]

Although the sun never set on the English empire, it likewise did not set on the problems that continually arose among the English and the native inhabitants of their imperial acquisitions. The English newspapers frequently reported violent attempts of the natives trying to wrest power from the English. These insurrections occurred in places far removed from England save for one—Ireland. Irish independence was an increasingly debated issue that gained popular momentum as the nineteenth century wore on. "This ill will characterizing Anglo-Irish relations in the late-nineteenth century, exacerbated by the rise of Fenianism and the debate over Home Rule, far surpassed the tensions that arose as a result of British rule elsewhere."[191] Victorian readers were aware of the tension in Ireland and the possibility of reverse colonization. Scores of Irish lived in England and were infiltrating the more influential circles of English society, especially in the arts. The long colonial relationship between Ireland and England is unique among those England maintained with its colonies.

Hundreds of years of imperial associations blurred the lines between colonizer and colonized which Valente concludes resulted in

> Ireland's dual status as partner in and victim of British colonial oppression [and] served to produce the most flagrant political oxymorons, like imperialist Home Rule, as straightforward common sense. The historian R. F. Foster notes, "The Irish were more politically conservative and imperialist than a people supposedly breaking the bonds of colonialism had any right to be"; and Stoker himself was not immune to this form of mystification.[192]

The confusion caused by attempting to articulate an Irish identity that separated itself from hundreds of years of English influence manifests itself in the unsettling figure of count Dracula and the martyred character of Quincey Morris. Dracula contains characteristics of both cultures in a most alarming manner. His home may reflect the Irish landscape and its big country houses, but his person reveals an affinity to rule rather than be ruled. He is a noble and aristocratic warrior who is historically a conqueror. "In many respects, Dracula represents a break from the Gothic tradition of vampires.... In Stoker's version of the myth, vampires are intimately linked to military conquest and to the rise and fall of empires."[193] He mirrors Western culture, especially the imperialistic conquests practiced by the English and, as Kiberd states, in "another kind of story, Dracula would indeed have been the hero."[194] Kiberd's observation is exemplified in how the British perceived the adventures of Sir Richard Francis Burton (1821–90),[195] whom Stoker knew through many dinners hosted by Irving. Burton knew over thirty languages and dialects, which was one reason he was recruited to be an intelligence officer because he could blend in so well.[196] "As the half–Persian, half–Arab cloth merchant Mirza Abdullah, he passed freely through the bazaar and into homes of Moslem Indians. Such an impersonation required an intimate knowledge of Islam."[197] Burton seems to have much in common with Dracula, especially when one considers the following story that Stoker retells in *Personal Reminiscences:*

> I remember when a lad hearing at a London dinner-party he told of his journey to Mecca ... he had to pass as a Muhammedan; the slightest breach of the multitudinous observances of that creed would call attention, and suspicion at such a time and place would be instant death. In a moment of forgetfulness, or rather inattention, he made some small breach of rule. He saw that a lad had noticed him and was quietly stealing away. He faced the situation at once, and coming after the lad in such a way as not to arouse his suspicion suddenly stuck his knife into his heart.... I asked him once about the circumstances.... He said it was quite true, and that it had never troubled him from that day to the moment at which he was speaking. Said he:
> "The desert has its own laws, and there—supremely of all the East—to kill is a small offence. In any case what could I do? It had to be his life or mine!"
> As he spoke the upper lip rose and his canine tooth showed its full length like the

gleam of a dagger. Then he went on to say that such explorations as he had undertaken were not to be entered lightly if one had qualms as to taking life.[198]

Burton studies another culture so that he can readily blend in and gain information that will probably be used in an attempt to subjugate its people. When there is a threat of being exposed, he kills without hesitation or remorse because he considers himself and his mission superior to the life of the country's native inhabitant. The English, much-admired Burton would have recognized a kindred spirit in Dracula. What prevents Dracula from being perceived as an admirable conqueror is his intention to take over England, which he nearly succeeds in doing.

He plans his invasion of England in painstaking detail and uses the English imperialistic superior attitude to his advantage. England's greatest weakness is its inability to believe that they can be invaded. An overconfident opponent is easier to defeat, particularly if the invader studies the culture and becomes more English than the English. As Arata explains, "Dracula's physical mastery of his British victims begins with an intellectual appropriation of their culture, which allows him to delve the workings of the 'native mind.'"[199] Language is key to successful intellectual appropriation. Dracula studies English in such great depth that Harker is surprised to see so many familiar English texts in the castle's library, including train schedules and maps. With the arrival of Harker, Dracula acquires the invaluable resource of "a native," and he drains Harker of all this valuable information while playing the role of a subservient host. As a result, Arata explains that Dracula achieves a status rarely if ever witnessed before in literature, especially reverse colonial literature.

> The truly disturbing notion is not that Dracula impersonates Harker, but that he does it so well. Here is the nub: Dracula can "pass." To impersonate an Englishman, and do it convincingly, is the goal of Dracula's painstaking research.... To understand how disquieting Dracula's talents are, we have only to remember that in Victorian texts non–Western "natives" are seldom—I am tempted to say never, since I have not come up with another example—permitted to "pass" successfully.[200]

Dracula comes dangerously close to succeeding in his plan to invade England, feed on its inhabitants, and repopulate it with his own kind. He is defeated not because of the superiority of the English but because of the combined powers of a foreign Catholic (Van Helsing) and a female of Irish immigrant descent (Mina). The "superstitions" associated with the Catholic Church provide the necessary weapons to fight the vampire—holy water, the cross, the consecrated host, and the wooden stake—and the insights of Mina, a symbol of the results of English colonization, allow the group to destroy Dracula and his threat to England. The irony of England's unlikely rescuers cannot be ignored, nor can the fact that one of the members of the group seeking to end Dracula's threat shares similar admirable as well as concerning traits, Quincey P. Morris.

Like Dracula, Morris contributes little actual writing to the narrative, so the clues to his identity are scattered throughout the text and are filtered through the point of view of another character. Like Dracula, he is not English but is also not associated with the East, as Dracula is. Instead, he is an American and a Texan. He possesses many of the characteristics that the English would have admired. While he is well-equipped to fit in English society through his associations with men like Godalming and Seward as well as being "really well educated and has exquisite manners,"[201] he chooses to use American "slang" because it amuses Lucy. He is respectable enough to court Lucy, and apparently the only one who receives a kiss from her. He is the most reserved of the men, his emotional moments are restricted to "pouring out a perfect torrent of love-making, laying his very heart and soul at [Lucy's] feet,"[202] choking up in Mina's presence about Lucy's death, and crying openly with the rest of the men when Mina requests that the group pity Dracula because someday she may need that pity, too.[203] He is a traveler, an adventurer, and the recognized leader among his friends Seward and Godalming.[204] Among the places he has been are South America, where he saw the effects of a vampire bat on a horse. He connects this experience to Lucy's condition after being her fourth blood donor, which makes him a more astute and unprejudiced observer than Seward. Later, he is also the first to perceive something more than lunacy in Renfield, "that he had some serious purpose."[205] He is also practical when he suggests that ordinary cabs would be much less conspicuous than Godalming carriages as they break into London residences to destroy the count's boxes of earth and suggesting Winchesters because "the Count comes from a wolf country."[206] He is brave because he patrols the grounds around Lucy's house, alone and all night, though he is not sure who or what he may have to fight against. He is also brave when he does know, taking the first watch outside the Harkers' bedroom to prevent any further attacks on Mina. He is loyal and supportive, staying close to Arthur as he leaves the deceased Lucy to attend to his father's funeral. He also is admired by other men in the novel. Van Helsing proclaims upon meeting him: "A brave man's blood is the best thing on this earth when a woman is in trouble. You're a man, and no mistake."[207] Given the above information, the reader is not surprised when, at the novel's end, that it is Morris who gives the ultimate sacrifice for the group's cause since his identity appears to be that of the ideal hero.

In addition to this picture of an ideal man, Quincey is also connected to a conquering spirit, much like Dracula. His American nationality is linked to expansionism and world power. When Renfield meets Quincey, he comments: "Mr. Morris, you should be proud of your great state. Its reception into the Union was a precedent which may have far-reaching effects hereafter, when the Pole and the Tropics may hold allegiance to the Stars and Stripes. The power of Treaty may yet prove a vast engine of enlargement, when the Monroe Doctrine takes its true place as a political."[208] Renfield, who could have made any remark to Quincey, chose to focus on America's penchant for acquiring territory, both past and future. Prior to this encounter, Seward records in his diary: "What a fine fellow is Quincey! I believe in my heart of hearts that he suffered as much about Lucy's death as any of us; but he bore himself through it like a moral Viking. If America can go on breeding men like that, she will be a power in the world indeed."[209] It is another past and future about territorial expansion. The past is the reference to Quincey as a "moral Viking," apparently meant as a compliment to him. Perhaps Seward is thinking more of the Vikings of legends rather than the Vikings in history. Regardless, that the word "Viking" is followed by "will be a world power indeed" indicates invasion and expansion. For the English, it should also indicate uneasiness. America had been a British colonial holding almost 125 years prior to the publication of *Dracula*, a text suggesting through the character of Quincey that the former colonies have now become a competitor on the world stage. The count was threatening England from the East and America, perhaps more subtly, from the West. When one further considers that Quincey's last name "Morris" is the Anglicized Ó Muirgheasa,[210] he had Irish roots like many other Americans. Many of these Irish-Americans supported Irish independence from England. If Quincey were one of these, he could be considered a threat to the England.

Quincey does have a few moments where he acts in some inexplicable ways that seem at odds with his character of a model man's man. First, when the group assembles for the first time to plan their strategy, he leaves the room to go outside to shoot at a bat he saw perched on the windowsill while he was inside the room. He misses the bat but shatters the window and endangers everyone in the room. It is an uncharacteristically reckless and illogical decision for his character, and he reports that he missed the huge bat.[211] Another curious incident occurs right after the group interrupts Dracula's attack on Mina. Mina is in a state of shock; Arthur runs from the room; Van Helsing is reviving Harker from his stupor; and Seward is looking out the window and sees "Quincey Morris run across the lawn and hide himself in the shadow of a great yew tree."[212] Arthur reports that there was no sign of Dracula in the asylum, but Dracula had burned all their written evidence. Van Helsing turns to Quincey and asks if he has anything to tell. His reply is cryptic, especially considering the circumstances:

> "A little," he answered. "It may be much eventually, but at present I can't say. I thought it well to know if possible where the Count would go when he left the house. I did not see him; but I saw a bat rise from Renfield's window, and flap westward. I expected to see him in some shape go back to Carfax; but he evidently sought some other lair. He will not be back tonight; for the sky is reddening in the east, and the dawn is close. We must work tomorrow!"
>
> He said the latter words through his shut teeth.[213]

Quincey's purposeful reticence is notable for two reasons. First, less than a page before, Van Helsing instructs both Arthur and Quincey: "We want no more concealments. Our hope now is in knowing all. Tell freely!"[214] But Quincey is clearly holding something back. What is even more interesting is that Quincey's unwillingness to tell all he knows is reminiscent of Renfield's a few chapters earlier when he tries to convince Seward to release him: "I am not at liberty to give you the whole of my reasons; but you may, I assure you, take it from me that they are good ones, sound and unselfish"[215] and follows up with "…if I were free to speak I should not hesitate a moment; but I am not my own master in the matter."[216] The reader soon learns that Renfield is prevented from speaking due to Dracula's power over him, and Dracula brutally deals with Renfield for telling as much as he did.

These two odd instances could be attributed to Stoker's original intention of having Quincey play a larger role in the novel, as indicated by his notes.[217] The explanation for Quincey's inconsistent behavior may have been part of one of his planned written contributions to the story, like Harker's recognizing the blonde vampire in Dracula's castle and the probable explanation for this detail being a reference to the excised material from the chapter that appeared as "Dracula's Guest." During the final editing before publication, some cuts could have been made that resulted in missing details to fill these gaps, or Stoker may not have written those parts at all. In addition to Quincey's initially planned larger role in the notes for *Dracula*, there are two interesting notations about the novel's end which concern Quincey. The notes show that on March 17, 1896, Stoker indicated that Morris seems to survive the climatic ending: "All arrive near sunset, wolves. Snow * Tzgany fight * volcano, red light—no scar."[218] However, this changes a few pages later in an undated but assumedly later note, which outlines an altered, more detailed ending:

Castle in sight—sun setting—time all important * at sunset Drac can fly. Makes stand. Quincey to rescue with maxim gun—storm building up—sun setting * victors hew top off box. Drac. Slain—mist melts—storm bursts on castle. Wild whirling figures of women on tower—obliterated by lightning. Quincey dies—as dying points to glow of red sunset hitting on Mina's face * no stain[219]

While some of the details change in the published ending—Quincey does not have a maxim gun in the final confrontation with the Szgany to gain access to the cart, and the vampire women had already been slain by Van Helsing—Quincey's death remains. It is a surprising choice given Stoker's admiration for America, the idealized man that he creates in Quincey, and the nature of the other characters who die in the novel. Quincey does not appear to fall into any of the categories of the other deceased characters of *Dracula*. He is not the older, infirm, parental figures, such as Mrs. Westenra, Lord Godalming (Arthur's father), Mr. Hawkins, and Mr. Swales. He is not a victim of Dracula like the crew of the *Demeter*, Lucy, Mrs. Westenra (dies of fright),[220] Mr. Swales (broken neck attributed to a sudden fright that caused a fall),[221] Renfield, or Petrof Skinsky ("throat had been torn open as if by some wild animal"[222]). He is not a vampire like Lucy, the three female vampires at Dracula's Castle, or Dracula. Like his identity itself, the purpose of Quincey's death is confusing.[223]

While Stoker seemed to admire America as depicted by Quincey, he ultimately rejected what America symbolizes as a solution for Irish-English relations. Quincey is an adventurer, brave, a leader, loyal to his friends, intuitive, practical, and open-minded. These are all traits that Stoker admired. However, he is the least emotional of the men, more American than Celtic, and Stoker hoped for a male ideal that combined a man's strength with a woman's heart. Quincey is also wealthy, though the source of that wealth is never revealed, so he is more Godalming's financial equal than any of the other middle-/upper-middle-class members of the group, but he lacks the aristocratic pedigree that would make his wealth respectable. His wealth, manners, education, and friendship with Godalming would have opened society doors for him in England, but families like the Westenras would desire their daughters to marry the Godalmings of society, not the dangerously charming, slang-talking Americans. This is illustrated by Lucy's rejection of Quincey's suit and her willingness to still kiss him. Finally, Quincey's symbolic association to America's emergence into a world power that would rival England makes him a threat. Quincey represents the many changes occurring in the world beyond London. It is why Stoker chose to end the novel the way he did. Quincey Morris dies on November 6, but Quincey Harker is born on that day,[224] and Harker notes: "His mother holds, I know, the secret belief that some of our brave friend's spirit has passed into him."[225] It is a very Celtic belief and would seem to indicate that the American part of Quincey's spirit will be tempered by his English family and perhaps his Irish heritage will exert itself further as a result of being mixed with the Irish Murray. It is a complicated compromise of identities, and it is regrettable that Stoker had not written a sequel to *Dracula* featuring Quincey Harker to see what kind of character emerged.

These many twists also reveal the nature of Stoker's personal awareness of his Irish identity. It is interesting to consider his position in society and where he allied himself politically. Stoker was a native-born Irishman. His Dublin, middle-class parents had distinct aspirations for their children's social status. Their eldest son, Dr. William Thornley Stoker, was knighted, and Stoker gained renown as the manager of England's most notable and first knighted actor, Henry Irving, who performed in London's most prestigious theater, the Lyceum. If one aspired to meet the illustrious Irving and socialize in his exclusive circle, it was important to gain the favor of Stoker. Stoker occupied one of the most enviable positions in England and enjoyed the benefits of it. Many perceived him as an Anglophile. In *Dracula*, England is saved from the threat of Dracula rather than victimized by it. Stoker himself had left Ireland to loyally serve English stage royalty as an unappreciated manager. After nearly thirty years of service, Stoker was not included in Irving's will and was physically depleted—he suffered his first stroke after he settled all the details surrounding Irving's death. Yet Stoker wrote a tremendous tribute to Irving in *Personal Reminiscences*.

Despite the appearance of embracing British culture at the expense of his Irish heritage, Stoker was still an outsider in London, because he was Irish. No matter who he knew, what he did, or how much he earned, being Irish meant he was not English. As Valente explains, "In the land of the Anglos [London], Stoker came to discover, Anglo-Irish usually translated as 'mere' Irish. Consequently, in *occupying* the metropolitan center he paradoxically came to *embody* the Celtic fringe."[226] "Even Stoker's university degree, the only one among the Lyceum company, failed to earn him the respectability he craved, mainly because it was conferred by an Irish institution (which might explain why he decided, at the age of thirty-nine, to secure an *English* barrister's license that he apparently never intended to use)."[227] Stoker sought acceptance from his British colleagues, but he was not willing to sacrifice his Irish heritage to gain it. In certain respects, like other notable Irish expatriates, Stoker became more Irish as a result of leaving Ireland. "Not only did he maintain social ties and mutually supportive relations with nationalist literati like Lady Jane Wilde and William

O'Brien but he also became a strong supporter of the Irish Literary Society, which carried the cultural nationalistic imprimatur of its founder, W. B. Yeats."[228] Yeats was part of the group headed by Justin McCarthy, close friends of Stoker's,[229] which assembled the ten volume collection of *Irish Literature* published in 1904. It included an excerpt from Stoker's *The Snake's Pass* that featured the gombeen man (money lender). It is an interesting choice since the collection includes Sir Richard F. Burton (1821–90) as an Irish writer and provides "The Preternatural in Fiction," "From the Essay on 'The Book of a Thousand Nights and a Night,'"[230] "A Journey in Disguise," and "From 'The Personal Narrative of a Pilgrimage to El Midnah and Mecca'"[231] as examples of his work—not exactly Irish-themed publications and from a writer born in England. When one considers that *Dracula* exhibits several features mentioned in Burton's "Preternatural" essay and the collection includes many examples of folklore, supernatural, superstitious, and nationalistic literature, it is surprising that an excerpt from *Dracula* was not included, especially since Stoker and McCarthy were good friends[232] so Stoker must have had some input on what would be included. Perhaps Stoker was as unaware of *Dracula*'s Irish literary merits as the editors were, which may be why they opted for the obviously Irish contents of *The Snake's Pass*.

Regardless of the selection, Stoker probably enjoyed being included in the collection alongside other past and present prestigious writers. He also did not limit his Irish support to literary endeavors. Although his name does not appear frequently in public in conjunction with the issue of Home Rule and Stoker "described himself as 'a philosophical Home-Ruler,'"[233] his commitment extended beyond the philosophical. His association with and support of it seems clear in the news reports of the time and, even more significantly, in his personal responses that were not recorded in the newspapers. On April 9, 1886, in the article "Home Rule for Ireland—Mr. Gladstone's Proposals," Stoker is specifically listed as a member of the packed house in attendance to hear the speech. The writer of the article described the scene: "A House thronged in every part listened with profound and unflagging interest to the speech, three hours and twenty minutes long, in which the Premier unfolded his Irish Proposals."[234] Stoker was a very busy man, so for him to have spent such an extensive amount of time listening to Gladstone talk about Home Rule means it must have been very important to him. His Irish political associations appeared in print at least twice more in the newspapers. In the *Glasgow Herald*'s March 22, 1888, edition a writer notes: "[George A.] Moore has become a fierce anti–Parnellite…. Oscar Wilde is the cheeriest and most pronounced of

Nationalists. In this respect, however, Oscar Wilde is not singular. It is the 'note' of a London Irishmen—even if Protestant and landlord bred—to be a Home Ruler—as, for example, Mr. Bram Stoker."[235] Stoker's name appears again in the June 24, 1892, article "Ulster Home Rulers in London," in which his name is listed as one of many who, unable to attend the meeting, sent a letter of apology to the organization.[236]

The minimal public attention to Stoker's politics is in keeping with his position at the Lyceum; he occupied himself behind the scenes while someone else held the audience's attention on stage. Paul Murray devotes a chapter to Stoker's politics where he provides helpful insights into Stoker's political thoughts and associations. Stoker knew William Gladstone through his frequent attendance at the Lyceum and supported him when Parnell politically attacked him.[237]

> By siding with Gladstone, he was aligning himself with Liberal opinion in England which decreed that Parnell's moral irregularity made impossible a continuation of the political alliance between Liberals and the Irish Parliamentary Party as long as Parnell remained its leader. The Party split on this issue, precipitating a deep and lasting rift in Irish political life. Stoker had friends on both sides of the divide but he was not a Parnell loyalist.[238]

One of Stoker's many influential friendships was with Justin McCarthy, "the Irish nationalist writer and politician who lived for many years in Cheyne Gardens, near Stoker."[239] Theirs was another of Stoker's lifelong friendships, just as his active participation in Home Rule.[240]

Perhaps the most obvious of all of Stoker's political actions was his speech. Barbara Belford asserts that "Stoker had a proper British accent, but often put on a Milesian brogue, for he believed with Shaw that 'it is a distinction to be an Irishman, and accordingly the Irish in England flaunt their nationality.'"[241] In England, speech indicates social standing better than any other physical manifestation. Anyone could buy the "right" clothes and live in the "right" neighborhood and belong to the "right" clubs, but where one came from was immediately evident by how one spoke. By completely altering one's speech, as George Bernard Shaw illustrated in *Pygmalion*, one could successfully "pass" in society. Stoker was obviously aware of this as a member of London society, a manager of a theater, and a writer. He was a careful observer of speech patterns as indicated in both numerous entries in *The Dublin Years The Lost Journal of Bram Stoker* and the four pages of words copied from F. K. Robinson's *A Glossary of Words Used in the Neighborhood of Whitby* (1876) in his *Notes for Dracula*.[242] Similarly, Count Dracula knows that his speech is the key to "passing" in London. Harker compliments the count's perfect English, but Dracula explains to his guest that he desires to learn more than the grammar and the words:

"Well I know that, did I move and speak in your London, none there are who would not know me for a stranger. That is not enough for me....I am content if I am like the rest, so that no man stops if he sees me, or pause in his speaking if he hear my words, to say, 'Ha, ha! A stranger!'.... You shall, I trust, rest here with me a while, so that by our talking I may learn the English intonation; and I would that you tell me when I make error, even of the smallest, in my speaking."[243]

Stoker again emphasizes the importance of speech using his publication of Irving as the most unusual vehicle. In 1906, Stoker published *The Personal Reminiscences of Henry Irving*, one of the most popular publications of his lifetime. Ironically, and perhaps intentionally, Stoker used the pages to recount a story from 1880 involving the usually nonpolitical Irving and himself debating the Home Rule issue. Irving decides to settle the disagreement by stopping a policeman on the Isle of Wight to ask his opinion.

Irving turned to me ... and said...: "...Here comes the Voice of England. Just listen to it and learn!" Then in a cheery, friendly voice he said to the invisible policeman:
"Tell me, officer, what is your opinion as to this trouble in Ireland?" The answer came at once, stern and full of pent-up feeling, and in an accent there was no possibility of mistaking:
"Ah, begob, it's all the fault iv the dirty Gover'mint!" His brogue might have been cut with a hatchet.[244]

Stoker made his point with Irving; England "was ... home to more Irishmen than Dublin."[245] Stoker knew the importance of speech in British society, but he consciously chose to call attention to his nationality rather than try to conceal it and fit in.

His position and his full awareness of it contribute to several instances of originality in the novel. As a solicitor, Harker is economically and socially the least prestigious of the male characters: Arthur Holmwood becomes Lord Godalming; Quincey Morris is a wealthy American; Dr. John Seward is a groundbreaking medical man who studied in Europe and was socially elevated enough to be the friend of Arthur; and Professor Abraham Van Helsing surpasses all in knowledge. Harker is an orphan and junior solicitor with his first assignment. Under normal conditions, Harker would never have socialized with Van Helsing, Seward, Morris, or Godalming, since he was not their equal. In fact, it is not until after Harker becomes a partner and Mr. Hawkins's heir that he meets Van Helsing, Seward, Morris, or Godalming. He experiences an unprecedented elevation in social status when he becomes a partner in the firm and inherits Mr. Hawkins's entire estate. Harker also demonstrates more courage and intelligence than anyone except for Mina and Van Helsing. He escapes Dracula's castle without any assistance, recovers from brain fever, follows the legal trail to locate Dracula's other property purchases, and strikes the initial blow leading to Dracula's physical destruction. Throughout these experiences, he shows himself to be superior in many respects to Godalming, Morris, and Seward. He also enjoys the singular status of having an exceptional wife in Mina and a son to carry on his name. As an English-degree-holding solicitor residing in London with an exceptional wife and son, a reputation for intelligence and courage, and a decided penchant for organization and writing memorandums, Harker has a great deal in common with Stoker. The only difference between them would be the occupational and social promotion Stoker permits Harker, an event only possible in fiction.

Stoker further reveals a personal identification in a rather surprising manner that fulfills the final criterion of Irish literature: passion. In *Reminiscences*, Stoker recounts in a moment of autobiography: "It is true that I had known weakness. In my babyhood I used, I understand, to be often at the point of death. Certainly till I was about seven years old I never knew what it was to stand upright."[246] Once he stood, Stoker did not seem to stop moving. He exhibited and exuded an astonishing passion for life. He was an excellent scholar, athlete, friend, and employee. When he committed himself to something or someone, he was nearly consumed. Stoker had a passion for his work that bordered on obsession. Belford emphasizes, in her biography, Stoker's "obsessive project" of *The Duties of Clerks of Petty Sessions in Ireland*, in which he meticulously researched every aspect of the book for over six months and reformed the clerks' duties into a more efficient and uniform system.[247] The reader will see the same obsessive quality in Mina and Van Helsing as they collect and organize every scrap of evidence. As a young man in Ireland, Stoker passionately pursued his dream of becoming more than just a civil servant, and realized it when Irving hired him as the manager of the Lyceum. Stoker's passion persisted in his work habits. He worked long hours to manage the theater but also possessed the energy to write. *Dracula* in particular exhibits his passionate pursuit of writing. He started researching the novel in 1890 and continued to revise and develop it for seven years, something he did not do with any of his other fictional works.

Stoker also exhibits the heroic passions that he gives to his male characters in *Dracula*. Van Helsing emphasizes the importance of strong men to carry out the tasks before them and would have welcomed the addition of Stoker to their heroic band of men. Stoker unabashedly describes himself as follows: "I was physically immensely strong. In fact I feel justified in saying I represented in my own person something of that aim of university education mens sana in corpore sano."[248] He heroically dove into the

Thames to save a man who was trying to commit suicide.[249] He embraced new opportunities for adventure like those offered by the trips to America. He was a "man's man," much like the one he depicts in the American character of Quincey Morris.

He was also emotionally effusive, like Lord Godalming, revealing his empathetic capacity long before creating Arthur's character. In his journal entry dated August 5, 1871, Stoker records:

> Men and women pass me every moment and as I glance into their faces I seem to see inmost yearning like my own. Some of the faces are marked by care & pain & the shadow of some great sorrow is over many such faces. I long to draw forwards and let them rest against my bosom where they may at least find a calm for a moment in the thought that there is a heart that feels with them....
>
> It makes me long, oh so much, for some shoulder on which to lay my own head and weep—and tell all my little pains and griefs....
>
> Will men ever believe that a strong man can have a woman's heart & the wishes of a lonely child? It may be so...[250]

After reading this entry, one cannot help but recall the scene where Mina comforts Lord Godalming:

> In an instant the poor dear fellow was overwhelmed with grief. It seemed to me that all he had of late been suffering in silence found a vent at once. He grew quite hysterical.... I felt an infinite pity for him, and opened my arms unthinkingly. With a sob he laid his head on my shoulder, and cried like a wearied child, whilst he shook with emotion....
>
> I felt this big sorrowing man's head resting on me, as though it were that of a baby that some day may lie on my bosom, and I stroked his hair as though he were my own child.[251]

Stoker realized his strong men with women's hearts and the dreams of a lonely child in the pages of *Dracula*, but he also recorded some emotionally important moments in his life.

Stoker's emotionally unguarded moments are not those one would expect, like the rush of emotion experienced when one marries or holds one's child for the first time. Stoker's most memorable experiences are well-recorded; the first is the often-quoted scene that was the beginning of Irving's and Stoker's long friendship. Stoker had written a favorable review of Irving's performance and was invited to dine with the actor. Irving recited Thomas Hood's poem "The Dream of Eugene Aram" as after-dinner entertainment, and, according to Stoker, it was quite a performance. After Irving delivers the stirring recitation, "he collapsed half fainting,"[252] and Stoker admits, "I burst into something like hysterics."[253] He immediately defends his response by extensively explaining that he "was no hysterical subject,"[254] but the fact remains that it happened and parallels the behavior of his male characters quite well. The other emotional experience often recalled by Stoker is the one elicited by Walt Whitman who, like Irving, Stoker greatly admired. Stoker corresponded with the poet for years, and, in 1884 during the theater company's tour of America, he finally met Whitman. Like his initial meeting of Irving, that with Whitman prompted an emotional response and left a lasting impression on Stoker.

> I found him [Whitman] all that I had ever dreamed of, or wished for in him: large-minded, broad-viewed, tolerant to the last degree; incarnate sympathy; understanding with an insight that seemed more than human.... No wonder that men opened their hearts to him—told him their secrets, their woes and hopes and griefs and loves! A man among men![255]

These genuine moments of feeling are mirrored on the pages of *Dracula* between and among its band of men and how they opened up to Mina.

It is also from *Dracula* that another aspect of passion emerges. Early psychoanalytic critics found Stoker's novel a wonderfully direct example of the applications of Freud, as Maurice Richardson's "The Psychoanalysis of Ghost Stories" showed:

> It is very remarkable how in *Dracula*, Stoker makes use of all the traditional mythical properties and blends them with a family type of situation of his own contriving that turns out to be a quite blatant demonstration of the Oedipus complex. From a Freudian standpoint—and from no other does the story really make any sense—it is seen as a kind of incestuous, necrophilous, oral-anal-sadistic all-in wrestling match.[256]

Here, passion in the form of nearly every sexual taboo known to the Victorian audience emerges, though Richardson is quick to add: "I doubt whether Stoker had any inkling of the erotic content of the vampire superstition."[257] Whether Stoker purposely set out to write a novel that would clearly illustrate Freud's research is difficult to say; however, the application of Freud's theories to Stoker's novel are evident. The detailed interpretations of Harker's seduction, Lucy's staking, and Mina's attack have prompted continuous and varied responses from all critical sectors regarding Stoker's sexual orientation and his view of women.

In regard to Stoker's personal perception of women, Carol A. Senf offers this observation:

> Familiar with the feminist movement and apparently supportive of women's struggles for professional equality, [Stoker] creates women characters who are the intellectual equals of the men in his novels; however he seems to have drawn the line at sexual equality, and he has his heroines choose the traditional roles of marriage and motherhood instead of careers.[258]

Susan Parlour agrees with Senf's view of Stoker and women, adding that "Stoker ... manipulates and exploits elements of Ireland's past and mingles them with England's contemporary concerns to create a more modern image of femininity than did his peers."[259] This modern image even extends to the female vampires. Senf observes that "Stoker's villainesses ... radiate sexuality,"[260] but Parlour interprets the sexually assertive female vampires as an original and positive feature: "In allowing the young women in the novel to transgress the clearly demarcated boundaries of sexual behavior and to engage with their sexuality in such an overtly explicit way, Stoker succeeds in breaking new ground in literature ... creat[ing] new viable visions of feminity which promote autonomy in both sexual and intellectual matters."[261] Nina Auerbach presents an additional view, noting that Stoker's female vampires, and especially Lucy, are more respectable in their transformed state.[262] "Far from personifying a reversion to woman-hating in late Victorian men, Lucy raises the tone of female vampirism by avoiding messy entanglements with mortals, directing her 'voluptuous wantoness' to her fiance alone.... As a vampire, Lucy the flirt is purified into Lucy the wife."[263] However, Lucy the wife is no exemplar of motherhood.

Auerbach's, Senf's, and Parlour's perceptions of the female characters, especially the vampiric ones, demonstrates the variety and complexity of Stoker's experiences with women. His mother, Charlotte, "appears to have been a powerful figure."[264] Her husband, Abraham, was nineteen years older than her twenty-five years when they married in 1844.[265] She raised their seven children in "a household ruled by a strong sense of moral righteous[ness]."[266] She was a feminist who argued publicly for women's rights, particularly for the poor, but reportedly was not as specifically concerned about her own two daughters' education.[267] Murray observes: "On the theme of sexual equality, she proved to be more progressive than her son would be more than a generation later."[268] The force of such a personality would be difficult to ignore and its influence was certainly felt in Stoker's fictional characters and also the women who formed important relationships in his life.

Stoker certainly seemed drawn to independent women who may not have always met the Victorian ideal. Two of his lifelong friends were actresses Genevieve Ward and Ellen Terry, whose lives were not that of a typical, respectable lady of the time. Terry's life prior to meeting Stoker was the stuff of sensational fiction:

At the age of sixteen she had contracted a short-lived marriage to the painter, G. F. Watts, after which she lived with the architect and designer, Edward Godwin, who became the father of her three children. After breaking up with Godwin, she returned to the stage to support her family. In 1877 she divorced and married the actor, Charles Kelly, essentially to provide a 'name' for her children. After a successful season at the

Court Theatre, she joined the then forty-year-old Irving as his leading lady at the Lyceum Theatre as it prepared to open under his management in 1878.[269]

Terry would become Irving's leading lady off the stage as well, despite Irving being married.

Genevieve Ward met Stoker prior to his Lyceum days, but he also met her through the theater in Dublin. Her story is even more colorful than Terry's. She was an American by birth but the Comtesse De Gerbel by marriage.

[I]n 1855 as a young girl, [Genevieve had] fallen in love with and married the Russian Count de Gerbel of Nicolaeiff in a civil ceremony in Nice. He attempted to use legal trickery to declare the marriage invalid but, through the medium of the Tsar was forced to marry her in a religious ceremony at Warsaw, her father packing a firearm in case he again had second thoughts. At the church door she bowed to him before parting; they were never to see each other again. She retained therefore a title but not a husband and developed a career, first as a singer and then as an actress.[270]

Both Ward and Terry achieved success on the stage and remained friends with Stoker throughout his lifetime. Another strong, successful woman whom Stoker knew was a banking heiress, Baroness Angela Georgina Burdett-Coutts. A philanthropist and regular theatergoer, she got to know both Stoker and his brother, Thornley. They were frequent guests at her gatherings and often supported her projects. While the baroness sounds like she was a typical aristocratic woman who gave her support and money to charitable causes, she scandalized society when in 1881, at the age of sixty-seven, she married thirty-year-old W. L. Ashmead Bartlett, who "took her name by royal license."[271]

Perhaps the most influential and speculated-about female relationship for Stoker was that with his wife, Florence Balcombe. More is known about Florence's prior or perhaps simultaneous courtship with Oscar Wilde than what led to her meeting and ultimately deciding to marry Stoker. As Belford describes:

If Stoker saw himself as "the most masculine man," then Florence Balcombe was his feminine counterpart. Eleven years younger, she was pretty but penniless.... Her dowry was ethereal beauty. Tall at five feet eight, with patrician profile, gray-blue eyes, and fine brown hair, she was fragile where he was robust, talkative where he was shy, curious where he was distracted. They made a striking couple. Everyone thought her admirable, but like Dracula's Lucy, she attracted too many promiscuous gazes.[272]

Although she did not bring any money to their marriage on December 4, 1878, in Dublin, nineteen-year-old Florence brought more than just her stunning beauty. She was a tremendous asset to him socially, exhibiting a "fierce devotion to Stoker."[273] She negotiated within the scrutinizing lens of society with grace and skill; she was a perfect hostess as well as guest. She found herself the object of W. S. Gilbert's attention, but no hint of scandal ever touched her. She also revealed an underlying steel to her surface fragility when she and Noel survived the sinking of the *Victoria* in 1887. As Murray concludes from one of her surviving letters to her mother: "The impression is of a woman who saw herself in partnership with her husband."[274] This partnership is best exhibited in her intelligent and skillful management of the household finances after Stoker became ill. She managed them so well that he left her an inheritance. And she managed it and his literary estate so well after his death that she left their son, Noel, with an even greater inheritance than Stoker had left her. Florence reflects many of the characteristics seen in Mina. She garnered the admiration of society for her appropriately feminine behavior, but she also proved to be her husband's equal and partner rather than his passive marital ornament.

Despite what appears to be a successful marriage, speculation surrounds Stoker's relationships with women, which prompts the introduction of another popular issue about his personal identity: his fidelity to his wife. Stoker's great-nephew, Daniel Farson, states in his biography of Stoker: "I know that he [Stoker] 'enjoyed' the reputation of being a 'womaniser,' reputedly famous for his sexual exploits. Certainly, he was obsessed by the ideal of the pure woman."[275] The remarks are highly suggestive, and Farson later uses them to lay the groundwork for his theory that Stoker actually died of tertiary syphilis, the cause of death barely concealed on his death certificate. The allegations were treated as fact in many subsequent studies and critiques of Stoker, but they should not be. Belford observes that "there is now sufficient medical opinion to cast doubt on syphilis as a cause of death or even a factor in Stoker's medical history,"[276] and further adds: "Being in a touring company provided abundant opportunity for dalliances, but Stoker must have been discreet—or uninvolved—to have left no whiff of gossip."[277] She makes an excellent point since, given Stoker's obsessive work ethic and penchant for letter-writing and saving everything, not one scrap of paper has yet surfaced to support the rumor that Stoker was anything but faithful to his wife.

The image of Stoker as the promiscuous husband has diminished, but the theory that he was a homosexual is still debated. This idea is based upon his correspondence with Walt Whitman, his unwavering attachment to Henry Irving, and the emotional excesses of the male characters in *Dracula*.

If a puppy could write with the fervor of its wagging tail, we might get something like Stoker's letter to Whitman. He describes himself artlessly, to Whitman....

What seeps through the coded diction of Stoker's letter is a cry of gratitude for a writer who has confronted his homosexuality.[278]

If Stoker was a homosexual and also knew it, he could never admit it without serious repercussions. He witnessed the complete destruction of his friend Oscar Wilde, who was tried, convicted, and sentenced for the crime of homosexuality in 1895. Wilde had been a frequent visitor to the Stoker home and intimately connected with the theater world, but Stoker did not mention him once in his tribute to Irving, because even the most remote connection to Wilde would be social suicide. An Irishman, like Wilde, Stoker was already an outsider in London, and he had no desire to be an outcast by having readers of *Dracula* see any evidence of anything even remotely homosexual within the pages of his novel.

Perhaps in an effort to distance himself from such allegations, Stoker expressed his sentiments about inappropriate reading material in a 1908 article entitled "The Censorship of Fiction." In it he asserts that "the measure of the ethics of the artist is expressed in the reticence shown in his work; and where such self-restraint exists there is no need for external compelling force."[279] Stoker continues: "It is through the corruption of individuals that the harm is done. A close analysis will show that the only emotions which in the long run harm are those arising from sex impulses."[280] Stoker was in earnest about protecting the public from reading sexually suggestive material and urges writers that they are their own best censors. It is ironic that the creator of *Dracula* could be so unaware of the possible interpretations ascribed to some of his most memorable and frequently quoted scenes. Among the suggestive scenes already quoted in this chapter, a discussion of Stoker and sex impulses is not complete without a reference to Arthur's graphic staking of Lucy using "a round wooden stake, some two and a half or three inches thick and about three feet long"[281] while Van Helsing, Seward, and Morris watch.

> The Thing [Lucy] in the coffin writhed; and a hideous, blood-curdling screech came from the opened red lips. The body shook and quivered and twisted in wild contortions; the sharp white teeth champed together till the lips were cut and the mouth was smeared with a crimson foam. But Arthur never faltered. He looked like a figure of Thor as his untrembling arm rose and fell, driving deeper and deeper the mercy-bearing stake, whilst the blood from the pierced heart welled and spurted up around it. His face was set, and high duty seemed to shine through it; the sight of it gave us courage, so that our voices seemed to ring through the little vault.[282]

The critical interpretations of this scene vary. "Lucy seems to be having the best orgasm in recorded history ... [and] is the sole beneficiary, either of a saved soul or a satiated body."[283] Other interpretations describe a less favorable experience for Lucy. Brigitte Boudreau in "Mother Dearest, Mother Deadliest: Object Relations Theory and the Trope of Failed Motherhood in *Dracula*" comments: "This scene resonates of an honor killing where the entire family stand as witnesses to the punishment of what is deemed a sexually liberated woman. Further, Arthur and the other men seem to gain a certain amount of satisfaction in destroying Lucy in a sexually-laden Manner."[284] Parlour offers: "The violence of Lucy's demise … is arguably in direct relation to the threat she poses to church and state, as she fails to conform to the sexual and social norms of the time."[285] Parlour later adds one of the most frequent interpretations of the disturbing scene:

> The violence of Lucy's "second death" is particularly brutal, whilst at the same time rendered overtly sexual. With all four men participating in her death and the weapon of choice being a stake, it is painted as an extreme violation of the female form, reminiscent of a gang-rape as patriarchal order strives to exert its dominance over the feminine's desire to be heard in society. The final blows delivered by Holmwood are recorded with an unrelenting and graphic realism, and the scene has a nightmarish quality to it.[286]

Though varied, all interpretations agree that the sexual aspects portrayed in the scene are impossible to ignore, prompting two immediate questions to any reader. First, if this is an example of Stoker exercising his reticence and self-restraint in his fiction, what would be the results if he allowed himself to be totally uncensored? The second question is what may have caused so many critics to examine and quote this particular scene: Why is the destruction of the much-loved Lucy so detailed, violent, and brutal in comparison to the centuries-old, seriously threatening Dracula? Stoker describes Dracula's death in three sentences:

> But, on the instant, came the sweep and flash of Jonathan's great knife. I [Mina] shrieked as I saw it shear through the throat; whilst at the same moment Mr. Morris's bowie knife plunged into the heart.
>   It was like a miracle; but before our very eyes, and almost in the drawing of a breath, the whole body crumbled into dust and passed from our sight.[287]

After the pages of the suspense-building chase, Dracula's "staking" scene is anticlimactic; it could easily be missed if one was a careless reader.

Questions like these, and the varied, thoughtful responses that make up the large body of criticism associated with Stoker and his work, are among the reasons that *Dracula* has remained in print since it was first published. Something about it resonates with the reader no matter from what era or culture or class, and, at the same time, something about it and its author remains elusive. *Dracula* is a complex novel that reflects the multiple sides to Stoker's identity. Kiberd explains that *Dracula* is a novel "where everybody turns into everyone else,"[288] a characteristic of identity attributed to Stoker. "His close friend Hall Caine observed that those who knew him only through the theatre hardly knew him at all. 'His true self was something quite unlike the personality which was seen in that environment.'"[289] Stoker's fluid identity was an effect of the time and place in which he lived. Fortunately for the Irish Gothic vampire, Stoker drew upon his life, his reading, and his environment to create a work and a character of such cultural importance that it accomplished more than even the Irish literary leaders had hoped for in a national literature. As explained by Auerbach:

> In his blankness, his impersonality, his emphasis on sweeping new orders rather than insinuating intimacy, Dracula *is* the twentieth century he still haunts. Not until the twentieth century was he reproduced, fetishized, besequeled, and obsessed over.... Dracula's disjunction from earlier, friendlier vampires makes him less a specter of an undead past than a harbinger of a world to come, a world that is our own.[290]

Over 100 years later, *Dracula* continues to prompt critical analysis and inspire popular culture, a trend that shows every sign of continuing through the twenty-first century and also reflects the importance of the Irish vampire.

6

The Irish Vampire
National, Literary, Personal
and Global Identity

FLUELLEN: Captain MacMorris, I think, look you, under your correction, there is not
many of your nation—
MACMORRIS: Of my nation? What ish my nation? Ish a villain and a bastard and a
knave and a rascal? What ish my nation? Who talks of my nation?—Shakespeare,
Henry V, Act III, Scene 3

King Henry V of England reigned from 1413 to 1422. Shakespeare's
Henry V (1598) was performed toward the end of Queen Elizabeth I's reign
(1558–1603), and the scene above shows the Welsh Fluellen and Irish Mac-
Morris having a brief disagreement that is settled by the English Gower
while the Scottish Jamy looks on. It is the only time that the characters of
MacMorris and Jamy are seen in the play, yet MacMorris's short speech
has attracted much critical attention. Though MacMorris "is the very
embodiment of the 'stage Irishman'; pugnacious and argumentative,
expressing all in repetitious 'mispronunciations,'"[1] he also represents the
greater issues of Irish national, literary, and personal identity in light of
the relationship of the Irish with England. MacMorris is clearly identified
as Irish in the play by other characters and through his distinctive speech.
However, he is a captain of the English army fighting for Henry V against
France, and his quick offense to Fluellen's reference to Ireland as his nation
implies that MacMorris considers himself an English subject, not an Irish
one. David Cairns and Shaun Richards emphasize the significance of Mac-
Morris within the play and Elizabethan foreign affairs:

> The resolution in the play is seen to be achieved by marriage rather than by massacre,
> by incorporation rather than by exclusion, but the inclusion of the Celts within the
> English State, of which the army is a paradigm, is as a result of an equally devastating
> act of cultural elision. The victims in the process of the march towards unity are those

who contradict, and so implicitly question, the dominance of the incorporating power. Shakespeare's work engages with the process of colonial discourse at the moment of its mobilization to deal with Ireland, but the position of the colonized, namely Macmorris, is seen as one of proud inclusion. In this sense, the play, despite its references to the slaughter of Irish rebels, is an idealization of an actuality which stubbornly refused to conform.[2]

Shakespeare wrote this play in the latter part of Elizabeth I's reign, during the initial stages of Irish colonization by the English. As Edward Said argued: "[The] age of imperialism is conventionally said to have begun in the late 1870s, with the scramble for Africa. Yet it seems to me to be perfectly clear that there are all sorts of cultural as well as political indications that it began a good deal earlier."[3] By the time Maturin began his literary career, Ireland had already experienced 200 years of colonial rule by England, and Irish independence was over 100 years away.

The Irish Gothic and the genre's development of the Irish vampire are critical aspects of the national, literary, and personal identity faced by the Irish as the result of English colonization. As noted earlier by McClelland, "Not only is the vampire effectively a mimetic double, he has no valid identity, no evident social position."[4] As illustrated through the biographies of Maturin, Le Fanu, and Stoker, the national identity of Ireland was especially unclear to those of the Anglo-Irish class. The options to effect change included revolution, politics, and literature. All three writers were highly unlikely as revolutionary leaders. Attempting a solution through political channels was a risky endeavor—Maturin could not negotiate the hierarchy of the church let alone that of the state; Le Fanu was nearly implicated in an uprising due to his political involvement; Stoker left Ireland's politics behind, preferring the English theater. Despite their occupations in other areas, they all actively wrote. Their literary aspirations may have been fueled in part by what Said identifies as the impetus for Yeats's writing:

> For Yeats the overlappings he knew existed between his Irish nationalism and the English cultural heritage that both dominated and empowered him as a writer were bound to cause an overheated tension, and it is the pressure of this urgently political and secular tension that one may speculate caused him to try to resolve it on a "higher," that is, nonpolitical level [in literature].[5]

The same may be said for Maturin, Le Fanu, and Stoker, but their nationalist opinions were expressed in a more subtle manner. Not only did each author choose literature over politics, but each settled on the Gothic genre when writing *Melmoth*, *Uncle Silas*, "Carmilla," and *Dracula*, forgoing the pursuit of a serious national literature consciously striven for by the leading Irish authors and also disregarding the more popular and lucrative genres of the period.

During Maturin's time, he saw the rise of the historical novel, a genre Sir Walter Scott popularized, and Maturin personally sought out Scott as his writing mentor. One of his reasons for seeking Scott's literary advice was indicated in an 1813 letter to Scott, explaining that Ireland was not known for literary talent: "[T]here is no excitement, no literary appetite or impulse in this Country, my most intimate acquaintances scarcely know that I have written, and they care as little as they know."[6] Given that Jonathan Swift, Laurence Sterne, Richard Brinsley Sheridan, Maria Edgeworth, and Lady Morgan either preceded or were contemporaries of Maturin, his statement to Scott is a little surprising, as is Maturin's statement to Scott in a subsequent letter: "There is no room for Irishmen in England."[7] However, when one considers that Maturin saw them as English authors, these remarks make more sense. He associated these successful authors with the English tradition rather than an Irish one. English publishers exerted their influence over Irish writers in regards to what was published. English publishers marketed to an English reading audience who had certain expectations and tastes when it came to their literature, especially when an Irish character appeared. This control became more defined in the generation following, as evidenced by Le Fanu's revisions of his Irish short stories into English novels. However, Le Fanu countered this influence with his own as an editor and owner of several Irish publications.

As Le Fanu began his literary career, the historical novel was already established in both England and Ireland; he started writing within the historical genre while pursuing a political position. However, when his political aspirations collapsed, he shifted his writing into the Gothic. Unlike Maturin, though, Le Fanu was very aware of Irish authors because he was an important participant in the developing national literature as an author and editor. Wayne E. Hall, in his *Dialogues in the Margin: A Study of the Dublin University Magazine*, and Joe Spence, in his essay "Nationality and Irish Toryism: The Case of *The Dublin University Magazine*, 1833–52," both show that the *Dublin University Magazine (D. U. M.)* was an important vehicle in the promotion and distribution of Irish writing. Despite the appearance of being associated with the elite members of Dublin society, the magazine actively pursued a policy of publishing a variety of writing submitted by an array of authors from all regions of Ireland. The "*D. U. M.* admitted local variation as evidence of nationality; it understood that only a province was uniform in character, while a nation thrived on the interplay of regional character."[8] As a result of their open-minded approach toward writers and their style and subjects, the magazine promoted Irish literature while maintaining a level of quality, as Spence explains:

At the end of its first year, 1833 was proclaimed a memorable year in the annals of literary Ireland, for it was felt that, from their sense of patriotism and public duty, the contributors of the *D. U. M.* had laid the foundations of a national "school of writing," and, celebrating its one-hundredth issue, in April 1841, the *D. U. M.* felt that it could boast that it had gone a long way towards "the creation of a literature which should be NATIONAL, without degenerating into PROVINCIALISM." In the same article, "nationality" was defined as a quality without which a people could not be great, no matter how vast their resources.[9]

Hall's in-depth analysis adds indisputable weight to the many contributions of the *Dublin University Magazine* to a national literature and further establishes Le Fanu's role within it. Hall notes Le Fanu's move away from historical writing, in his own fiction, and shift of the magazine, under his editorship, away from political matters. Le Fanu's personal journey into the realm of Irish Gothic fiction meant that "he could present the internal doubts, the confusions, the fears of many Protestants about the legitimacy and authority of their ascendancy status…. Le Fanu managed to draw from [Gothic conventions] a psychological depth that makes his works seem in many respects more modern than that of any other writer for the DUM."[10] Le Fanu's writings during this time "reveal a part of his own nature just as they reveal a part of his whole Anglo-Irish class."[11] As an editor, Le Fanu also influenced the shape of Irish literature. Hall explains the significance of Le Fanu's editorial tenure by concluding, "Once Le Fanu gave over the editorship in June 1869 to Charles Frederick Adams, the DUM entered into a generally depressing period, closing out its existence with what Michael Sadleir terms 'years of melancholy ineffectiveness.'"[12] An Irish national identity was being explored through a literary identity in Le Fanu's writing and his editorial decisions. Le Fanu's seemingly non-political choices as an editor were reflected in his writing as his career progressed.

Le Fanu's "Carmilla" is a distinctly Gothic text that makes no reference to Ireland yet, as seen in Chapter 4, the story may be read as a colonial text. Even though Stoker was aware of the issues dominating Irish politics, when he read "Carmilla" he was influenced less by the subtle implications and more by the vampire tale. This is not surprising since Stoker had no interest in securing a political office, preferring the fantastical environment of the theater and the influence he held there. Despite the prestige of his position, Stoker pursued writing because he desired an identity separate from that of Irving and the theater. He accomplished this goal by writing *Dracula*, which not only illustrates all the qualities of a national literature, but also "is less the culmination of a tradition than the destroyer of one"[13] that served to define a myth for the twentieth century.

The analysis of these three writers has prompted interesting results.

Raymond McNally posed the question: "Why do Irish authors so dominate the Gothic in English literature?"[14] He devotes many pages to discussing Irish Gothic writers in order to answer this question. He notes the "traditionally strong element"[15] of fantasy found in Irish folktales and the tremendous impact of imperialism and explains:

> What makes the Gothic of these writers Irish is that there is generally no interest in past medieval times; instead, as W. J. McCormack points out, "Irish gothic fiction is remarkably explicit in the way it demonstrates its attachment to history and to politics" … It is my theory that there was no interest in medieval horrors in Ireland because the horrors of the day sufficed.[16]

McNally is referring to the horrors that resulted from several hundred years of colonization by its English neighbors, which saw its origins in the time Shakespeare wrote *Henry V* and oddly foreshadowed the turmoil that followed. This is why the vampire continues to manifest itself: "There are many reasons why the vampire has remained in our conscious thought over time, but one common element to almost all cases is fear."[17] Everyone understands fear, and centuries after the events that prompted Shakespeare to write *Henry V*, Stephen Dedalus remarks for the generations: "History … is a nightmare from which I am trying to awake."[18] The results of this nightmare are summarized by Luke Gibbons in "Culture, History and Irish Identity":

> Ireland is a First World country, but with a Third World memory. It is with this paradox that many of the essays in the present book deal: the dislocations between periphery and centre, the country and the city, tradition and modernity. Though it is usual to present these as opposites, both the strengths and weaknesses of Irish culture derive from its confounding of such neat polarities.[19]

Nowhere else is this "confounding" more evident than in Irish Gothic literature and its vampire. The Irish Gothic writers were in the midst of this history. For them, writing was an attempt to make sense of the events that were occurring and articulate them in terms of their nation and themselves. It is difficult to possess a national identity when the country's inhabitants are unsure of their personal identities. As Terry Eagleton aptly explains, "Nobody can live in perpetual deferment of their sense of selfhood, or free themselves from bondage without a strongly affirmative consciousness of who they are."[20] This theme of identity surfaces repeatedly in the literature of the colonized, as the generations following the one that was conquered seek to define who they are in terms other than those provided by their conquerors.

Ireland's unique colonial relationship with England provides the background for the development of the Irish vampire. As McClelland notes:

"Whatever other themes they may address, tales about vampires are on some level always about the relationship between violence, social cohesion, and justice."[21] The English families sent to Ireland to occupy and manage the daily governmental affairs for the English crown found themselves in an awkward position in subsequent generations. The Irish viewed them as English, the English viewed them as Irish, and they themselves more readily identified themselves as Irish with English affiliations. The Anglo-Irish naturally had complex identity issues throughout the nineteenth century. Maturin, Le Fanu, and Stoker are representative of this inner and outward conflict and convey it through their writing. Their solutions to these problems lie in who they were but also in what they wrote about the Irish vampire.

Maturin does not completely break with established English Gothic traditions in *Melmoth the Wanderer* to create a separate genre; he subtly adapts it. The result was a paradoxical type of writing that was both original and imitative. Maturin worked within the formula of the English Gothic and, in doing so, altered it. Le Fanu read Maturin and learned from him. He continued the process of literary adaptation begun by Maturin, taking larger risks that resulted in more significant changes. Le Fanu benefited from his position in publishing and his association with politics as he altered the English Gothic tradition. He was restricted by his contracts to avoid setting his novels in Ireland, but he still managed to convey a recognizable Irish landscape, and he connected the vampire to it. By the time Stoker published *Dracula*, the English Gothic genre had undergone complete reverse colonization, which is why this novel offers the greatest challenges of interpretation. Like his title character, Stoker was extremely adept at transforming himself to suit the situation. He was an Irishman in London who was frequently reminded that he "was not a standard issue middle-class Anglo-Irish Protestant ... but an interethnic Anglo-Celt and hence a member of a conquering and a conquered race, a ruling and a subject people, an imperial and an occupied."[22] Irish Gothicism, and more specifically the Irish vampire, addressed issues that were often not spoken of in polite society. Stoker's characters continually emphasize the "etiquette of silence" in the novel. Topics that could potentially damage one's reputation are not discussed and studiously ignored. Stoker shows the devastating effects of such a dangerous policy. Dracula nearly succeeds in his plan to dominate England, not because of his superiority, but because the characters are unwilling to initially communicate with each other to allow for the possibility of the impossible.

Due to the contributions of Stoker, Le Fanu, and Maturin to Irish

Gothic literature, an enduring myth of the Irish vampire was born with distinctive origins in the Irish imagination. But the Irish Gothic did not end with these writers. It continued to be shaped and adapted by writers who published works after these three, including Somerville and Ross's *Big House of Inver* (1925), Aidan Higgins's *Langrishe, Go Down* (1966), John Banville's *Birchwood* (1973), and William Trevor's *Fools of Fortune* (1983). Perhaps, though, the most amazing characteristic of Irish writing is its diversity. The Irish literary talent that emerged in the twentieth and twenty-first centuries is nothing short of extraordinary. The number of novelists, short story writers, poets, dramatists, script writers, film directors, and lyricists is staggering. Their capacity for originality far exceeds the Irish national literary criteria as seen in the banned fiction of James Joyce and Edna O'Brien. A review of the Field Day anthologies' various tables of contents provide an impressive list of authors. Irish writers have established themselves nationally and internationally. The stage Irishman still appears, but he is accompanied by a diverse array of other Irish characters—some stock, but others unique. Maturin, Le Fanu, and Stoker would also have been pleased to see their influences on some of these writers and how they continued to reshape the Irish Gothic to reflect the nation and themselves.

There remain only three final remarks before ending this book. The theme of reverse colonization that Stoker alluded to in *Dracula* has become a reality in the myth of the Irish vampire Dracula and the countless variations and applications stemming from it. Leonard Wolf devotes an entire chapter of his study to list the wide range of authors who feature a vampire in their fiction, among them, Stephen King, Chelsea Quinn Yarbo, and Anne Rice[23]; M. R. James, F. Marion Crawford, and E. F. Benson[24]; Mary Wilkins Freeman, Edith Wharton, Fritz Leiber, John Cheever, and Joyce Carol Oates[25]; C. L. Moore, Leslie Roy Carter, and Suzy McKee Charnas[26]; Hans Heinz Ewers, Roger Zelazny, and Tanith Lee[27]; Ray Bradbury, Laura Anne Gilman, and Jewelle Gomez[28]; and Charles Beaumont, Woody Allen, and Frederic Brown.[29] Since Wolf's publication, even more may be added such as Charlaine Harris's Sookie Stackhouse series, from which the extremely popular HBO *True Blood* series began in 2008, and Stephenie Meyer's *Twilight* series, which also prompted an equally popular series of films closely based on the books.

In addition to literary influences, Wolf also provides a comprehensive list of films and plays featuring Stoker's vampire. The twenty-nine film versions of *Dracula* end with Francis Ford Coppola's 1992 production.[30] The list naturally does not include the film adaptation of Anne Rice's *Interview with a Vampire*, produced in 1994, but it is a natural inclusion since it clearly transformed the vampire into her own distinct creation. However, it is necessary to note that the box-office hit was directed by the celebrated Irish filmmaker Neil Jordan, who, in a 1995 interview, explains his own *Dracula* connection: "I've always liked Gothic horror. I grew up close to Bram Stoker's house in Dublin and I remember cycling past it on my way into town and thinking it was the scariest house ever—I'd never seen a creepier place. I also loved horror movies, because they give you the opportunity to go to these dark places you'll never see—the nightworld of the dead."[31] In the same interview, Jordan discussed his then-current project, *Michael Collins.* When asked why he would make a film on Collins, Jordan replied: "Collins has become almost a mythic figure in Irish history, and you're able, through a single character, to tell the whole story of the contradictions of the Irish relationship to England and the paradoxes of the uses of violence."[32] Jordan's insights into both Gothic and Irish history make one wonder what he would do if given the opportunity to direct Stoker's *Dracula.*

The vampire is not limited to just film, stage, and literary appearances. One of the more recent and well-known adaptations of the Irish vampire is on the American television series *Buffy the Vampire Slayer* and its spin-off, *Angel.* As the title indicates, Buffy is a female vampire hunter, a character reminiscent of Mina Murray Harker. Buffy also has a small band of friends who assist her, headed by the paternal figure of Rupert Giles, an Englishman who is in America (similar to the Dutch Abraham Van Helsing, who travels to England to lead a band of vampire hunters there). During its seven-season run, the series devoted an entire episode to Buffy actually facing Stoker's legendary Count Dracula.

Angel also contains Irish vampire connections. The most obvious association is that the vampire Angel has his human origins in eighteenth-century Galway, Ireland. His father is a wealthy, and very possibly Anglo-Irish, landlord. When Angel becomes a vampire in the mid-eighteenth century, his first victims are his family. He then wanders the world like Melmoth, only he is much more effective in taking the lives and souls of others (until a gypsy curse returns his soul in the late nineteenth century). With a soul not only comes tremendous guilt from generations of killing that must be expiated but also a loss of his identity. His soul gives him a conscience that separates him from other vampires, but his soul does not make him human, so he still remains apart from people.

As exemplified with Angel, and the numerous films, television shows, and other works of fiction currently available, vampires of the twenty-first century will adapt themselves to the time, place, and culture from which they emerge.[33] Their persistence is difficult to ignore; a more serious study of Stoker's text is needed. Stoker, and by association Le Fanu and Maturin, are serious subjects of study for scholars of Irish literature because they offer an opportunity to study the culture from which they were produced. However, as McNally illustrates, it may take time for students of Irish Gothic and vampire literature to be received as scholars:

> [A]s a Dracula expert, I am frequently asked, "are there really such things as vampires?" Or, more poignantly, "Do you believe in vampires?" To which I often reply, "What do you think I am anyway? I'm a teacher, not a preacher." In my life I have never met an undead, so until I do, I cannot personally believe in such a thing. But I do listen when other people tell me that vampires exist, because they are usually describing something that is real to them, so I try to figure out what they mean. It's like detective work. Some people still like to believe in Santa Claus and the Easter Bunny. They need myths.[34]

This is lightly put, but essentially fitting when the pervasiveness of the vampire and its ramifications are considered.

This text set out to analyze as a group three Irish authors who are frequently discussed individually. Each has already been referenced in prior studies about the Irish Gothic, and Stoker and Le Fanu are also regularly cited in works relating to vampires. This study takes the available research and vampire folklore a few steps further. First, it considers Maturin, Le Fanu, and Stoker together in their development of an Irish vampire and progression of the Irish Gothic. Next, it establishes the importance of each author's work in relation to a developing national literature that is vying for expression against a complex colonial situation, exacerbated by the writers' membership in the less readily defined status and position of the Anglo-Irish class as it changed throughout the nineteenth century. Maturin, Le Fanu, and Stoker also changed the vampire of regional folklores into an international, mythical figure. From the nineteenth-century Irish Gothic emerged the Irish vampire, a fascinating addition to a richly imaginative Irish literature, which already contained a long list of notable character creations.

Chapter Notes

Preface

1. D. "On Vampyrism," *New Monthly Magazine and Literary Journal* [London] 7.25 (Jan. 1823): 140–49. Web, *ProQuest*, 3 June 2015: 140.

2. Paul Barber, *Vampires, Burial, and Death: Folklore and Reality* (New Haven: Yale University Press, 1988), vii. Print.

3. When I passed my dissertation defense in March 2004, my final copy listed seventy-four cited works as references. This revision of that dissertation cites over 230 sources. This number of sources scarcely includes all possible texts on the subject, but it does illustrate the continued and growing interest in this topic.

4. Jarlath Killeen, "Irish Gothic: A Theoretical Introduction," *Irish Journal of Gothic and Horror Studies* 1 (30 Oct. 2006): n.p. Web, irishgothichorrorjouranl.homestead.com, 2 July 2015.

5. Richard Haslam, "Irish Gothic: A Rhetorical Hermeneutics Approach," *Irish Journal of Gothic and Horror Studies* 2 (17 March 2007): n.p. Web, irishgothichorrorjouranl.homestead.com, 2 July 2015.

6. Jarlath Killeen, "Irish Gothic Revisited," *Irish Journal of Gothic and Horror Studies* 4 (6 Aug. 2008): n.p. Web, irishgothichorrorjouranl.homestead.com, 2 July 2015.

7. W. J. McCormack, ed. "Irish Gothic and After (1820–1945)," *The Field Day Anthology of Irish Writing*, Vol. II, ed. Seamus Deane (Derry, Ireland: Field Day, 1991), 831–54. Print.

8. Stoker was not initially motivated to write due to the pressure of finances, but after Irving was compelled to close the Lyceum Theatre, he relied much more on his publications to pay the household bills.

Chapter 1

1. Dr. Pierart, as quoted in Dudley Wright, *Vampires and Vampirism: Legends from Around the World* (Maple Shade, NJ: Lethe Press, 1914, 2001), 197. Print.

2. "The Travels of Three English Gentlemen, from Venice to Hamburgh, being the Grand Tour of Germany, in the Year 1734. MS Never Before Published," *The Harleian Miscellany; or, a Collection of Scarce, Curious, and Entertaining Pamphlets and Tracts, as Well in Manuscript and in Print, Found in the Late Earl of Oxford's Library, Interspersed with Historical, Political, and Critical Notes*, Vol. XI (London: Robert Dutton, 1810), 218–355. Web, Penn State Interlibrary Loan, 8 June 2016, 231–32.

3. Nina Strochlic, "Bulgaria's Vampire Graveyards," *Daily Beast*, 15 Oct. 2014: n.p. Web, *NewsBank*, 20 June 2016.

4. *Ibid.*

5. The use of both pronouns is due to my research findings disagreeing with those like Dudley Wright in *Vampires & Vampirism: Legends from Around the World*: "Vampire lore is, in general, confined to stories of resuscitated corpses of male human beings" (6).

6. Emphasis on "overview"—the research on vampire folklore and archaeology is not only currently vast but continually grows due to regular discoveries being made. While I cannot thoroughly cover all the stories from all cultures and times, I will try to refer the reader to texts which do in my footnotes and bibliography.

7. Many of the eighteenth- and nineteenth-century studies on vampires began their works with a dictionary definition of "vampire," and while I did not realize it initially, my use of the prestigious and authoritative *OED* perpetuates this traditional start.

8. "vampire, n," *OED Online*, Oxford University Press, June 2016. Web, 17 June 2016.

9. "Foreign News," *Grub Street Journal* [London, England], 16 March 1732: n.p. Web, *British Newspapers 1600–1950*, 17 June 2016.

10. The article, "Foreign Advices for March, 1732," *Gentleman's Magazine; or, Monthly Intelligencer* 2.15 (March 1732): 681, appeared while searching *ProQuest British Periodical Review* on 21 June 2015, but the magazine only indicates a month while the newspaper provides the date so, depending upon when the magazine appeared in March, it could precede the newspaper's use of "vampyre."

11. Katharina Wilson in her article "The History of the Word 'Vampire'" also addresses the appearance of the word "vampire" in print not only in English but also in other languages, including French and German.

12. "vampire, n.," *OED Online*.

13. Katharina Wilson, "The History of the Word 'Vampire,'" *Journal of the History of Ideas* 46.4 (1985): 577–83. Web, *JSTOR*, 28 June 2016.

14. Wilson cites many excellent sources for the curious reader to pursue. A few others one may wish to consult are: Malcolm Burr, "Notes on the Origin of the Word Vampire"; Peter Mario Kreater, "The Name of the Vampire"; and Brian Cooper, "The Word Vampire: Its Slavonic Form and Origin."

15. Brian Cooper, "The Word 'Vampire': Its Slavonic Form and Origin," *Journal of Slavic Linguistics* 13.2 (2005): 251–70. Web, *JSTOR*, 28 June 2016: 256; and Bruce McClelland, *Slayers and Their Vampires: A Cultural History of Killing the Dead* (Ann Arbor: University of Michigan Press, 2006), 1987. Print.

16. McClelland, 31–32.

17. Dudley Wright, *Vampires and Vampirism: Legends from Around the World*. 1914 (Maple Shade, NJ: Lethe Press, 2001), 6–7. Print. Clive Leatherdale in *Dracula: The Novel & the Legend* claimed that "perhaps the most ancient sources of vampire belief stem from the Orient," 17.

18. Thompson's work listed in Wright's bibliography.

19. J. Gordon Melton, "Babylon and Assyria, Vampires in Ancient," *The Vampire Book: The Encyclopedia of the Undead* (Detroit, MI: Visible Ink Press, 1999), 27. Print.

20. *Ibid.*, 28

21. Leah Rediger Schulte, "Lilith," *The Oxford Encyclopedia of Women in World History* (Oxford: Oxford University Press, 2008). *Oxford Reference*. 2008. Date accessed 11 July 2016.

22. *Ibid.* According to Schulte, the story of

Lilith being Adam's wife "does not appear until the Talmudic period (second to fifth centuries)." Lilith's only reference in Isaiah 34:14 dates to around the eighth century BCE (*Saint Joseph Personal Size Edition of the New American Bible* [New York: Catholic Book Publishing, 1970], 824. Print.)

23. Melton, 422.

24. Schulte, "Lilith."

25. David Leeming, "Gilgamesh," *The Oxford Companion to World Mythology* (Oxford: Oxford University Press, 2005). *Oxford Reference*. 2006. Date accessed 11 July 2016.

26. Matthew Beresford, *From Demons to Dracula: The Creation of the Modern Vampire Myth* (London: Reaktion Books, 2008, 2011), 27–28. Print.

27. Geoffrey Keating, *The General History of Ireland*. 1629–31, Vols. I and II, translated by Dermod O'Connor (Dublin: James Duffy, 1841), 21. Print.

28. *Ibid.*, 56–57.

29. *Ibid.*, 84.

30. *Ibid.*

31. *St. Joseph Personal Size Edition of the New American Bible*, 12

32. *Genesis* 10:5

33. Keating, 86.

34. John Cuthbert Lawson, *Modern Greek Folklore and Ancient Greek Religion: A Study in Survivals* (Cambridge: Cambridge University Press, 1910), 451. Print.

35. *Ibid.*, 444.

36. *Ibid.*, 451–52.

37. *Ibid.*, 450.

38. Vampires' inability to cross water is well-known in vampire folklore and perhaps best demonstrated in Greece where transporting suspected vampires to islands effectively contained the threat, resulting in the Greek island of "Santorini [as] the most famous haunt of *vrykolakes* in the whole of Greece" (Lawson, 436).

39. "Partholanus died in the plains of Moynealta, where he was buried" (Keating, 87).

40. Beresford, 62.

41. Wright, 169.

42. Beresford, 20.

43. Dudley Wright, *Vampires and Vampirism: Legends from Around the World* (Maple Shade, NJ: Lethe Press, 1914, 1924), 110. Print.

44. McClelland, 58.

45. Lawson, 375.

46. *Ibid.*, 376.

47. Food and the tools used to grow them can also become vampiric, according to Beres-

ford's research: "according to various superstitions, objects such as agricultural tools or other inanimate objects can turn into vampires if left outside on the eve of a full moon" (9), and "Tatomir Vukanovic stated that Serbian gypsies believe that pumpkins and watermelons can become vampires if kept for more than 10 days (10).

48. Keating determines that Partholanus died in 1986 BCE (87).

49. Keating, 87.

50. Retold by Lawson, 174.

51. Wright, 152.

52. Keating, 90–99.

53. *Ibid.*, 100. Keating states: "if we believe some antiquaries, [they settled] in Boeotia; others say that they came to Athens, and settled near the city of Thebes; yet the truest account is, that they landed in Achaia, a country of Greece, that borders upon Boeotia, and near it stands the city of Thebes."

54. Keating, 100–101.

55. Beresford, 66.

56. *Ibid.*

57. Beresford, "The Dangerous Dead," 9–11.

58. Wright, 112.

59. It should be noted that all methods appearing in this chapter met with varying degrees of success when it came to ridding the community of the vampire; however, the one method that almost always was effective was total cremation.

60. Barber, 63.

61. 7

62. Beresford, 20.

63. McClelland, 72.

64. *Ibid.*, 73.

65. *Ibid.*

66. Wright, 66.

67. Beresford, 11. At this point, I must echo McClelland's conclusion about folkloric vampires' confusion by crossroads, digging themselves deeper in the grave, and distracted easily by seeds: "vampires are considered very gullible, if not downright stupid" (70).

68. "It will be remembered that it was at one time the practice in England to bury suicides at the four cross-roads" (Wright, 12).

69. Beresford, 49.

70. Wright, 156–57.

71. Léon Wieger, *Chinese Tales of Vampires, Beasts, Genies and Men*, translated by Derek Bryce (Somerset, UK: Llanerch Press, 1909, 2011), 123. Print.

72. *Ibid.*, 17–19.

73. Saint Clair, Stanislaus Graham Bower, and Charles A. Brophy, *A Residence in Bulgaria* (Memphis, TN: General Books, LLC, 1869, 2012), 17. Print.

74. Wright, 107. Note: "favorite" and "forever" were edited to reflect current American spelling.

75. *Ibid.*, 149.

76. "BUFFY—Trust me: only someone who's been living underground for ten years would think that was the look." Joss Whedon, "Welcome to the Hellmouth," *Buffy the Vampire Slayer, the Script Book Season One, Volume One* (New York: Pocket Books, 2000), 47. Print.

77. Barber, 2.

78. Beresford, 104.

79. Wright, 107.

80. Lawson, 387.

81. Wright, 174.

82. Leatherdale, 17.

83. Wright, 173.

84. Richard F. Burton, *Vikram and the Vampire, or Tales of Hindu Devilry* (London: Longmans, Green, and Co., 1870). Web, *Hathitrust*, 18 July 2016: 46–47.

85. Leatherdale, 17.

86. McClelland, 67.

87. Quoted in Lawson, 364–65.

88. St. Clair and Brophy, 17.

89. *Ibid.*

90. Barber, 44; and Beresford, 103.

91. Wright, 108.

92. The third letter of this word was unclear in the digital text so unsure if it is "Cajchaw," "Calchaw," or "Caichaw." Barber's translation of the actual report filed by government investigators that Paole was attacked "near Gossowa in Turkish Serbia" (16).

93. "Foreign News," *Grub Street Journal* [London, England] 16 March 1732: n.p. Web, *British Newspapers 1600–1950.* 17 June 2016.

94. Barber, 6.

95. *Ibid.*

96. Clive F. Ross, "The Croglin Vampire," *Tomorrow: World Digest of Psychical Research and Occult Studies* Spring 1963: 103–109. Interlibrary loan. Received electronically 4 Feb. 2016; and Lionel and Patricia Fanthorpe, *The Big Book of Mysteries* (Toronto: Dundurn Press, 2010), 260–67. Print.

97. The family is never named in Hare's story, but Ross learns the family's name in his research (108).

98. The first names of the Croglin renters appear in the Fanthorpe's book (261), but it is unclear where they found the information.

99. Unless otherwise noted, assume that the story is paraphrased from Augustus Hare, *Peculiar People: The Story of My Life*. Eds. Anita Miller and James Papp (Chicago: Academy Chicago Publishers, 1896–1900, 2007), 192–96. Print.

100. Hare, 194.

101. *Ibid.*

102. *Ibid.*, 196.

103. *Ibid.*

104. Henry More, *An Antidote Against Atheism; Or, An Appeal to the Naturall Faculties of the Minde of Man, Whether There Be Not a God*, second edition (London: J. Flesher, 1655). Web, *Hathitrust*, 18 July 2016. More credits the written account of Martinus Weinrichius, a physician and philosopher from Silesia for this story and attests to his credibility as well as the story being true (209).

105. *Ibid.*, 209. More is actually this precise as to when the event occurred.

106. *Ibid.*, 208. Yes, the pagination is backward, but this is the page number printed on the page.

107. *Ibid.*

108. *Ibid.*, 210.

109. More's text has "onely blew marks," I updated the spelling for clarity (212).

110. More, 211–12.

111. *Ibid.*, 212.

112. *Ibid.*, 212–13.

113. *Ibid.*, 213.

114. P. G. Walsh and M. J. Kennedy, eds, "Introduction," *William of Newburgh: The History of English Affairs Book II* (Cambridge: Cambridge University Press, 2007), 1. Print.

115. Andrew Joynes, *Medieval Ghost Stories: An Anthology of Miracles, Marvels and Prodigie* (Suffolk, England: Boydell Press, 2001, 2006), 123. Print.

116. The summary is from Joynes, 139–41.

117. *Ibid.*, 139–40.

118. *Ibid.*, 141.

119. W[alter] S[cott], "Abstract of the Eyrbiggia-Saga; Being the Early Annals of that District of Iceland Lying Around the Promontory Called Snaefells," *Illustrations of Northern Antiquities, From the Earlier Teutonic and Scandinavian Romances; Being an Abstract of the Books of Heroes, and Nibelungen Lay*, eds. Henry W. Weber and Robert Jamieson (Edinburgh, Scotland: John Ballantyne, 1814), 475–513. Web, *Hathitrust*, 25 May 2016: 497. Scott indicates in a footnote that this manner of death referred to is probably suicide.

120. *Ibid.*, 498.

121. *Ibid.*

122. Wieger, 11.

123. *Ibid.*, 17.

124. Wieger, "A Vampire Kills Three Sleeping Men," 27–29.

125. *Ibid.*, 27.

126. *Ibid.*, 28.

127. *Ibid.*, 29.

128. Joseph Dunn, "Book of Armagh, The," *Catholic Encyclopedia*, 1996–2016. Web, www.catholic.com, 24 July 2016.

129. John Waller, ed., "Irish Popular Superstitions," *Dublin University Magazine* (June 1849): 707–718. Web, *ProQuest*, 24 July 2016: 707–708.

130. *Ibid.*: 543–60. Web, *ProQuest*, 24 July 2016: 553.

131. Beresford, "The Dangerous Dead," 8.

132. P. W. Joyce, *The Origin and History of Irish Names of Places*, second edition, enlarged and corrected (Dublin: McGlashan and Gill, 1870). Web, *Hathitrust*, 24 June 2016: 319–20.

133. Bob Curran, "Was Dracula an Irishman?" *History Ireland* 8.2 (2000): 12–15.

134. *Ibid.*, 12.

135. *Ibid.*

136. Beresford, "Dangerous Dead," 9

137. Eoin Burke-Kennedy, "4,000-Year-Old Laois Bog Body Turns Out to Be World's Oldest, *Irish Times* 3 Aug. 2013: 5. Web, *ProQuest Historical Newspapers*, 1 July 2016.

138. *Ibid.*, 5.

139. *Ibid.*

Chapter 2

1. James Joyce, *A Portrait of the Artist as a Young Man* (New York: Viking, 1916). Web, *Hathitrust*, 31 July 2015. Stephen Dedalus in his April 26 entry: "I go to encounter for the millionth time the reality of experience and to forge in the smithy of my soul the uncreated conscience of my race" (299).

2. W[illiam] P[atrick] Ryan, *The Irish Literary Revival: Its History, Pioneers, and Possibilities* (London: Ward and Downey, [1894]). Web, *Hathitrust*, 24 July 2015: p. v.

3. William Butler Yeats, "Ireland and the Arts," *Essays and Introductions* (Dublin: Gill and Macmillan, 1961), 203–10. Print.

4. Charles Welsh, "Foreword," *Irish Literature*, Vol. I, ed. Justin McCarthy (Philadelphia: John D. Morris, 1904), xvii–xxv. Web, *Hathitrust*, 10 June 2015: xix.

5. *Ibid.*, xvii.

6. Justin McCarthy, ed. *Irish Literature*,

Vols. I—10 (Philadelphia: John D. Morris, 1904). Web, *Hathitrust*,10 June 2015: 1927.

7. A "gombeen man" is essentially an Irish money lender

8. Maurice Francis Egan, "Irish Novels," *Irish Literature*, Vol. V, ed. Justin McCarthy (Philadelphia: John D. Morris, 1904), vii–xvii. Web, *Hathitrust*, 10 June 2015: vii.

9. Justin McCarthy, ed., *Irish Literature*, 3556.

10. Le Fanu's youngest child, George, was listed in Ryan's account among the artistic professional members of the Society: "G. Brinsely Lefanu [*sic*] (son of the author of "Shemus [*sic*] O'Brien)" (124).

11. According to Paul Murray's biography, *From the Shadow of Dracula: A Life of Bram Stoker*: "Stoker formed a close literary and political friendship with Justin McCarthy" (144–45).

12. Raymond T. McNally, "Bram Stoker and Irish Gothic," *The Fantastic Vampire: Studies in the Children of the Night Selected Essays from the Eighteenth International Conference on the Fantastic in the Arts*, ed. James Craig Holte (Westport, CT: Greenwood, 2002), 11–21.

13. Leonard Wolf, *Dracula: The Connoisseur's Guide* (New York: Broadway, 1997), 142. Print.

14. Leven M. Dawson, "*Melmoth the Wanderer*: Paradox and the Gothic Novel," *Studies in English Literature 1500–1900* 8 (1968): 621–32.

15. Fred Botting, *Gothic* (London: Routledge, 1996), 105. Print.

16. Muriel E. Hammond, "C. R. Maturin and *Melmoth the Wanderer*," *English* 11 (1956): 97–101

17. Diane D'Amico, "Feeling and Conception of Character in the Novels of Charles Robert Maturin," *Massachusetts Studies in English* 9.3 (1984): 41–54.

18. Heinz Kosok, "Charles Robert Maturin and Colonialism," *Massoud*: 228–33. Print.

19. Dale Kramer, *Charles Robert Maturin* (New York: Twayne, 1973). 141.

20. Jarlath Killeen, "Irish Gothic: A Theoretical Introduction," *Irish Journal of Gothic and Horror Studies* 1 (30 Oct. 2006): n.p. Web, irishgothichorrorjouranl.homestead.com, 2 July 2015.

21. Christina Morin, *Charles Robert Maturin and the Haunting of Irish Romantic Fiction* (Manchester: Manchester University Press, 2011), 149. Print.

22. Jim Kelly, *Charles Maturin Authorship, Authenticity and the Nation* (Dublin: Four Courts Press, 2011), 150. Print.

23. James M. Cahalan, *The Irish Novel: A Critical History* (Boston: Twayne, 1988), 8. Print.

24. W[illiam] P[atrick] Ryan, *The Irish Literary Revival: Its History, Pioneers, and Possibilities* (London: Ward and Downey, [1894]). Web, *Hathitrust*, 24 July 2015: 64.

25. *Ibid.*, 66–67.

26. *Ibid.*, 68.

27. Justin McCarthy, "Irish Literature," *Irish Literature*, Vol. I, ed. Justin McCarthy (Philadelphia: John D. Morris, 1904. vii–xvi. Web, *Hathitrust*, 10 June 2015: xiv.

28. Charles Welsh, "Foreword," *Irish Literature*, Vol. I, ed. Justin McCarthy (Philadelphia: John D. Morris, 1904), xvii–xxv. Web, *Hathitrust*, 10 June 2015: xvii–xviii.

29. *Ibid.*, xviii.

30. *Ibid.*, xx.

31. *Ibid.*, xxiii.

32. Aside from the omission of Maturin, two included authors were a complete surprise: Fitz-James O'Brien (1828–1862) and Sir Richard Burton (1821–1890). Burton is English, not Irish, although his biography in the collection states he was born in Tuam, County Galway (McCarthy, 403). O'Brien was born in Ireland, but the editors' selection of an excerpt of "The Diamond Lens" has two serious objections which oddly escaped the attention of the editors. First, the story's publication by O'Brien was clouded in accusations that he plagiarized his deceased English friend, William North (1824–54), a charge which has merit. If the editors were not aware of this scandal, they certainly violated their goal of not offending "the taste of any class or creed" by choosing the one section of the story that says: "There was but one step to be taken,—to kill Simon. After all, what was the life of a little peddling Jew in comparison with the interests of science?" (McCarthy, 2595).

33. McCarthy, "Irish Literature," xi.

34. *Ibid.*

35. Egan, vii–viii.

36. *Ibid.*, viii.

37. *Ibid.*, xiv. Egan later remarks that Griffin's "The Half Sir" would have been botched by the Banims because it would have been "seen as through a glass darkly" (xv), probably an unintentional allusion to Le Fanu who is not mentioned at all in the essay, but it is frustrating nonetheless.

38. Douglas Hyde, "Early Irish Literature," *Irish Literature*, Vol. II, ed. Justin McCarthy (Philadelphia: John D. Morris, 1904), vii–xx. Web, *Hathitrust*,10 June 2015: vii.

39. *Ibid.*, ix.

40. *Ibid.*, viii. *Melmoth the Wanderer*'s wildness and strangeness was often commented upon by its reviewers, as will be seen.

41. *Ibid.*, xx.

42. Thomas Flanagan, *The Irish Novelists 1800–1850* (New York: Columbia University Press, 1959), viii. Print.

43. *Ibid.*, 7.

44. *Ibid.*, 16.

45. *Ibid.*, 334.

46. *Ibid.*, 335.

47. James M. Cahalan, *Great Hatred, Little Room: The Irish Historical Novel* (Syracuse: Syracuse University Press, 1983), 7. Print.

48. *Ibid.*, 19.

49. Cahalan, *The Irish Novel: A Critical History*, xvii.

50. Cahalan, *The Irish Novel*, xviii.

51. Quoted in Cahalan, *The Irish Novel*, xix.

52. Quoted in Benedict Kiely, "Foreword," *Fairy and Folk Tales of Ireland*, ed. W. B. Yeats (New York: Collier, 1986), ix–xx. Print.

53. Daniel Murphy, "Foreword," *Cuchulain of Muirthemne: The Story of the Red Branch of Ulster Arranged and Put into English by Lady Gregory* (Buckinghamshire, England: Colin Smythe, 1990), 7–10. Print.

54. William Butler Yeats, "The Celtic Element in Literature," *Essays and Introductions* (Dublin: Gill and Macmillan, 1961), 173–88. Print.

55. *Ibid.*, 184.

56. *Ibid.*, 185.

57. McNally, 13.

58. John Morrill, "Cromwell, Oliver (1599–1658)," *Oxford Dictionary of National Biography*, eds. H. C. G. Matthew and Brian Harrison (Oxford: Oxford University Press, 2004), online edition, ed. David Cannadine, Sept. 2015. Web, 29 July 2016. "[I]t is overwhelmingly likely that the malarial fevers that had troubled him [Cromwell] at time[s] of stress ever since the early 1630s came back to haunt him and triggered a chest infection and pneumonia from which he died … he died at Whitehall at three in the afternoon on 3 September 1658."

59. *Ibid.* "For the first 200 years after the conquest [of Ireland] he had been subsumed in Catholic—at least in English-language Catholic—writing in a long list of English men

of violence, and in ascendancy writing his religious fanaticism relegated him to a status far below that of King Billy. But with the recovery of Irish-language folklore in the nineteenth century, and with the emergence of a new kind of Irish nationalism, Cromwell was demonized."

60. Cahalan, *Great Hatred*, 25.

61. Curran, "Was Dracula an Irishman?" 12.

62. McNally, 13.

63. Le Fanu's *Carmilla* was first serialized in *The Dark Blue*, December 1871–March 1872, before it became part of the anthology, *In a Glass Darkly* (1872).

Chapter 3

1. *The Correspondence of Sir Walter Scott and Charles Robert Maturin with a Few Other Allied Letters*, eds. Fannie Elizabeth Ratchford and William Henry McCarthy (Austin: University of Texas Press, 1937), 24. Print.

2. John B. Harris, *Charles Robert Maturin: The Forgotten Imitator* (New York: Arno, 1980), 3. Print.

3. Quoted in William Monck Mason, *The History and Antiquities of the Collegiate and Cathedral Church of St. Patrick, near Dublin from its Foundation in 1190 to the year 1819* (Dublin: W. Folds, 1820). Web, *Hathitrust*, 12 May 2015: 445.

4. Harris, 6.

5. "Conversations of Maturin—No.1," *New Monthly Magazine and Literary Journal* 19.73 (Jan. 1827): 401–11. Web, *ProQuest*, 15 May 2015: 403.

6. Niilo Idman, *Charles Robert Maturin: His Life and Works* (London: Constable, 1923), 214. Print.

7. "Memoir of Charles Robert Maturin," *Melmoth the Wanderer*, Vol. 1 (1820), Charles Robert Maturin (London: Richard Bentley and Son, 1892), vii–xxvii. Web, *Hathitrust*, 13 June 2015: iii.

8. *Ibid.*, ix.

9. Michael Osborne, *The Maturin and Johnston Families in Ireland*, 2015. Web, www.maturin.org.uk, 27 May 2015.

10. *Ibid.*

11. *Ibid.*

12. According to Osborne's research, Gabriel's release was quite exceptional since he was one of only six ministers in his prison to have been released during Louis XIV's lifetime; not even Gabriel's other surviving companion was released.

13. Osborne, *The Maturin and Johnston Families in Ireland.*
14. *Ibid.*
15. *Ibid.*
16. Brigid O'Mullane, "The Huguenots in Dublin: Part I (Continued)," *Dublin Historical Record* 8.4 (Sept.–Nov. 1946): 121–34. Web, *JSTOR*, 27 May 2015: 121–26.
17. "Conversations of Maturin—No. 1," 403.
18. "Conversations of Maturin—No. II," *New Monthly Magazine and Literary Journal* 19.73 (Jan. 1827): 570–77. Web, *ProQuest*, 15 May 2015: 570; Bernard Nicholas Schilling, *Charles Robert Maturin: A Biographical and Critical Study,* dissertation (Chicago: University of Chicago, June 1928), 3. Print.
19. Kevin Brennan, "Charles Robert Maturin (1782–1824): Forgotten Irish Novelist," *Dublin Historical Record* 32.4 (Sept. 1979): 135–41. Web, *JSTOR*, 25 May 2015: 136; "Memoranda of Maturin," *Douglas Jerrold's Shilling Magazine Vol. 3 January–June* (London: Punch Office, 1846), 125–34. Web, *Hathitrust*, 7 June 2015; Osborne, *The Maturin and Johnston Families in Ireland.* Idman does not directly reference Maturin's siblings in his text but includes them in the "Notes" at the end of his work, saying: "According to a family pedigree, particulars of which have kindly been communicated to me by Miss Sybil Maturin, he [Maturin] had two brothers: William and Henry, and three sisters: Fidelia, Emma, and Alicia" but also notes the discrepancy in Maturin's reported biographical information, "which goes to show that the information furnished by the Magazines is, in general, to be taken with some reserve" (312–13).
20. [Alaric Watts], "Memoir of the Rev. C. R. Maturin," *New Monthly Magazine and Universal Register* 11.62 (March 1819): 165–67. Web, *ProQuest*, 15 May 2015: 165. Although Watts's name is not attached to the original publication of the memoir in the *New Monthly Magazine*, his son quotes him in his biography of his father: "I have … no distinct recollection of the occasion of my introduction to this remarkable man; but I have little doubt that it originated in my having written a memoir of him in the first series of the *New Monthly Magazine*, to accompany a fantastic-looking portrait of him in that periodical" (Watts, *Alaric Watts, A Narrative of his Life,* 64).
21. Michael Osborne, *The Maturin and Johnston Families in Ireland.*
22. "Charles Robert Maturin," Ancestrywww: n.p. 1997–2015. Web, 15 May 2015.
23. "Conversations of Maturin—No. II," 574.
24. Idman, 6.
25. *The Correspondence of Sir Walter Scott and Charles Robert Maturin with a Few Other Allied Letters,* 4.
26. "Conversations of Maturin—No II," 574.
27. "Memoranda of Maturin," 129.
28. Hammond, 97.
29. *The Correspondence of Sir Walter Scott and Charles Robert Maturin,* 4.
30. Watts, "Memoir of the Rev. C. R. Maturin," 165.
31. "Memoranda of Maturin," 129.
32. Watts, "Memoir of the Rev. C. R. Maturin," 165.
33. *The Correspondence of Sir Walter Scott and Charles Robert Maturin with a Few Other Allied Letters,* 4.
34. "Memoir of Charles Robert Maturin," x.
35. "Conversations of Maturin—No. I," 411.
36. Watts, "Memoir of the Rev. C. R. Maturin," 167.
37. Idman, 10.
38. "Conversations of Maturin—No. I," 411.
39. Charles Robert Maturin, *Sermons* (London: Archibald Constable, 1819), 176. Print.
40. *The Correspondence,* Letter III, 9.
41. Harris, 8. Michael Osborne's website contains a detailed explanation of this event.
42. "Biographical Particulars of Celebrated Persons Lately Deceased," *New Monthly Magazine and Literary Journal* 15.49 (Jan. 1825): 39–43. Web, *ProQuest*, 15 May 2015: 41.
43. Brennan, 136. A certain amount of credence is added to this assertion of the defaulting debtor being Maturin's brother. Several sources indicate that the person was a "relative" and in Michael Osborne's meticulously researched genealogy of the Maturins, Maturin's youngest brother, Henry, is the only one of his siblings who cannot be accounted for.
44. Watts, "Memoir of the Rev. C. R. Maturin," 166.
45. *The Correspondence,* Letter VIII, 20.
46. [Robert Charles Maturin], *The Milesian Chief A Romance by the Author of Montorio and The Wild Irish Boy,* Vol. 1 (London: Henry Colburn, 1812). Web, *Hathitrust,* 4 June 2015: iii.
47. *The Correspondence,* Letter VIII, 20.
48. "Memoir of Charles Robert Maturin," xii.
49. *The Correspondence,* Letter XXXVII, 66.
50. Mrs. Hughes [Mary Ann Watts], *Letters and Recollections of Sir Walter Scott,* eds. Horace

Hutchinson (London: Smith, Elder, 1904). Web, *Hathitrust*, 13 June 2015: 283.

51. "Art III *Fatal Revenge; or, the Family of Montorio,*" *Quarterly Review* 3.6 (May 1810): 339–47. Web, *ProQuest*, 12 May 2015.

52. *The Correspondence*, Letter I, 6.

53. Watts, "Memoir of the Rev. C. R. Maturin," 167.

54. "Recollections of Maturin—No. III," *New Monthly Magazine and Literary Journal* 20.79 (July 1827): 146–52. Web, *ProQuest*, 15 May 2015: 146.

55. William Upcott, Frederic Shoberl, and John Watkins, *A Biographical Dictionary of the Living Authors of Great Britain and Ireland* (London: Henry Colburn, 1816). Web, *Hathitrust*, 13 June 2015: 246.

56. "Memoir of Charles Robert Maturin," x.

57. "Rev. C. R. Maturin," *Gentlemen's Magazine; and Historical Chronicle* (Jan. 1825): 84–85. Web, *ProQuest*, 25 May 2015: 85.

58. "Dramatic Necrology," *Drama, or, The Theatrical Pocket Magazine* 7.7 (April 1825): 393–405. Web, *ProQuest*, 26 May 2015: 399.

59. *Ibid.*, 400.

60. "Memoranda of Maturin," 129–30.

61. Idman, 129.

62. *The Correspondence*, Letter III, 9.

63. *Ibid.*, Letter III,10.

64. *Ibid.*, Letter IV, 12.

65. Quoted in Harris, 9.

66. *The Correspondence*, Letter V, 14–15.

67. Harris, 9.

68. "Biographical Particulars of Celebrated Persons Lately Deceased," 43.

69. "Memoir of Charles Robert Maturin," xxiv.

70. *Recollections of a Ramble, During the Summer of 1816 in a Letter to a Friend* (London: Smith and Elder, 1817). Web, *Hathitrust*, 13 June 2015: 5.

71. "Recollections of Maturin, No. IV," *New Monthly Magazine and Literary Journal* 20.79 (Jul. 1827): 370–76. Web, *ProQuest*, 15 May 2015: 374.

72. Willem Scholten, *Charles Robert Maturin, the Terror-Novelist* (New York: Garland, 1933, 1980), 51. Print.

73. "Recollections of Maturin, No. IV," 374.

74. Idman, 12.

75. *Ibid.*, 131.

76. "Conversations of Maturin—No. II," 575.

77. Idman, 196.

78. "Memoranda of Maturin," 132.

79. Sharon Ragaz, "Maturin, Archibald Constable, and the Publication of *Melmoth the Wanderer*," *Review of English Studies* 57.230 (June 2006): 359–73. Web, *JSTOR*, 27 May 2015: 369.

80. Maturin, *Sermons,*162.

81. Barbara T. Gates, "Blue Devils and Green Tea: Sheridan Le Fanu's Haunted Suicides," *Studies in Short Fiction* 24 (1987): 15–23.

82. Ragaz, 361–362.

83. "Memoranda of Maturin," 127.

84. *The Correspondence,* Letter LVII, 97.

85. Charles Robert Maturin, "Charles Robert Maturin Curate of St. Peter's, Dublin and Henrietta, His Widow," 25 Sept. 1822–23, Nov. 1824, MS Archives of the Royal Literary Fund: Archives of the Royal Literary Fund 472, World Microfilms. Web, *Nineteenth Century Collections Online*, 26 May 2015.

86. "London," *Edinburgh Magazine and Literary Miscellany* 13 (Nov. 1823): 617–18. Web, *ProQuest*, 8 June 2015: 617.

87. "Monthly List of Publications," *British Critic* 22 (July 1824): 109–11. Web, *ProQuest*, 8 June 2015: 109.

88. *The Correspondence,* Letter LXI, 102.

89. Rev. C[harles] R[obert] Maturin, *Five Sermons on the Errors of the Roman Catholic Church Preached in St. Peter's Church, Dublin,* second edition (Dublin: William Curry, Jun, & Company, 1826) Web, *Hathitrust*, 8 June 2015: 85–86.

90. Maturin, *Five Sermons,* 93–94.

91. Thomas Landseer, ed. *Life and Letters of William Bewick (Artist),* Vol. 1 (Safari Press, 2008), 210–14. Print.

92. Harris, 335.

93. Idman, 308.

94. "Marriages and Deaths," *Liverpool Mercury* 12 Nov. 1824: 159. Web, *19th Century British Newspapers*, 15 May 2015: 159.

95. "Memoir of Charles Robert Maturin," xxvii.

96. The *Athenaeum* reports in its 19 Nov. 1870 issue the sale of Bewick's works by Messrs Watson and Bowman of Darlington, in Haughton House, Haughton-le-Skerme. Among the long list of items are "[a] series of chalk drawings, portraits, by Bewick, of notabilities of his youth and manhood, recording his practice of portrait-painting, is more interesting; they sold as follows: ...the Rev. C. R. Maturin, of 'barrel-organ' fame 38s; Sir W. Scott, taken at Abbotsford, 7l; ...Lady Morgan, 13s; ...D. O'Connell, 10s" (662).

97. Landseer, 254–55.

98. *The Correspondence,* Letter LXII, 102–103.

99. *Ibid.,* 103.

100. Maturin, "Charles Robert Maturin Curate of St. Peter's."

101. Quoted in Landseer, 230.

102. "Memoranda of Maturin," 131–32.

103. Maturin, *Sermons,* 173.

104. *Ibid.,* 30.

105. *Ibid.,* 40.

106. Idman, 10.

107. *Ibid.,* 129.

108. "Remarks on 'Melmoth,'" *New Monthly Magazine and Universal Register* 14.83 (Dec. 1820): 662–68. Web, *ProQuest,* 15 May 2015: 662.

109. "On the Writings of Mr. Maturin, and More Particularly His 'Melmoth,'" *London Magazine* 3.17 (May 1821): 514–24. Web, *ProQuest,* 15 May 2015: 518–19.

110. "Art VIII Melmoth the Wanderer, a Tale," *Literary and Scientific Repository, and Critical Review* 2.4 (1 April 1821): 364. Web, *ProQuest,* 15 May 2015.

111. "Conversations of Maturin—No. II," 576.

112. *Ibid.,* 404.

113. "Recollections of Maturin—No. III," 146.

114. *The Correspondence,* Letters LII and LIII, 87–90.

115. Harris, 251.

116. "Art I—*Melmoth the Wanderer,*" *Quarterly Review* 24.48 (Jan. 1821): 303–311. Web, *ProQuest,* 15 May 2015: 305.

117. "Art II—*Melmoth the Wanderer: a Tale,*" *Port-Folio* 11.2 (June 1821): 277. Web, *ProQuest,* 15 May 2015.

118. "Art I—*Melmoth the Wanderer,*" 310–11.

119. "On the Writings of Mr. Maturin," 515.

120. Charles Robert Maturin, *Melmoth the Wanderer* (Oxford: Oxford University Press, 1820, 1989), 5.

121. Edgar A. Poe, "Letter to Mr.—," *Poems,* second edition (New York: Elam Bliss, 1831), 2–29. Print.

122. Poe, 20.

123. Maturin, *Sermons,* 34.

124. David Punter, *The Literature of Terror: A History of Gothic Fictions from 1765 to the Present Day,* Vol. 1 (London: Longman, 1996), 59. Print.

125. *Ibid.,* 59.

126. *Ibid.,* 60.

127. *The Correspondence,* Letter V, 14.

128. Punter, 124.

129. "Melmoth the Wanderer, &c," *Black-wood's Edinburgh Magazine* 8.44 (Nov. 1820): 161–68. Web, *ProQuest,* 15 May 2015: 162.

130. Maturin, *Sermons,* 192.

131. Idman, 198. Interestingly, Polidori's vampire also inspired Uriah Derick D'Arcy to write *The Black Vampyre; A Legend of St. Domingo* (New York: Printed for the Author, 1819). Reviews from the time it was published indicate that it is a satire on Polidori's vampire.

132. Kramer, 98.

133. Veronica M. S. Kennedy, "Myth and the Gothic Dream: C. R. Maturin's *Melmoth the Wanderer,*" *Pacific Coast Philology* 4 (1969): 41–47.

134. Kennedy, 41.

135. Amy Elizabeth Smith, "Experimentation and 'Horrid Curiosity' in Maturin's *Melmoth the Wanderer,*" *English Studies* 74.6 (Dec. 1993): 524–35. Web, *Academic Search Complete,* 25 May 2015: 524.

136. McClelland, 62.

137. Kennedy, 47.

138. "Melmoth the Wanderer, &c," 161.

139. Idman, 8.

140. Jim Kelly, *Charles Maturin Authorship, Authenticity and the Nation* (Dublin: Four Courts Press, 2011), 161. Print.

141. Kelly, 162.

142. Maturin, *Melmoth,* 543.

143. Kelly, 166.

144. Charles Welsh, "Irish Fairy and Folk Tales," *Irish Literature,* Vol. III, ed. Justin McCarthy (Philadelphia: John D. Morris, 1904), xvii–xxiv. Web, *Hathitrust,* 10 June 2015: xvii–xviii.

145. W[illiam] B[utler] Yeats, ed. *Fairy and Folk Tales of Ireland* (New York: Collier Books, 1888, 1892, 1986), 383. Print.

146. Bob Curran, *Bloody Irish: Celtic Vampire Legends* (Dublin: Merlin, 2002), 1. Print.

147. Curran, "Was Dracula an Irishman?" 14.

148. Maturin, *Melmoth,* 20.

149. *Ibid.,* 22.

150. *Ibid.,* 26.

151. *Ibid.,* 27.

152. *Ibid.,* 87.

153. *Ibid.,* 90.

154. *Ibid.,* 91.

155. *Ibid.,* 94.

156. D'Amico, 51.

157. Margot Gayle Backus, *The Gothic Family Romance: Heterosexuality, Child Sacrifice, and the Anglo-Irish Colonial Order* (Durham: Duke University Press, 1999), 114. Print.

158. Maturin, *Sermons*, 181–82.
159. *Ibid.*
160. "Memoir of Charles Robert Maturin," xxvi.
161. Terry Eagleton, "Form and Ideology in the Anglo-Irish Novel," Massoud, 135–46. Print.
162. McClelland, 24.
163. Harris, 293.
164. *Ibid.*, 11.
165. *Ibid.*, 13.
166. Kelly, 20.
167. Morin, 147.
168. Ragaz, 368.
169. "Melmoth the Wanderer, &c," 163. It is important to note Sharon Ragaz's statement that *Melmoth the Wanderer* "is the product of an extended process of collaboration, negotiation, procrastination and accident [between Maturin, Constable, and their printer], complicated on either side by each participant's evolving sense of professional standing, reputation and obligation at a time when the literary marketplace was rapidly changing" (372).
170. D'Amico, 50.
171. *Ibid.*, 52.
172. McCarthy, viii.
173. C. L. Innes, *Woman and Nation in Irish Literature and Society, 1880–1935* (Athens: University of Georgia Press, 1993), 2. Print.
174. *Ibid.*
175. Maturin, *Sermons*, 185.
176. [Charles Robert Maturin], *Fatal Revenge; or the Family of Montorio A Romance by Dennis Jasper Murphy*, Vol. 1 (London: Longman, Hurst, Rees, and Orme, 1807). Web, *Hathitrust*, 4 June 2015: viii.
177. [Charles Robert Maturin], *The Wild Irish Boy A Romance by the Author of Montorio*, Vol. 1 (London: Longman, Hurst, Rees, and Orme, 1808). Web, *Hathitrust*, 4 June 2015: vi.
178. Maturin, *The Milesian Chief*, v.
179. [Charles Robert Maturin], *Women; or Pour et Contre A Tale by the Author of "Bertram," &c.*, Vol. 1 (Edinburgh: Archibald Constable, 1818). Web, *Hathitrust*, 4 June 2015: iv.
180. Maturin, *Melmoth*, 5.
181. Morin, 132–33.
182. D'Amico, 51.
183. Morin, 149.
184. Quoted in Harris, 24.
185. Cahalan, *The Irish Novel*, 32.
186. Morin, 182.
187. *Ibid.*
188. Punter, 124, 129.

189. Idman, 212.
190. Julian Moynahan, "The Politics of Anglo-Irish Gothic: Maturin, Le Fanu, and 'The Return of the Repressed,'" *Studies in Anglo-Irish Literature*, ed. Heinz Kosok (Bonn: Bouvier, 1982), 43–53. Print.
191. The 1852 version of the play has three acts, as opposed to a later two-act version from 1856. The only version I found of the 1852 edition was from the University of South Florida Libraries, Special Collections, and this will be the version that I will cite.
192. Maturin, *Melmoth*, 18.
193. *Ibid.*, 20.
194. *Ibid.*
195. James Malcolm Rymer, *Varney the Vampire; or, The Feast of Blood*, Introduction by Curt Herr (Crestline, CA: Zittaw Press, 1847, 2008), 35. Print.
196. *Ibid.*
197. *Ibid.*, 43.
198. *Ibid.*
199. Curt Herr provides helpful footnotes throughout the edition of *Varney* published in 2008 by Zittaw Press. One of the many is on page 67, when Runnagate suddenly becomes Marmaduke. Herr informs the reader that Rymer was writing at least nine other series while writing *Varney*, so consistency of details was not prevalent in the serials.
200. *Ibid.*, 53.
201. *Ibid.*, 54.
202. *Ibid.*, 93.
203. *Ibid.*, 748.
204. *Ibid.*
205. *Ibid.*
206. The first scene is set in June 1660, but the dialogue is quickly indicates that the date is August 15.
207. Dion Boucicault, *The Vampire, A Phantasm*, 1852, transcription by Matthew Knight, Assistant Director of Special Collections, Assistant Librarian. University of South Florida Libraries. Transcript emailed to author 20 May 2016.
208. Boucicault, "The Second Drama."
209. *Ibid.*
210. *Ibid.*
211. Rymer, 37.
212. *Ibid.*
213. Kennedy, 43.

Chapter 4

1. Victor Sage, "Irish Gothic: C. R. Maturin and J. S. LeFanu," *A Companion to the*

Gothic, ed. David Punter (Oxford: Blackwell, 2001), 81–93. Print.

2. F. S. L. Lyons, "A Question of Identity: A Protestant View," *Irish Times* 9 Jan. 1975: n.p. Web, Interlibrary loan, 19 June 2015.

3. Cahalan, *Great Hatred*, 19.

4. For a thorough biographical account of Le Fanu, see W. J. McCormack's *Sheridan Le Fanu.*

5. William Richard Le Fanu, *Seventy Years of Irish Life, Being Anecdotes and Reminiscences* (New York: Macmillan, 1893). Web, *Hathitrust*, 10 June 2015: 1.

6. W. J. McCormack, *Sheridan Le Fanu* (Guernsey, Channel Islands: Guernsey, 1997), 18. Print.

7. *Ibid.*, 19.

8. Le Fanu, *Seventy Years*, 7.

9. Isaac Butts, "Irish Tranquility," *Dublin University Magazine* 9.53 (May 1837): 577–86. Web, *ProQuest British Periodicals*, 16 June 2015: 586.

10. McCormack, *Sheridan Le Fanu*, 27.

11. *Ibid.*

12. *Ibid.*

13. "The Bishop of Exeter's Charge," *Belfast News-Letter* 24 June 1845: n.p. Web, *British Newspapers 1600–1950*, 10 June 2015.

14. McCormack, *Sheridan LeFanu*, 33.

15. *Ibid.*, 39.

16. Le Fanu, *Seventy Years*, 65.

17. Butts, 580.

18. Le Fanu, *Seventy Years*, 150.

19. *Ibid.*, 149.

20. McCormack, *Sheridan Le Fanu*, 90.

21. E. F. Bleiler, ed., "Introduction," *Ghost Stories and Mysteries*, by J. S. LeFanu (New York: Dover, 1975), v–ix. Print.

22. Richard Davenport-Hines, *Gothic: Four Hundred Years of Excess, Horror, Evil, and Ruin* (New York: North Point, 1999), 254. Print.

23. McCormack, *Sheridan Le Fanu*, 115.

24. Le Fanu, *Seventy Years*, 177.

25. McCormack, *Sheridan Le Fanu*, 115.

26. Le Fanu, *Seventy Years*, 106–107.

27. T. W. Moody, and F. X. Martin, *The Course of Irish History*, revised and enlarged fourth edition (Cork: Mercier, 1990), 274. Print.

28. D. George Boyce, *Nineteenth-Century Ireland: The Search for Stability* (Dublin: Gill and Macmillan, 1990), 109. Print.

29. Le Fanu, *Seventy Years*, 178.

30. Cahalan, *The Irish Novel*, 72.

31. W. J. McCormack, "Introduction," *Uncle Silas*, by Sheridan Le Fanu (Oxford: Oxford University Press, 1981), vii–xx.

32. McCormack, "Introduction," *Uncle Silas*, i.

33. McCormack, *Sheridan Le Fanu*, 123.

34. *Ibid.*, 126.

35. *Ibid.*, 127.

36. Quoted in McCormack, *Sheridan Le Fanu*, 62.

37. *Ibid.*, 128.

38. *Ibid.*, 295.

39. Wayne E. Hall, *Dialogues in the Margin: A Study of the* Dublin University Magazine (Washington: Catholic University Press, 1999), 208. Print.

40. McCormick, *Sheridan Le Fanu*, 138.

41. S. M. Ellis, "Joseph Sheridan LeFanu," *Bookman* (Oct. 1916): 15–21. Web, *ProQuest British Periodical Review*, 16 June 2015: 20.

42. McCormack, *Sheridan Le Fanu*, 197.

43. *Ibid.*

44. Ellis, 20.

45. Ellis, "Joseph Sheridan LeFanu," 20.

46. Michael Begnal, *Joseph Sheridan LeFanu* (Lewisburg: Bucknell University Press, 1971), 82. Print.

47. Quoted in Brian Showers, "A Void Which Cannot Be Filled Up: Obituaries of J. S. Le Fanu," *Reflections in a Glass Darkly: Essays on J. Sheridan Le Fanu*, eds. Gary William Crawford, Jim Rockhill, and Brian J. Showers (New York: Hippocampus Press, 2011), 72–83.

48. *Ibid.*, 73–74.

49. *Ibid.*, 77.

50. Quoted in Brian J. Showers, "Deciphering the Bennett/Le Fanu Capstone," *Le Fanu Studies* 4.1 (May 2009): n.p. Web, www.lefanustudies.com, 10 June 2015.

51. McCormack, *Sheridan Le Fanu*, 270–71.

52. *Ibid.*, 269.

53. *Ibid.*, 271.

54. Quoted in McCormack, *Sheridan Le Fanu*, 270.

55. McCormack, *Sheridan Le Fanu*, 274–76.

56. *Ibid.*, 277–89.

57. Hall, p.194.

58. Stephen Colclough, "J. Sheridan Le Fanu and the 'Select Library of Fiction': Evidence from Four Previously Unpublished Letters," *Publishing History* 60 (2006): 5–19. Web, Penn State ILL, 31 Oct. 2014.

59. McCarthy, *Irish Literature*, 1927.

60. Joseph Sheridan Le Fanu, "Passage in the Secret History of an Irish Countess," *Dublin University Magazine* 12 (1838): 502–19.

61. Kathleen Costello-Sullivan, ed. *Carmilla by Joseph Sheridan Le Fanu: A Critical Edition*

(Syracuse: Syracuse University Press, 2013), xiii. Print.

62. Le Fanu, "Passage," 506.

63. Joseph Sheridan Le Fanu, "Carmilla," *In a Glass Darkly* (London: Peter Davies, 1872, 1929), 291–382. Print.

64. Wolf, 95.

65. Robert Smart, "Postcolonial Dread and the Gothic: Refashioning Identity in Sheridan Le Fanu's *Carmilla* and Bram Stoker's *Dracula*," *Transnational and Postcolonial Vampires: Dark Blood*, eds. Tabish Khair, et. al. (New York: Palgrave Macmillan, 2013), 10–45. Web, Penn State ILL, 20 Oct. 2014: 13.

66. Davenport-Hines, 254.

67. Sage, 90.

68. Patrick Diskin, "Poe, Le Fanu and the Sealed Room Mystery," *Notes and Queries* 13 (1965): 337–39.

69. Peter Penzoldt, "From *The Supernatural in Fiction* [1952]," *Reflections in a Glass Darkly: Essays on J. Sheridan Le Fanu*, eds. Gary William Crawford, Jim Rockhill, and Brian Showers (New York: Hippocampus Press, 2011), 108–126. Print.

70. Begnal, 72–73.

71. Joseph Sheridan Le Fanu, *Uncle Silas*, ed. W. J. McCormack (Oxford: Oxford University Press, 1864, 1981), 60. Print.

72. Hall, 209.

73. Le Fanu, *Uncle Silas*, 255.

74. *Ibid.*, 291–92.

75. *Ibid.*, 295.

76. *Ibid.*, 414.

77. *Ibid.*, 417.

78. Nina Auerbach, *Our Vampires, Ourselves* (Chicago: University of Chicago Press, 1995), 41. Print.

79. Backus, 127.

80. Hall, 199.

81. Cahalan, *The Irish Novel,* 74.

82. Backus, 128.

83. Although he did not live in the country, Le Fanu was also a tenant of an "absentee" landlord while living at Merrion Square. When George Bennett retired to Shropshire with his two unmarried daughters in the summer of 1851, the Le Fanus moved into the big house, paying £22 10s per annum to his brother-in-law, John, who inherited the house when George died (Showers, "Deciphering the Bennett/Le Fanu Capstone"). Le Fanu quickly became in debt to John for the rent (McCormack, *Sheridan Le Fanu,* 135).

84. Paul E. Davis, "Dracula Anticipated: The 'Undead' in Anglo-Irish Literature," *The*

Universal Vampire: Origins and Evolution of a Legend, eds. Barbara Brodman and James E. Doan (Madison, NJ: Fairleigh Dickinson University Press, 2013), 17–31. Print.

85. Le Fanu, *Carmilla,* 296.

86. *Ibid.*

87. *Ibid.*, 313.

88. *Ibid.*, 43.

89. Jarlath Killeen, "An Irish *Carmilla*?" *Carmilla by Joseph Sheridan Le Fanu: A Critical Edition*, ed. Kathleen Costello-Sullivan (Syracuse: Syracuse University Press, 2013), 99–109. Print.

90. Renee Fox, "*Carmilla* and the Politics of Indistinguishability," *Carmilla by Joseph Sheridan Le Fanu: A Critical Edition*, ed. Kathleen Costello-Sullivan (Syracuse: Syracuse University Press, 2013), 110–21. Print.

91. "Foreign Advices for March, 1732," *Gentleman's Magazine; or, Monthly Intelligencer* 2.15 (March 1732): 681. Web, *ProQuest British Periodical Review*, 21 June 2015; "Foreign News," *Grub Street Journal* [London, England] 16 March 1732: n.p. Web, *British Newspapers 1600–1950*, 17 June 2016.

92. Curran in his article spells this *dearg-diúlaí*, defining it as "a drinker of human blood" (12).

93. Curran, "Was Dracula an Irishman?" 14.

94. Montague Summers, *The Vampire in Lore and Legend* (Mineola, New York: Dover, 1929, 2013), 117. Print.

95. Dudley Wright, *Vampires and Vampirism: Legends from Around the World* (Maple Shade, NJ: Lethe Press, 1914, 2001), 50. Print.

96. Summers, 117.

97. S. E. Ellis, *Wilkie Collins, Le Fanu, and Others* (Freeport, NY: Books for Libraries Press, 1931, 1968), 140–91. Print.

98. Ellis, *Wilkie Collins, Le Fanu, and Others* 154.

99. "Draoideachta: The Magic of the Ancient Irish," *Dublin University Magazine* 63.374 (Feb. 1864): 148–55. Web, *ProQuest British Periodicals,* 21 June 2015: 149.

100. Le Fanu, *Carmilla,* 318.

101. Le Fanu, *Uncle Silas,* 219.

102. *Ibid.*, 60.

103. *Ibid.,*. 424.

104. *Ibid.*, 423.

105. Davenport-Hines, 255.

106. Backus, 132.

107. Le Fanu, *Carmilla,* 297.

108. Jarlath Killeen, "In the Name of the Mother: Perverse Maternity in 'Carmilla,'"

Reflections in a Glass Darkly: Essays on J. Sheridan Le Fanu, eds. Gary William Crawford, Jim Rockhill, and Brian J. Showers (New York: Hippocampus Press, 2011), 363–84. Print.

109. Le Fanu, *Carmilla,* 314.

110. Fox, 113–14.

111. Killeen, "In the Name of the Mother: Perverse Maternity in 'Carmilla,'" 366–67.

112. *Ibid.,* 367.

113. Le Fanu, *Carmilla,* 366.

114. Killeen, "In the Name of the Mother," 377–79.

115. *Ibid.,* 367.

116. Boucicault has the vampire Alan Raby use this stigma of insanity in the Third Drama, Scene II of *The Vampire, A Phantasm* (1852) to separate Ada from her love who recoils from her and apologizes to Raby.

117. Smart, 25.

118. McClelland, 24.

119. Begnal, 81.

120. Le Fanu, *Uncle Silas,* 131.

121. *Ibid.*

122. Quoted in Ellis, *Wilkie Collins, Le Fanu, and Others,* 164–65.

123. Joe Spence, "Nationality and Irish Toryism: The Case of *The Dublin University Magazine,* 1833–52," *Journal of Newspaper and Periodical History* 4.3 (1988): 2–17.

124. *Le Fanu's Gothic: The Rhetoric of Darkness* (New York: Palgrave Macmillan, 2004), 5.

125. McCormack, *Sheridan Le Fanu,* 202.

126. *Ibid.,* 203.

127. Le Fanu, *Uncle Silas,* 112–13.

128. McCormack, *Sheridan Le Fanu* 129.

129. Auerbach, 44.

130. Penzoldt, p. 112.

131. *Ibid.,* 114.

132. *Ibid.,* 115.

133. *Ibid.,* 116.

134. *Ibid.,* 118.

135. *Ibid.,* 124–25.

136. *Ibid.,* 125.

137. Carol A. Senf, "Women and Power in 'Carmilla.'" *Le Fanu Studies* 10.1 (May 2015): n.p. Web, Lefanustudies.com, 11 June 2015.

138. McCormack, *Sheridan Le Fanu,* 122.

139. The thought that Susanna may have committed suicide first occurred to me when I was reviewing materials published since 2004. In a footnote in Francoise Dupeyron-Lafay's "Victorian Gothic Fiction as a Ghost: Immortality and the Undead in Joseph Sheridan Le Fanu's *Uncle Silas* (1864)," he notes: "Le Fanu became a student and follower of Swedenborg's mystic, esoteric thought in the 1860s after his

depressive wife committed suicide in 1858" (58). Other sources that could link to and further develop this idea also appeared, so I decided to include them all in the revision.

140. Quoted in McCormack, *Sheridan Le Fanu,* 298.

141. McCormack, *Sheridan Le Fanu* 127.

142. Quoted in McCormack, *Sheridan Le Fanu* 133.

143. McCormack, *Sheridan Le Fanu,* 129.

144. Quoted in McCormack, *Sheridan Le Fanu* 293.

145. *Ibid.,* 295.

146. Showers, "Deciphering the Bennett/Le Fanu Capstone."

147. McCormack, *Sheridan Le Fanu,* 60.

148. "A Glimpse of the Supernatural in the Nineteenth Century," *Dublin University Magazine* 58.347 (Nov. 1861): 620–29. Web, *ProQuest British Periodicals,* 15 June 2015: 629.

149. Much has been said by many biographers that Le Fanu had an interest in the supernatural but not in the séances popular at the time. As noted by S. M. Ellis: "Although the supernatural was his obsessing passion, he apparently never embraced any of the visionary doctrines concerned with magic and intercourse with spirits ... the anaemic and mild manifestations of ordinary spiritualism had no attraction for him: his imagination soared to terrific horrors far beyond spirit rappings and writings and faint manifestations" ("Joseph Sheridan Le Fanu," 20). One surprising piece of biographical information that surfaced during my research, possibly explaining his lack of interest in spiritualism, appeared in a letter from Mrs. Emma L. Darton in the April 1909 edition of the *Journal of the Society for Psychical Research.* She recounted her story of seeing an apparition and added: "I do not feel certain that any of my relations in the present generation have had any experiences of the kind, but my grandfather, Joseph Sheridan Le Fanu, the novelist, used to assert that he saw this sort of thing constantly" (quoted in Lang, 71).

150. "A Glimpse," 628.

151. Bleiler, xi.

152. Begnal, 80.

153. Bleiler, xiii.

154. Wolf, 111.

155. Helen Conrad-O'Briain, "Providence and Intertextuality: Le Fanu, M. R. James, and Dorothy Sayers' *The Nine Tailors," Irish Journal of Gothic and Horror Studies* 9 (2 Oct. 2011): n.p. Web, irishgothichorrorjournal.homestead.com, 2 July 2015.

156. McCormack, *Uncle Silas* xix.

157. Austin Clarke, "Yeats and Le Fanu," *Times Literary Supplement* 12 Dec. 1968: 1409.

158. David Annwn, "Dazzling Ghostland: Sheridan Le Fanu's Phantasmagoria," *Irish Journal of Gothic and Horror Studies* 6 (8 Jul. 2009): n.p. Web, irishgothichorrorjournal.homestead.com, 2 July 2015.

Chapter 5

1. "*Dracula* by Bram Stoker," *Academy Fiction Supplement* (12 June 1897): 11. Web, *ProQuest British Periodicals*, 4 July 2015.

2. "Novels and Stories," *National Observer and British Review of Politics, Economics, Literature, Science, and Art* 18.450 (3 July 1897): 334. Web, *ProQuest British Periodicals*, 4 July 2015.

3. "New Fiction," *Saturday Review of Politics, Literature, Science, and Art* 84.2175 (3 July 1897): 21. Web, *ProQuest British Periodicals*, 4 July 2015.

4. Quoted in Daniel Farson, *The Man Who Wrote Dracula: A Biography of Bram Stoker* (New York: St. Martin's, 1975), 162–63. Print.

5. Bram Stoker, *Personal Reminiscences of Henry Irving* (New York: Macmillan, 1906), 31–32. Print.

6. Dick Collins, "The Devil and Daniel Farson: How Did Bram Stoker Die?" *Journal of Dracula Studies* 10 (2008): 1–9. Web, Draculastudies.web.kutztown.edu: 8.

7. Collins, 8–9.

8. Barbara Belford, *Bram Stoker: A Biography of the Author of Dracula* (Cambridge, MA: Da Capo, 1996), 30. Print.

9. *Ibid.*, 31.

10. *Ibid.*, 34.

11. Paul Murray, *From the Shadow of Dracula: A Life of Bram Stoker* (London: Jonathan Cape, 2004), 109. Print.

12. Belford, 25.

13. In *Bram Stoker's Notes for Dracula A Facsimile Edition*, annotated and transcribed by Robert Eighteen-Bisang and Elizabeth Miller, the Methodology section indicates that "it is not possible to determine when most of the Notes were written" (9), but the earliest of the dates in the notes—8 March 1890 (17)—is used for the basis of determining when Stoker began to plan *Dracula*. However, an entry dated 5 August 1871 in *The Dublin Years The Lost Journal of Bram Stoker*, edited by Elizabeth Miller and Dacre Stoker, records a thought that reminds one of the scene in *Dracula* where Mina comforts Arthur (133–34).

14. Belford, 279.

15. Murray, 213.

16. Belford, 291.

17. Paul Murray provides an excellent account of Irving's imprudent financial and production decisions at this time and shows that "Stoker did stand up to Irving when necessary and that his advice was sound" (215).

18. Belford, 300–302.

19. Murray, 235.

20. *Ibid.*, 235–36.

21. Belford, 304–305.

22. According to Dick Collins, "This cannot have been a major cerebrovascular incident, and it is more to have been what is called today a transient ischemic attack—a momentary lack of blood to the brain. A TIA is often caused by high blood pressure, or occurs more often in hypertensive people. We should note also that strokes, and heart attacks, and migraines, for that matter, tend to come on not in the thick of stress but after that stress has gone" (6).

23. Belford, 311.

24. Often described as a hero-worshipping tribute to Irving, Murray offers a much more interesting reading of Stoker's *Personal Reminiscences*: "One of Stoker's main objectives was to explain how Irving came to such a tragic end while upholding the actor's national iconic status and defending his role in Irving's affairs. Yet, for a supposed work of hagiography, there was little real warmth towards its subject.... Stoker's portrait of the great actor in decline in his later years, while not truly unvarnished, was sufficiently revealing to have been uncomfortable to contemporaries" (236–37).

25. Murray, 247.

26. Belford, 311.

27. Quoted in Belford, 315.

28. Quoted in Murray, 266.

29. The Archives for The Royal Literary Fund were accessed online and, even with technical assistance, I cannot say for certain that this word is "shows."

30. Same technical issue with "divine" as indicated in previous footnote.

31. Abraham Stoker, "Abraham Stoker 1847–1912. 'Bram Stoker,'" 20 Feb. 1911–9 March 1911, MS Archives of The Royal Literary Fund Archives of The Royal Literary Fund 2841, World Microfilms. Web, *Nineteenth Century Collections Online*, 26 May 2015.

32. Collins, 1.

33. Farson, 233–34.

34. Belford, 321.

35. Murray, 268–70.

36. Murray, 269.
37. Collins, 9.
38. According to Stephen Morley's "Historical UK Inflation and Price" calculator, £4723 in 1912 would equal approximately £470,000.00 in 2013.
39. "Stoker, Abraham otherwise Bram," *England and Wales, National Probate Calendar (Index of Wills and Administrations)*, 287. Web, Ancestrywww, 5 July 2015.
40. Belford, 323.
41. "Mr. Bram Stoker's Library," *Times* [London, England] 8 July 1913: 11. Web, *Times Digital Archives 1785–1985*, 8 July 2015: "Messrs. Sotheby sold yesterday the collection of printed books and manuscripts of the late Mr. Bram Stoker, 211 lots realizing £400 12s."
42. "Books and Manuscripts," *Anthenaeum* 4473 (19 July 1913): 64. Web, *ProQuest British Periodicals*, 8 July 2015: "On Monday and Tuesday, the 7th and 8th inst. Messrs. Sotheby sold books and manuscripts, including the library of the late Bram Stoker.... The total of the sale was 5,367*l* 17s."
43. Belford, 325.
44. Murray, 272.
45. "Wills and Bequests," *Times* [London, England] 26 July 1937: 14. Web, *Times Digital Archives 1785–1985*, 8 July 2015.
46. Murray, 273.
47. Susan Parlour, "Vixens and Virgins in the Nineteenth-Century Anglo-Irish Novel: Representations of the Feminine in Bram Stoker's *Dracula*," *Journal of Dracula Studies* 11 (2009): 61–80. Web, Penn State Interlibrary Loan, 8 July 2015: 62.
48. Belford, 50–51.
49. *Ibid.*, 59–60.
50. Bram Stoker, *Dracula*, eds. Nina Auerbach and David Skal (New York: W. W. Norton, 1897,1997), 1–327. Print.
51. Bram Stoker, *Bram Stoker's Notes for Dracula A Facsimile Edition*, annotated and transcribed by Robert Eighteen-Bisang and Elizabeth Miller (Jefferson, NC: McFarland, 2008), 15, 17, 29. Print.
52. *Ibid.*, 29.
53. Murray, 239.
54. Murray, 132.
55. Belford, 264.
56. Davis, 28.
57. Jane Stoddard, "Interview with Bram Stoker About *Dracula*," *Journal of Dracula Studies* 6 (2004): n.p. Reprinted from *British Weekly* 1 Jul. 1897: 185. Penn State Interlibrary Loan (ILL), 10 July 2015.

58. Le Fanu, *Uncle Silas*, 189–90.
59. Stoker, *Dracula*, 22.
60. *Ibid.*, 24.
61. *Ibid.*, 22.
62. Davis, 27.
63. Botting, 146–47.
64. Davis, 27.
65. The American Quincey P. Morris and Arthur Holmwood (Lord Godalming) are not included in this list because, although they are part of the group and often featured as taking active roles in the novel, they do not contribute a significant amount of first-person writing to the assembled text. Quincey writes one brief note to Arthur (25 May), congratulating him on his engagement to Lucy and extending a dinner invitation with Seward and himself to celebrate. Arthur writes two telegrams (May 26 and Sept. 1) and one letter to Seward (Aug. 31) asking his help with Lucy.
66. Malcolm Smith, "Dracula and the Victorian Frame of Mind," *Trivium* 24 (1989): 76–97.
67. Carol A. Senf, *Science and Social Science in Bram Stoker's Fiction* (Westport, CT: Greenwood Press, 2002), 18.
68. *Ibid.*, 131.
69. Belford, 269.
70. David J. Skal, "'His Hour Upon the Stage': Theatrical Adaptations of *Dracula*," Auerbach and Skal, 371–81. Print.
71. Wolf, 151.
72. Boucicault's vampire, Alan Raby, is closest to resembling Dracula. He is a soldier and a leader, demonstrates his ruthlessness and commitment to the cause by killing his own brothers, plans and manipulates to achieve his goals, and his victims are women.
73. Stephen Arata, "The Occidental Tourist: *Dracula* and the Anxiety of Reverse Colonization," *Victorian Studies* 33 (1990): 621–45.
74. Le Fanu, *Carmilla*, 315.
75. Stoker, *Dracula*, 267.
76. Arata, 637.
77. Botting, 147.
78. Backus, 111.
79. Botting, 146.
80. Stoker, *Dracula*, 32.
81. *Ibid.*
82. *Ibid.*, 40.
83. Auerbach, 79.
84. Stoker, *Dracula*, 42.
85. *Ibid.*
86. Le Fanu, *Carmilla*, 318.
87. *Ibid.*, 335–36.
88. Stoker, *Dracula*, 42–43.

89. *Ibid.*, 43.
90. Auerbach, 83–84.
91. *Ibid.*, 71.
92. Stoker, *Dracula,*123.
93. Declan Kiberd, "Undead in the Nineties: Bram Stoker and *Dracula,*" *Irish Classics* (Cambridge: Harvard University Press, 2001), 379–98. Print.
94. *Ibid.*, 389.
95. *Ibid.*
96. Stoker, *Dracula,* 197.
97. *Ibid.*, 204.
98. *Ibid.*, 99–100.
99. *Ibid.*, 155.
100. *Ibid.*, 157.
101. *Ibid.*, 147
102. *Ibid.*, 152.
103. *Ibid.*,192.
104. *Ibid.*, 193.
105. Robert Smart, in his essay, "Postcolonial Dread and the Gothic: Refashioning Identity in Sheridan Le Fanu's *Carmilla* and Bram Stoker's *Dracula,*" writes that "Lucy Westenra is "also Irish, by the way, from County Roscommon" (28). This parenthetical statement was not cited, so it is uncertain how Smart arrived at this conclusion. However, when checking Dennis Walsh's "Old Irish-Gaelic Surnames" list, Murray *and* Morris (Ó Muirgheasa) were listed, but no Westenra.
106. Stoker, *Dracula,* 203.
107. Kiberd, 390.
108. Elizabeth Miller and Dacre Stoker, eds., *The Dublin Years The Lost Journal of Bram Stoker* (London: Robson Press, 2012), 134. Print.
109. Kiberd, 390.
110. Carol A. Senf, "'Dracula': Stoker's Response to the New Woman," *Victorian Studies* 26 (1982): 33–49.
111. McClelland, 60.
112. Stoker, *Dracula,* 207.
113. Kiberd, 390.
114. Stoker, *Dracula,* 88.
115. *Ibid.*, 89.
116. *Ibid.*
117. *Ibid.*
118. *Ibid.*, 155.
119. *Ibid.*, 203.
120. *Ibid.*, 86–87.
121. *Ibid.*, 165.
122. *Ibid.*, 226.
123. Senf, "'Dracula': Stoker's Response to the New Woman," 48.
124. Smart, 28.
125. Stoker, *Dracula,* 168.
126. *Ibid.*, 208.

127. *Ibid.*, 213–14.
128. *Ibid.*, 214.
129. *Ibid.*, 247. This scene may also be another original addition to vampire mythology. The vampire folklore from the first chapter indicated that vampires were created from circumstances like sudden death, an animal crossing a corpse, or being a vampire's victim. However, my research has not, to date, uncovered the specific method of blood exchange between the vampire and his victim as seen between Dracula and Mina in order to make a vampire. Also, no scenes like this appear in Maturin's, Polidori's, Rymer's, Boucicault's, or Le Fanu's stories.
130. Stoker, *Dracula,* 194.
131. *Ibid.*, 253.
132. Kiberd, 390.
133. Stoker, *Dracula,* 269.
134. McClelland, 7.
135. Grigore Nandris, "The Historical Dracula: The Theme of His Legend in the Western and in the Eastern Literature of Europe," *Comparative Literature* 3 (1966): 367–96.
136. Also noted by Eighteen-Bisang and Miller: "Many scholars consider this book Stoker's most important source, for it is most likely where he discovered the name 'Dracula'" (Stoker, *Bram Stoker's Notes,* 245).
137. Stoker, *Bram Stoker's Notes,* 245. For a more thorough explanation, read Elizabeth Miller's *Dracula: Sense and Nonsense.*
138. Stoker, *Bram Stoker's Notes,* 121.
139. *Ibid.*, 211.
140. *Ibid.*, 129.
141. *Ibid.*, 186–93.
142. *Ibid.*, 304–305.
143. Patrick Johnson, "Count Dracula and the Folkloric Vampire: Thirteen Comparisons," *Journal of Dracula Studies* 3 (2001): 33–41. Web, Penn State Interlibrary Loan, 8 July 2015: 37.
144. Johnson, 40.
145. *Ibid.*, 41.
146. *Ibid.*, 37.
147. Belford, 18.
148. *Ibid.*, 59.
149. Lady Wilde, *Ancient Legends, Mystic Charms, and Superstitions of Ireland,* Vol. 2 (London: Ward and Downey, 1887). Web, *Hathitrust,* 15 July 2015: 103.
150. Wilde, Vol. 2, 109.
151. Lady Wilde, *Ancient Legends, Mystic Charms, and Superstitions of Ireland,* Vol. 1 (London: Ward and Downey, 1887). Web, *Hathitrust,* 15 July 2015: 31.
152. Wilde, Vol. 2, 208.

153. Waller, "Irish Popular Superstitions" (May 1849), 553.

154. Yeats, *Fairy and Folk Tales of Ireland*, 383.

155. Wilde, Vol. 1, 209.

156. Lady Augusta Gregory, *Cuchulain of Muirthemne: The Story of the Men of the Red Branch of Ulster Arranged and Put into English* (Buckinghamshire, England: Colin Smythe, 1990), 142. Print.

157. Stoker, *Dracula*, 60.

158. Curran, "Was Dracula an Irishman?" 13–14.

159. Joseph Valente, *Dracula's Crypt: Bram Stoker, Irishness, and the Question of Blood* (Urbana: University of Illinois Press, 2002), 135. Print.

160. Moody and Martin, 123.

161. Dennis Walsh in "Old Irish-Gaelic Surnames" gives Valente's spelling and also Ó Muireachaidh.

162. Valente, 66.

163. Seamus Deane, "Introduction," Deane, 3–19. Print.

164. Valente, 93.

165. Quincey Morris's anglicized Irish last name, American birth, death, and "rebirth" in Quincey Harker offers several intriguing interpretive possibilities that will be examined later. I hesitate to include Lucy since all genealogical Irish surname sources that have been consulted thus far do not list any Westenras, from County Roscommon or otherwise.

166. McNally, 18–19.

167. Valente, 93.

168. Smith, 84.

169. The drawing is reproduced on a non-paginated page with other illustrations inserted in Chapter 10: Political Animal.

170. Stoker, *Dracula*, 3.

171. McNally, 18.

172. Valente, 51.

173. McNally, 16.

174. M., "Immigration of Irish Authors," *New Monthly Magazine and Literary Journal* 23.91 (July 1828): 140–45. Web, *ProQuest*, 15 May 2015: 140.

175. *Ibid.*, 141.

176. *Ibid.*

177. *Ibid.*, 142.

178. *Ibid.*, 141.

179. *Ibid.*, 142.

180. *Ibid.*, 143.

181. *Ibid.*

182. *Ibid.*

183. *Ibid.*, 144.

184. *Ibid.*

185. *Ibid.*

186. *Ibid.*, 145.

187. *Ibid.*

188. *Ibid.*

189. Patrick Brantlinger, *Rule of Darkness: British Literature and Imperialism, 1830–1914* (Ithaca: Cornell University Press, 1988), 233. Print.

190. Arata, 623.

191. *Ibid.*, 633.

192. Valente, 23.

193. Arata, 627.

194. Kiberd, 391.

195. Multiple sources verify Burton's birthplace at Torquay, Devonshire, England, so it is quite puzzling that he is not only included in the *Irish Literature* collection but that his biography in Volume 1 indicates that he was born in Tuam, County Galway (McCarthy 403). Tuam, as Murray indicates in Stoker's biography, was where Burton's "paternal grandfather had been the Church of Ireland rector and owner of an estate" (178).

196. Joan Corwin, "Richard F. Burton," *Victorian Prose Writers Before 1867*, Vol. 55, ed. William B. Thesing (Detroit, MI: Gale Research, 1987), 25–40. Web, *Gale Dictionary of Literary Biography*, 19 July 2015: 28.

197. *Ibid.*, 29.

198. Stoker, *Personal Reminiscences*, 358–359. Burton is certainly a candidate for part of the inspiration that became the character of Dracula. Stoker records his first impression of Burton when he saw him in a carriage with Irving on August 13, 1878: "[T]he man riveted my attention. He was dark, and forceful, and masterful, and ruthless. I have never seen so iron a countenance" (*Personal Reminiscences* 350). Paul Murray not only makes the connection between Dracula and Burton (177–79), but he also notes that Alfred, Lord Tennyson "may, to some degree, have been a model for the character of Dracula" since Stoker also draws attention to his canine tooth as he does with Burton's (117).

199. Arata, 634.

200. *Ibid.*, 638–39.

201. Stoker, *Dracula*, 59.

202. *Ibid.*

203. *Ibid.*, 269.

204. *Ibid.*, 266.

205. *Ibid.*, 218.

206. *Ibid.*, 282.

207. *Ibid.*, 136.

208. *Ibid.*, 215.

209. *Ibid.*, 156.
210. Dennis Walsh, "Old Irish-Gaelic Surnames," *Ireland's History in Maps*, 1996–2009. Web, www.rootsweb.ancestry.com, 16 July 2015.
211. Stoker, *Dracula*, 213.
212. *Ibid.*, 248.
213. *Ibid.*, 250.
214. *Ibid.*, 249.
215. *Ibid.*, 216.
216. *Ibid.*, 217.
217. Stoker, *Bram Stoker's Notes*, 29–31, 53, 63–67, 73–77, 81–83.
218. *Ibid.*, 113.
219. *Ibid.*, 117.
220. Stoker, *Dracula*, 134.
221. *Ibid.*, 85.
222. *Ibid.*, 303.
223. He is an American, an experienced adventurer, who brought a Winchester to what appeared to be a knife fight and yet ends up being fatally stabbed. Harker, the solicitor, passes through the Szgany unchallenged (Stoker, *Dracula*, 324).
224. A year later? Two? All the reader knows is that seven years after their ordeal, the Harkers have a son who was born on the anniversary of Quincey's death, so at the very most, the boy could only be six years old when Harker writes his undated note.
225. Stoker, *Dracula*, 326.
226. Valente, 38.
227. *Ibid.*, 28.
228. *Ibid.*, 39.
229. Murray, 144–45.
230. McCarthy, 404.
231. *Ibid.*, 408.
232. It is interesting to note that McCarthy died within four days of his close friend, on April 24, 1912.
233. Murray, 139.
234. "Home Rule for Ireland—Mr. Gladstone's Proposals," *Birmingham Daily Post* 9 April 1886: n.p. Web, *British Newspapers 1600–1950*, 8 July 2015.
235. "Our London Correspondence—Rejection of Mr. Parnell's Arrears Bill," *Glasgow Herald* 22 March 1888: n.p. Web, *Nineteenth Century British Newspapers*, 18 July 2015.
236. "Ulster Home Rulers in London," *Freeman's Journal and Daily Commercial Advertiser* [Dublin, Ireland] 24 June 1892: n.p. Web, *Nineteenth Century British Newspapers*, 8 July 2015.
237. Murray, 139.
238. *Ibid.*
239. *Ibid.*, 145.

240. *Ibid.*, 144.
241. Belford, 99.
242. Stoker, *Notes for Dracula*, 142–49.
243. Stoker, *Dracula*, 26.
244. Stoker, *Personal Reminiscences*, 344.
245. Belford, 91.
246. Stoker, *Personal Reminiscences*, 31.
247. Belford, 78.
248. Stoker, *Personal Reminiscences*, 32.
249. Belford, 136.
250. Miller and Stoker, 132–34.
251. Stoker, *Dracula*, 203.
252. Stoker, *Personal Reminiscences*, 30.
253. *Ibid.*, 31.
254. *Ibid.*, 30.
255. Quoted in Farson, 21.
256. Maurice Richardson, "The Psychoanalysis of Ghost Stories," *Twentieth Century* 66 (1959): 419–31.
257. *Ibid.*, 429.
258. Senf, "'Dracula': Stoker's Response to the New Woman," 38.
259. Parlour, 62.
260. Senf, "'Dracula': Stoker's Response to the New Woman," 39.
261. Parlour, 63.
262. Auerbach, 79.
263. *Ibid.*, 79–80.
264. Lisa Hopkins, *Bram Stoker: A Literary Life* (New York: Palgrave Macmillan, 2007), 23. Print.
265. Murray, 13.
266. *Ibid.*
267. *Ibid.*, 14.
268. *Ibid.*, 16.
269. *Ibid.*, 102.
270. *Ibid.*, 59.
271. *Ibid.*, 141.
272. Belford, 83.
273. Murray, 80.
274. *Ibid.*
275. Farson, 212.
276. Belford, 122.
277. *Ibid.*
278. Wolf, 126.
279. Bram Stoker, "The Censorship of Fiction," *Nineteenth Century and After* 64 (1908): 479–87.
280. *Ibid.*, 483.
281. Stoker, *Dracula*, 190.
282. *Ibid.*, 193.
283. George Stade, "Dracula's Women," *Partisan Review* (1986): 200–15.
284. Brigitte Boudreau, "Mother Dearest, Mother Deadliest: Object Relations Theory and the Trope of Failed Motherhood in *Dracula*,"

Journal of Dracula Studies 11 (2009): 5–22. Penn State Interlibrary Loan.
285. Parlour, 64.
286. *Ibid.*, 66.
287. Stoker, *Dracula*, 325.
288. Kiberd, 389.
289. Belford, 126–27.
290. Auerbach, 63.

Chapter 6

1. David Cairns and Shaun Richards. "What Ish My Nation?" *Post-Colonial Studies Reader*, eds. Bill Ashcroft, Gareth Griffiths, and Helen Tiffin (London: Routledge, 1995), 178–80.
2. Cairns and Richards, 180.
3. Edward W. Said, "Yeats and Decolonization," Deane, 69–95. Print.
4. McClelland, 24.
5. Said, 80.
6. *The Correspondence*, Letter III, 10.
7. *The Correspondence*, Letter V, 14.
8. Spence, 5.
9. *Ibid.*, 9.
10. Hall, 195.
11. *Ibid.*, 216.
12. *Ibid.*, 217.
13. Auerbach, 63.
14. McNally, 12.
15. *Ibid.*, 13.

16. *Ibid.*
17. Beresford, 10.
18. James Joyce, *Ulysses* (New York: Vintage, 1922, 1986), 28. Print.
19. Luke Gibbons, "Introduction: Culture, History and Irish Identity," *Critical Conditions: Field Day Essays—Transformations in Irish Culture* (Cork: Cork University Press, 1996), 3–22. Print.
20. Terry Eagleton, "Nationalism: Irony and Commitment," Deane, 23–39. Print.
21. McClelland, 30.
22. Valente, 4.
23. Wolf, 185.
24. *Ibid.*, 195.
25. *Ibid.*, 196.
26. *Ibid.*, 197.
27. *Ibid.*
28. *Ibid.*, 198.
29. *Ibid.*
30. There are, of course, many films, as any internet search will show.
31. Quoted in Colin Lacey, "Interview with the Vampire Maker," *Irish America* 11 (1995): 36.
32. Quoted in Lacey, 36.
33. One of the more interesting shifts is away from fear and to a heroic, compassionate, sympathetic, and prom-datable vampire.
34. McNally, 19–20.

Bibliography

Annwn, David. "Dazzling Ghostland: Sheridan Le Fanu's Phantasmagoria." *Irish Journal of Gothic and Horror Studies* 6 (8 July 2009): n.p. Web. irishgothichorrorjournal.home-stead.com. 2 July 2015.

Arata, Stephen. "The Occidental Tourist: *Dracula* and the Anxiety of Reverse Colonization." *Victorian Studies* 33 (1990): 621–45.

"Art I—*Melmoth the Wanderer.*" *Quarterly Review* 24.48 (Jan. 1821): 303–11. Web. *ProQuest.* 15 May 2015.

"Art II—*Melmoth the Wanderer: a Tale.*" *Port-Folio* 11.2 (June 1821): 277. Web. *ProQuest.* 15 May 2015.

"Art III *Fatal Revenge; or, the Family of Montorio.*" *Quarterly Review* 3.6 (May 1810): 339–47. Web. *ProQuest.* 12 May 2015.

"Art VIII Melmoth the Wanderer, a Tale." *Literary and Scientific Repository, and Critical Review* 2.4 (1 April 1821): 364. Web. ProQuest. 15 May 2015.

Auerbach, Nina. *Our Vampires, Ourselves.* Chicago: University of Chicago Press, 1995. Print.

_____, and David Skal, eds. *A Norton Critical Edition Bram Stoker's* Dracula. New York: Norton, 1997. Print.

Backus, Margot Gayle. *The Gothic Family Romance: Heterosexuality, Child Sacrifice, and the Anglo-Irish Colonial Order.* Durham: Duke University Press, 1999. Print.

_____. "The Outsider." Review of Joseph Valente's *Dracula's Crypt: Bram Stoker, Irishness, and the Question of Blood. Irish Literary Supplement* Fall (2003): 27.

Barber, Paul. *Vampires, Burial, and Death: Folklore and Reality.* New Haven: Yale University Press, 1988. Print.

Begnal, Michael. *Joseph Sheridan LeFanu.* Lewisburg: Bucknell University Press, 1971. Print.

Belford, Barbara. *Bram Stoker: A Biography of the Author of* Dracula. Cambridge, MA: Da Capo, 1996. Print.

Beresford, Matthew. "The Dangerous Dead: The Early Medieval Deviant Burial at Southwell, Nottinghamshire in a Wider Context." *MBArchaeology Local Heritage Series*, No. 3 (Oct. 2012): 1–16. Web. http://www.mbarchaeology.co.uk/. 30 June 2016.

_____. *From Demons To Dracula: The Creation of the Modern Vampire Myth.* 2008. London: Reaktion Books, 2011. Print.

"Biographical Particulars of Celebrated Persons Lately Deceased." *New Monthly Magazine and Literary Journal* 15.49 (Jan. 1825): 39–43. Web. *ProQuest.* 15 May 2015.

"The Bishop of Exeter's Charge." *Belfast News-Letter* 24 June 1845: n.p. Web. *British Newspapers 1600–1950.* 10 June 2015.

Bleiler, E. F., ed. Introduction. *Ghost Stories and Mysteries.* J. S. Le Fanu. New York: Dover, 1975. v–ix. Print.

"Books and Manuscripts." *Anthenaeum* 4473 (19 July 1913): 64. Web. *ProQuest British Periodicals*. 8 July 2015.

Botting, Fred. *Gothic*. London: Routledge, 1996. Print.

Boucicault, Dion. *The Vampire, A Phantasm*. 1852. Transcribed by Matthew Knight, Assistant Director of Special Collections, Assistant Librarian. University of South Florida Libraries. Transcript emailed to author 20 May 2016.

Boudreau, Brigitte. "Mother Dearest, Mother Deadliest: Object Relations Theory and the Trope of Failed Motherhood in *Dracula*." *Journal of Dracula Studies* 11 (2009): 5–22. Penn State Interlibrary Loan.

Boyce, D. George. *Nineteenth-Century Ireland: The Search for Stability*. Dublin: Gill and Macmillan, 1990. Print.

Brantlinger, Patrick. *Rule of Darkness: British Literature and Imperialism, 1830–1914*. Ithaca: Cornell University Press, 1988. Print.

Brennan, Kevin. "Charles Robert Maturin (1782–1824): Forgotten Irish Novelist." *Dublin Historical Record* 32.4 (Sept. 1979): 135–41. Web. *JSTOR*. 25 May 2015.

Burke-Kennedy, Eoin. "4,000-Year-Old Laois Bog Body Turns Out to Be World's Oldest." *Irish Times* 3 Aug. 2013: 5. Web. *ProQuest Historical Newspapers*. 1 July 2016.

Burr, Malcolm. "Notes on the Origin of the Word Vampire." *Slavonic and East European Review* 28 (1 Jan. 1949): 306–307. Web. *MLA International Bibliography*. 25 June 2016

Burton, Richard F. *Vikram and the Vampire, or Tales of Hindu Devilry*. London: Longmans, Green, and Co., 1870. Web. *Hathitrust*. 18 July 2016.

Butts, Isaac, ed. "Irish Tranquility." *Dublin University Magazine* 9.53 (May 1837): 577–86. Web. *ProQuest British Periodicals*. 16 June 2015.

Cahalan, James M. *Great Hatred, Little Room: The Irish Historical Novel*. Syracuse: Syracuse University Press, 1983. Print.

_____. *The Irish Novel: A Critical History*. Boston: Twayne, 1988. Print.

Cairns, David, and Shaun Richards. "What Ish My Nation?" *The Post-Colonial Studies Reader*. Eds. Bill Ashcroft, Gareth Griffiths, and Helen Tiffin. London: Routledge, 1995. 178–80.

Calmet, Dom Augustin. *Dissertations Upon the Apparitions of Angels, Daemons, and Ghosts and Concerning the Vampires of Hungary, Bohemia, Moravia, and Silesia*. Translated from French. London: M. Cooper, 1769. Web. *Hathitrust*. 21 June 2015.

"Charles Robert Maturin." *Ancestry.com*. n.p. 1997–2015. Web. 15 May 2015.

Clarke, Austin. "Yeats and Le Fanu." *Times Literary Supplement* 12 Dec. 1968: 1409.

Colclough, Stephen. "J. Sheridan Le Fanu and the 'Select Library of Fiction': Evidence from Four Previously Unpublished Letters." *Publishing History* 60 (2006): 5–19. Web. Penn State ILL. 31 Oct. 2014.

Collins, Dick. "The Devil and Daniel Farson: How Did Bram Stoker Die?" *Journal of Dracula Studies* 10 (2008): 1–9. Web. Draculastudies.web.kutztown.edu.

Conrad-O'Briain, Helen. "Providence and Intertextuality: Le Fanu, M. R. James, and Dorothy Sayers' *The Nine Tailors*." *Irish Journal of Gothic and Horror Studies* 9 (2 Oct. 2011): n.p. Web. irishgothichorrorjournal.homestead.com. 2 July 2015.

"Conversations of Maturin—No.1" *New Monthly Magazine and Literary Journal* 19.73 (Jan. 1827): 401–411. Web. *ProQuest*. 15 May 2015.

"Conversations of Maturin—No. II." *New Monthly Magazine and Literary Journal* 19.73 (Jan. 1827): 570–77. Web. *ProQuest*. 15 May 2015.

Cooper, Brian. 'The Word "Vampire": Its Slavonic Form and Origin." *Journal of Slavic Linguistics* 13.2 (2005): 251–70. Web. *JSTOR*. 28 June 2016.

The Correspondence of Sir Walter Scott and Charles Robert Maturin with a Few Other Allied Letters. Eds. Fannie Elizabeth Ratchford and William Henry McCarthy. Austin: University of Texas Press, 1937. Print.

Corwin, Joan. "Richard F. Burton." *Victorian Prose Writers Before 1867*. Vol. 55. Ed. William

B. Thesing. Detroit, MI: Gale Research, 1987. 25–40. Web. *Gale Dictionary of Literary Biography.* 19 July 2015.

Costello-Sullivan, Kathleen, ed. *Carmilla by Joseph Sheridan Le Fanu: A Critical Edition.* Syracuse: Syracuse University Press, 2013. Print.

Curran, Bob. *Bloody Irish: Celtic Vampire Legends.* Dublin: Merlin, 2002. Print.

_____. "Was Dracula an Irishman?" *History Ireland* 8.2 (2000): 12–15.

D. "On Vampyrism." *New Monthly Magazine and Literary Journal* [London] 7.25 (Jan. 1823): 140–49. Web. *ProQuest.* 3 June 2015.

D'Amico, Diane. "Feeling and Conception of Character in the Novels of Charles Robert Maturin." *Massachusetts Studies in English* 9.3 (1984): 41–54.

D'Arcy, Uriah Derick. *The Black Vampyre; A Legend of St. Domingo.* New York: Printed for the Author, 1819. Penn State University Interlibrary Loan.25 May 2016.

Davenport-Hines, Richard. *Gothic: Four Hundred Years of Excess, Horror, Evil, and Ruin.* New York: North Point, 1999. Print.

Davis, Paul E. "Dracula Anticipated: The Undead' in Anglo-Irish Literature." *The Universal Vampire: Origins and Evolution of a Legend.* Eds. Barbara Brodman and James E. Doan. Madison, NJ: Fairleigh Dickinson University Press, 2013. 17–31. Print.

Dawson, Leven M. "*Melmoth the Wanderer*: Paradox and the Gothic Novel." *Studies in English Literature 1500–1900* 8 (1968): 621–32.

Deane, Seamus. "Introduction." Deane. 3–19. Print.

_____, ed. *Nationalism, Colonialism, and Literature.* Minneapolis: University of Minnesota Press, 1990. Print.

Diskin, Patrick. "Poe, Le Fanu and the Sealed Room Mystery." *Notes and Queries* 13 (1965): 337–39.

"*Dracula* by Bram Stoker." *The Academy Fiction Supplement* (12 June 1897): 11. Web. *ProQuest British Periodicals.* 4 July 2015.

"Dramatic Necrology." *The Drama, or, The Theatrical Pocket Magazine* 7.7 (April 1825): 393–405. Web. *ProQuest.* 26 May 2015.

"Draoideachta: The Magic of the Ancient Irish." *Dublin University Magazine* 63.374 (Feb. 1864): 148–55. Web. *ProQuest British Periodicals.* 21 June 2015.

Dunn, Joseph. "Book of Armagh, The." *Catholic Encyclopedia.* 1996–2016. Web. www.cath olic.com. 24 July 2016.

Dupeyron-Lafay, Francoise. "Victorian Gothic Fiction as a Ghost: Immortality and the Undead in Joseph Sheridan Le Fanu's *Uncle Silas* (1864)." *Fastitocalon: Studies in Fantasticism Ancient to Modern* 1.1 (2010): 55–68. Web. Penn State Interlibrary Loan. 31 Oct. 2014.

Eagleton, Terry. "Form and Ideology in the Anglo-Irish Novel." Massoud. 135–46. Print.

_____. "Nationalism: Irony and Commitment." Deane. 23–39. Print.

Egan, Maurice Francis. "Irish Novels." *Irish Literature.* Vol. V. Ed. Justin McCarthy. Philadelphia: John D. Morris, 1904. Vii–xvii. Web. *Hathitrust.* 10 June 2015.

Ellis, S. M. "Joseph Sheridan LeFanu." *Bookman* (Oct. 1916): 15–21. Web. *ProQuest British Periodical Review.* 16 June 2015.

_____. *Wilkie Collins, Le Fanu, and Others.* 1931. Freeport, NY: Books for Libraries Press, 1968. 140–91. Print.

"Fairy Mythology of Ireland." *Dublin University Magazine* 63.378 (June 1864): 646–58. Web. *ProQuest British Periodicals.* 21 June 2015.

Fanthorpe, Lionel, and Patricia. *The Big Book of Mysteries.* Toronto: Dundurn Press, 2010. 260–67. Print.

Farson, Daniel. *The Man Who Wrote* Dracula*: A Biography of Bram Stoker.* New York: St. Martin's, 1975. Print.

Flanagan, Thomas. *The Irish Novelists 1800–1850.* New York: Columbia University Press, 1959. Print.

"Foreign Advices for March, 1732." *Gentleman's Magazine; or, Monthly Intelligencer* 2.15 (March 1732): 681. Web. *ProQuest British Periodical Review.* 21 June 2015.

"Foreign News." *Grub Street Journal* [London, England] 16 March 1732: n.p. Web. *British Newspapers 1600–1950.* 17 June 2016.

Fox, Renee. "*Carmilla* and the Politics of Indistinguishability." *Carmilla by Joseph Sheridan Le Fanu: A Critical Edition.* Ed. Kathleen Costello-Sullivan. Syracuse: Syracuse University Press, 2013. 110–21. Print.

Gates, Barbara T. "Blue Devils and Green Tea: Sheridan Le Fanu's Haunted Suicides." *Studies in Short Fiction* 24 (1987): 15–23.

Gibbons, Luke. "Introduction: Culture, History and Irish Identity." *Critical Conditions: Field Day Essays—Transformations in Irish Culture.* Cork: Cork University Press, 1996. 3–22. Print.

"A Glimpse of the Supernatural in the Nineteenth Century." *Dublin University Magazine* 58.347 (Nov. 1861): 620–29. Web. *ProQuest British Periodicals.* 15 June 2015.

"Glimpses of Celtic and Anglo-Saxon Literature." *Dublin University Magazine* 64.381 (Sept. 1864): 298–307. Web. *ProQuest British Periodicals.* 21 June 2015.

Gregory, Lady Augusta. *Cuchulain of Muirthemne: The Story of the Men of the Red Branch of Ulster Arranged and Put into English.* Buckinghamshire, England: Colin Smythe, 1990. Print.

Hall, Wayne E. *Dialogues in the Margin: A Study of the* Dublin University Magazine. Washington: Catholic University Press, 1999. Print.

Hammond, Muriel E. "C. R. Maturin and *Melmoth the Wanderer.*" *English* 11 (1956): 97–101.

Hare, Augustus. *Peculiar People: The Story of My Life.* 1896–1900. Eds. Anita Miller and James Papp. Chicago: Academy Chicago Publishers, 2007. 192–96. Print.

Harris, John B. *Charles Robert Maturin: The Forgotten Imitator.* New York: Arno, 1980. Print.

Haslam, Richard. "Irish Gothic: A Rhetorical Hermeneutics Approach." *Irish Journal of Gothic and Horror Studies* 2 (17 March 2007): n.p. Web. irishgothichorrorjouranl.homestead.com. 2 July 2015.

Herr, Curt. "Introduction—Born from Stinking Streets: The Rise of Penny Fiction." *Varney the Vampire; or, The Feast of Blood.* James Malcolm Rymer. Crestline, CA: Zittaw Press, 2008. 9–27. Print.

Holy Bible, King James Version. Grand Rapids, MI: Zondervan, 1994. Print.

"Home Rule for Ireland—Mr. Gladstone's Proposals." *Birmingham Daily Post* 9 April 1886: n.p. Web. *British Newspapers 1600–1950.* 8 July 2015.

Hopkins, Lisa. *Bram Stoker: A Literary Life.* New York: Palgrave Macmillan, 2007. Print.

Hughes, Mrs. [Mary Ann Watts]. *Letters and Recollections of Sir Walter Scott.* Ed. Horace Hutchinson. London: Smith, Elder, 1904. Web. *Hathitrust.* 13 June 2015.

Hyde, Douglas. "Early Irish Literature." *Irish Literature.* Vol. II. Ed. Justin McCarthy. Philadelphia: John D. Morris, 1904. vii–xx. Web. *Hathitrust.* 10 June 2015.

Idman, Niilo. *Charles Robert Maturin: His Life and Works.* London: Constable, 1923. Print.

Innes, C. L. *Woman and Nation in Irish Literature and Society, 1880–1935.* Athens: University of Georgia Press, 1993. Print.

Johnson, Patrick. "Count Dracula and the Folkloric Vampire: Thirteen Comparisons." *Journal of Dracula Studies* 3 (2001): 33–41. Web. Penn State Interlibrary Loan. 8 July 2015.

Joyce, James. *A Portrait of the Artist as a Young Man.* New York: Viking, 1916. Web. *Hathitrust.* 31 July 2015.

_____. *Ulysses.* 1922. New York: Vintage, 1986. Print.

Joyce, P. W. *The Origin and History of Irish Names of Places.* 2nd ed., enl. and corr. Dublin: McGlashan and Gill, 1870. Web. *Hathitrust.* 24 June 2016.

Joynes, Andrew, comp. and ed. *Medieval Ghost Stories: An Anthology of Miracles, Marvels and Prodigies.* 2001. Suffolk, England: Boydell Press, 2006. Print.

Keating, Geoffrey. *The General History of Ireland.* 1629–31. Vols. I and II. Translated by Dermod O'Connor. Dublin: James Duffy, 1841. Print.

Kelly, Jim. *Charles Maturin Authorship, Authenticity and the Nation.* Dublin: Four Courts Press, 2011. Print.

Kennedy, Veronica M. S. "Myth and the Gothic Dream: C. R. Maturin's *Melmoth the Wanderer.*" *Pacific Coast Philology* 4 (1969): 41–47.

Kiberd, Declan. "Undead in the Nineties: Bram Stoker and *Dracula.*" *Irish Classics.* Cambridge: Harvard University Press, 2001. 379–98. Print.

Kiely, Benedict. Foreword. *Fairy and Folk Tales of Ireland.* Ed. W. B. Yeats. New York: Collier, 1986. ix–xx. Print.

Killeen, Jarlath. *Gothic Ireland Horror and the Irish Anglican Imagination in the Long Eighteenth Century.* Dublin: Four Courts Press, 2005. Print.

_____. "In the Name of the Mother: Perverse Maternity in 'Carmilla.' *Reflections in a Glass Darkly: Essays on J. Sheridan Le Fanu.* Eds. Gary William Crawford, Jim Rockhill, and Brian J. Showers. New York: Hippocampus Press, 2011. 363–84. Print.

_____. "An Irish *Carmilla?*" *Carmilla by Joseph Sheridan Le Fanu: A Critical Edition.* Ed. Kathleen Costello-Sullivan. Syracuse: Syracuse University Press, 2013. 99–109. Print.

_____. "Irish Gothic: A Theoretical Introduction." *Irish Journal of Gothic and Horror Studies* 1 (30 Oct. 2006): n.p. Web. irishgothichorrorjouranl.homestead.com. 2 July 2015.

_____. "Irish Gothic Revisited." *Irish Journal of Gothic and Horror Studies* 4 (6 Aug. 2008): n.p. Web. irishgothichorrorjouranl.homestead.com. 2 July 2015.

Kosok, Heinz. "Charles Robert Maturin and Colonialism." Massoud. 228–33. Print.

Kramer, Dale. *Charles Robert Maturin.* New York: Twayne, 1973. Print.

Kreater, Peter Mario. "The Name of the Vampire: Some Reflections on Current Linguistic Theories on the Word Vampire." *Vampires: Myths and Metaphors of Enduring Evil.* Ed. Peter Day. New York: Rodopi, 2006. 251–70. Print.

Lacey, Colin. "Interview with the Vampire Maker." *Irish America* 11 (1995): 36.

Landseer, Thomas, ed. *Life and Letters of William Bewick (Artist).* Vol. 1. : Safari Press, 2008. Print.

Lang, Andrew. "'Spirit Hands.' Suggestion and Dogs." *Journal of the Society for Psychical Research Volume XIV 1909–1910.* London: The Society's Rooms, 1910. 65–72. Web. *Hathitrust.* 10 June 2015.

Lawson, John Cuthbert. *Modern Greek Folklore and Ancient Greek Religion: A Study in Survivals.* Cambridge: Cambridge University Press, 1910. Print.

Le Fanu, Joseph Sheridan. "Carmilla." *In a Glass Darkly.* 1872. London: Peter Davies, 1929. 291–382. Print

_____. "Passage in the Secret History of an Irish Countess." *Dublin University Magazine* 12 (1838): 502–519.

_____. *Uncle Silas.* 1864. Ed. W. J. McCormack. Oxford: Oxford University Press, 1981. Print.

Le Fanu, William Richard. *Seventy Years of Irish Life, Being Anecdotes and Reminiscences.* New York: Macmillan, 1893. Web. *Hathitrust.* 10 June 2015.

Leatherdale, Clive. *Dracula the Novel and the Legend: A Study of Bram Stoker's Gothic Masterpiece.* Revised edition. Brighton, East Sussex: Desert Island Books, 1993. Print.

Leeming, David. "Gilgamesh." *The Oxford Companion to World Mythology.* Oxford: Oxford University Press, 2005. *Oxford Reference.* 2006. Date accessed 11 July 2016.

"Legendary Fictions of the Irish Celts." *Dublin University Magazine* 69.409 (Jan. 1867): 84–86. Web. *ProQuest British Periodicals.* 21 June 2015.

"London." *Edinburgh Magazine and Literary Miscellany* 13 (Nov. 1823): 617–18. Web. *ProQuest.* 8 June 2015.

Lyons, F. S. L. "A Question of Identity: A Protestant View." *Irish Times* 9 Jan. 1975: n.p. Web. Interlibrary loan. 19 June 2015.

M. "Immigration of Irish Authors." *New Monthly Magazine and Literary Journal* 23.91 (July 1828): 140–45. Web. *ProQuest.* 15 May 2015.

"Marriages and Deaths." *Liverpool Mercury* 12 Nov. 1824: 159. Web. *19th Century British Newspapers.* 15 May 2015.

Marryat, Florence. *The Blood of the Vampire.* 1897. Kansas City: Valancourt Press, 2009. Print.

Mason, William Monck. *The History and Antiquities of the Collegiate and Cathedral Church of St. Patrick, near Dublin from its Foundation in 1190 to the year 1819.* Dublin: W. Folds, 1820. Web. *HathiTrust.* 12 May 2015.

Massoud, Mary, ed. *Literary Inter-Relations: Ireland, Egypt, and the Far East.* Gerrards Cross, England: Smythe, 1996. Print.

Maturin, Charles Robert. "Charles Robert Maturin Curate of St. Peter's, Dublin and Henrietta, His Widow." 25 Sept. 1822–23, Nov. 1824. MS Archives of the Royal Literary Fund: Archives of the Royal Literary Fund 472. World Microfilms. Web. *Nineteenth Century Collections Online.* 26 May 2015.

[Maturin, Charles Robert]. *Fatal Revenge; or the Family of Montorio A Romance by Dennis Jasper Murphy.* Vol. 1 London: Longman, Hurst, Rees, and Orme, 1807. Web. *Hathitrust.* 4 June 2015.

Maturin, Rev. C[harles] R[obert]. *Five Sermons on the Errors of the Roman Catholic Church Preached in St. Peter's Church, Dublin.* 2nd edition. Dublin: William Curry, Jun, & Company, 1826. Web. *Hathitrust.* 8 June 2015.

Maturin, Charles Robert. *Melmoth the Wanderer.* 1820. Oxford: Oxford University Press, 1989.

[Maturin, Charles Robert]. *The Milesian Chief A Romance by the Author of Montorio and The Wild Irish Boy.* Vol. 1. London: Henry Colburn, 1812. Web. *Hathitrust.* 4 June 2015.

_____. *Sermons.* London: Archibald Constable, 1819. Print.

[Maturin, Charles Robert]. *The Wild Irish Boy A Romance by the Author of Montorio.* Vol. 1 London: Longman, Hurst, Rees, and Orme, 1808. Web. *Hathitrust.* 4 June 2015.

[Maturin, Charles Robert]. *Women; or Pour et Contre A Tale by the Author of "Bertram," &c.* Vol. 1. Edinburgh: Archibald Constable, 1818. Web. *Hathitrust.* 4 June 2015.

Mayo, Herbert. *Letters on the Truths Contained in Popular Superstitions.* 1849. Delhi, India: Facsimile Publisher, 2016. Print.

McCarthy, Justin. "Irish Literature." *Irish Literature.* Vol. I. Ed. Justin McCarthy. Philadelphia: John D. Morris, 1904. vii–xvi. Web. *Hathitrust.* 10 June 2015.

_____, ed. *Irish Literature.* Vols. I –10. Philadelphia: John D. Morris, 1904. Web. *Hathitrust.* 10 June 2015.

McClelland, Bruce. *Slayers and Their Vampires: A Cultural History of Killing the Dead.* 2006. Ann Arbor: University of Michigan Press, 2009. Print.

McCormack, W. J. "Introduction." *Uncle Silas.* Sheridan Le Fanu. Oxford: Oxford University Press, 1981. vii–xx. Print.

_____, ed. "Irish Gothic and After (1820–1945)." *The Field Day Anthology of Irish Writing.* Vol. II. Ed. Seamus Deane. Derry, Ireland: Field Day, 1991. 831–54. Print.

_____. *Sheridan Le Fanu.* Guernsey, Channel Islands: Guernsey, 1997. Print.

McNally, Raymond T. "Bram Stoker and Irish Gothic." *The Fantastic Vampire: Studies in the Children of the Night Selected Essays from the Eighteenth International Conference on the Fantastic in the Arts.* Ed. James Craig Holte. Westport, CT: Greenwood, 2002. 11–21.

"Melmoth the Wanderer, &c." *Blackwood's Edinburgh Magazine* 8.44 (Nov. 1820): 161–68. Web. *ProQuest.* 15 May 2015.

Melton, J. Gordon. *The Vampire Book: The Encyclopedia of the Undead.* Detroit, MI: Visible Ink Press, 1999. Print.

"Memoir of Charles Robert Maturin." *Melmoth the Wanderer.* 1820. Vol. 1. Charles Robert Maturin. London: Richard Bentley and Son, 1892. vii–xxvii. Web. *Hathitrust.* 13 June 2015.

"Memoranda of Maturin." *Douglas Jerrold's Shilling Magazine Vol. 3 January—June.* London: Punch Office, 1846. 125–34. Web. *Hathitrust.* 7 June 2015.

Middleton, Jessie Adelaide. *Another Grey Ghost Book, with a Chapter on Prophetic Dreams and a Note on Vampires.* London: Eveleigh Nash, 1914. Print.

Miller, Elizabeth, and Dacre Stoker, eds. *The Dublin Years: The Lost Journal of Bram Stoker.* London: Robson Press, 2012. Print.

"Monthly List of Publications." *British Critic* 22 (July 1824): 109–11. Web. *ProQuest.* 8 June 2015.

Moody, T. W., and F. X. Martin. *The Course of Irish History.* Revised and enlarged, 4thed. Cork: Mercier, 1990. Print.

More, Henry. *An Antidote Against Atheism; Or, An Appeal to the Naturall Faculties of the Minde of Man, Whether There Be Not a God.* 2d ed. London: J. Flesher, 1655. Web. *Hathitrust.* 18 July 2016.

Morely, Stephen. "Historical UK Inflation and Price." Web. *Safalra's Website. Safalra.com.* 31 July 2015.

Morin, Christina. *Charles Robert Maturin and the Haunting of Irish Romantic Fiction.* Manchester: Manchester University Press, 2011. Print.

Morrill, John. "Cromwell, Oliver (1599–1658)." John Morrill *Oxford Dictionary of National Biography.* Eds. H. C. G. Matthew and Brian Harrison. Oxford: Oxford University Press, 2004. Online ed. Ed. David Cannadine. Sept. 2015. Web. 29 July 2016.

Moynahan, Julian. "The Politics of Anglo-Irish Gothic: Maturin, Le Fanu, and 'The Return of the Repressed.'" *Studies in Anglo-Irish Literature.* Ed. Heinz Kosok. Bonn: Bouvier, 1982. 43–53. Print.

"Mr. Bram Stoker's Library." *Times* [London, England] 8 July 1913: 11. Web. *Times Digital Archives 1785–1985.* 8 July 2015.

Murphy, Daniel. "Foreword.". *Cuchulain of Muirthemne. The Story of the Red Branch of Ulster Arranged and Put into English by Lady Gregory.* Buckinghamshire, England: Colin Smythe, 1990. 7–10. Print.

Murray, Paul. *From the Shadow of Dracula: A Life of Bram Stoker.* London: Jonathan Cape, 2004. Print.

Nandris, Grigore. "The Historical Dracula: The Theme of His Legend in the Western and in the Eastern Literature of Europe." *Comparative Literature* 3 (1966): 367–96.

"New Fiction." *Saturday Review of Politics, Literature, Science, and Art* 84.2175 (3 July 1897): 21. Web. *ProQuest British Periodicals.* 4 July 2015.

"Novels and Stories." *National Observer and British Review of Politics, Economics, Literature, Science, and Art* 18.450 (3 July 1897): 334. Web. *ProQuest British Periodicals.* 4 July 2015.

O'Mullane, Brigid. "The Huguenots in Dublin: Part I (Continued)." *Dublin Historical Record* 8.4 (Sept.–Nov. 1946): 121–34. Web. *JSTOR.* 27 May 2015.

'On the Writings of Mr. Maturin, and More Particularly His "Melmoth."' *London Magazine* 3.17 (May 1821): 514–24. Web. *ProQuest.*15 May 2015.

Osborne, Michael. *The Maturin and Johnston Families in Ireland.* 2012. Web. www.maturin. org.uk. 27 May 2015.

"Our London Correspondence—Rejection of Mr. Parnell's Arrears Bill." *Glasgow Herald* 22 March 1888: n.p. Web. *Nineteenth Century British Newspapers.* 18 July 2015.

Parlour, Susan. "Vixens and Virgins in the Nineteenth-Century Anglo-Irish Novel: Representations of the Feminine in Bram Stoker's *Dracula.*" *Journal of Dracula Studies* 11 (2009): 61–80. Web. Penn State Interlibrary Loan. 8 July 2015.

Penzoldt, Peter. "From *The Supernatural in Fiction.* [1952]" *Reflections in a Glass Darkly: Essays on J. Sheridan Le Fanu.* Eds. Gary William Crawford, Jim Rockhill, and Brian Showers. New York: Hippocampus Press, 2011. 108–126. Print.

Poe, Edgar A. "Letter to Mr.—." *Poems.* 2nd ed. New York: Elam Bliss, 1831. 2–29. Print.

Punter, David. *The Literature of Terror: A History of Gothic Fictions from 1765 to the Present Day.* Volume 1. London: Longman, 1996. Print.

Ragaz, Sharon. "Maturin, Archibald Constable, and the Publication of *Melmoth the Wanderer.*" *Review of English Studies* 57.230 (June 2006): 359–73. Web. *JSTOR.* 27 May 2015.

"Recollections of Maturin—No. III." *New Monthly Magazine and Literary Journal* 20.79 (July 1827): 146–52. Web. *ProQuest.* 15 May 2015.

"Recollections of Maturin, No. IV." *New Monthly Magazine and Literary Journal* 20.79 (July 1827): 370–76. Web. *ProQuest.* 15 May 2015.

Recollections of a Ramble, During the Summer of 1816 in a Letter to a Friend. London: Smith and Elder, 1817. Web. *Hathitrust.* 13 June 2015.

'Remarks on "Melmoth."' *New Monthly Magazine and Universal Register* 14.83 (Dec. 1820): 662–68. Web. *ProQuest*. 15 May 2015.

"Rev. C. R. Maturin." *Gentlemen's Magazine; and Historical Chronicle* (Jan. 1825): 84–85. Web. *ProQuest*. 25 May 2015.

Richardson, Maurice. "The Psychoanalysis of Ghost Stories." *Twentieth Century* 66 (1959): 419–31.

Ross, F. Clive. "The Croglin Vampire." *Tomorrow: World Digest of Psychical Research and Occult Studies* Spring 1963: 103–109. Interlibrary loan. Received electronically 4 Feb. 2016.

Ryan, W[illiam] P[atrick]. *The Irish Literary Revival: Its History, Pioneers, and Possibilities.* London: Ward and Downey, [1894]. Web. *Hathitrust*. 24 July 2015.

Rymer, James Malcolm. *Varney the Vampire; or, The Feast of Blood.* 1847. Introduction by Curt Herr. Crestline, CA: Zittaw Press, 2008. Print.

Sage, Victor. "Irish Gothic: C. R. Maturin and J. S. LeFanu." *A Companion to the Gothic*. Ed. David Punter. Oxford: Blackwell, 2001. 81–93. Print.

_____. *Le Fanu's Gothic: The Rhetoric of Darkness.* New York: Palgrave Macmillan, 2004.

Said, Edward W. "Yeats and Decolonization." Deane. 69–95. Print.

Saint Clair, Stanislaus, Graham Bower, and Charles A. Brophy. *A Residence in Bulgaria.* 1869. Memphis, TN: General Books, LLC, 2012. Print.

Saint Joseph Personal Size Edition of the New American Bible. New York: Catholic Book Publishing, 1970. Print.

"Sale of William Bewick's Works." *Athenaeum* 19 Nov. 1870: 662. Web. *ProQuest*. 12 July 2015.

Schilling, Bernard Nicholas. *Charles Robert Maturin: A Biographical and Critical Study.* Dissertation. Chicago: University of Chicago, June 1928. Print.

Scholten, Willem. *Charles Robert Maturin, the Terror-Novelist.* 1933. New York: Garland, 1980. Print.

Schulte, Leah Rediger. "Lilith." *The Oxford Encyclopedia of Women in World History*. Oxford: Oxford University Press, 2008. *Oxford Reference*. 2008. Date accessed 11 July 2016

Schumann, Nancy. "Women with Bite: Tracing Vampire Women from Lilith to *Twilight*." *The Universal Vampire: Origins and Evolution of a Legend*. Eds. Barbara Brodman and James E. Doan. Madison, NJ: Fairleigh Dickinson University Press, 2013. 109–120. Print.

S[cott], W[alter]. "Abstract of the *Eyrbiggia-Saga*; Being the Early Annals of that District of Iceland Lying Around the Promontory Called Snaefells." *Illustrations of Northern Antiquities, From the Earlier Teutonic and Scandinavian Romances; Being an Abstract of the Books of Heroes, and Nibelungen Lay*. Eds. Henry W. Weber and Robert Jamieson. Edinburgh, Scotland: John Ballantyne, 1814. 475–513. Web. *Hathitrust*. 25 May 2016.

Senf, Carol A. "'Dracula': Stoker's Response to the New Woman." *Victorian Studies* 26 (1982): 33–49.

_____. *Science and Social Science in Bram Stoker's Fiction.* Westport, CT: Greenwood Press, 2002.

_____. 'Women and Power in "Carmilla."' *Le Fanu Studies* 10.1 (May 2015): n.p. Web. *Lefanustudies.com* 11 June 2015.

Shakespeare, William. *Henry V. The Complete Works.* Eds. Stanley Wells and Gary Taylor. Oxford: Clarendon, 1986. 637–71.

Showers, Brian J. "Deciphering the Bennett/Le Fanu Capstone." *Le Fanu Studies* 4.1 (May 2009): n.p. Web. www.lefanustudies.com. 10 June 2015.

_____. "A Void Which Cannot Be Filled Up: Obituaries of J. S. Le Fanu." *Reflections in a Glass Darkly: Essays on J. Sheridan Le Fanu*. Eds. Gary William Crawford, Jim Rockhill, and Brian J. Showers. New York: Hippocampus Press, 2011. 72–83.

Skal, David. J. "'His Hour Upon the Stage': Theatrical Adaptations of *Dracula*." Auerbach and Skal. 371–81. Print.

Smart, Robert. "Postcolonial Dread and the Gothic: Refashioning Identity in Sheridan Le Fanu's *Carmilla* and Bram Stoker's *Dracula*." *Transnational and Postcolonial Vampires: Dark Blood.* Eds. Tabish Khair, et. al. New York: Palgrave Macmillan, 2013. 10–45. Web. Penn State ILL. 20 Oct. 2014.

Smith, Amy Elizabeth. "Experimentation and 'Horrid Curiosity' in Maturin's *Melmoth the Wanderer*." *English Studies* 74.6 (Dec. 1993): 524–35. Web. *Academic Search Complete*. 25 May 2015.

Smith, Malcolm. "Dracula and the Victorian Frame of Mind." *Trivium* 24 (1989): 76–97.

Spence, Joe. "Nationality and Irish Toryism: The Case of *The Dublin University Magazine*, 1833–52." *Journal of Newspaper and Periodical History* 4.3 (1988): 2–17.

Stade, George. "Dracula's Women." *Partisan Review* (1986): 200–215.

Stoddard, Jane. "Interview with Bram Stoker About *Dracula*." *Journal of Dracula Studies* 6 (2004): n.p. Reprinted from *British Weekly* 1 July 1897: 185. Penn State Interlibrary Loan (ILL). 10 Jul. 2015.

Stoker, Abraham. "Abraham Stoker 1847–1912. 'Bram Stoker.'" 20 Feb. 1911–9 March 1911. MS Archives of the Royal Literary Fund Archives of The Royal Literary Fund 2841. World Microfilms. Web. *Nineteenth Century Collections Online*. 26 May 2015.

"Stoker, Abraham otherwise Bram." *England and Wales, National Probate Calendar (Index of Wills and Administrations)*: 287. Web. *Ancestry.com*. 5 July 2015.

Stoker, Bram. *Bram Stoker's Notes for Dracula A Facsimile Edition.* Annotated and transcribed by Robert Eighteen-Bisang and Elizabeth Miller. Jefferson, NC: McFarland, 2008. Print.

_____. "The Censorship of Fiction." *Nineteenth Century and After* 64 (1908): 479–87.

_____. *Dracula.* 1897. Eds. Nina Auerbach and David Skal. New York: W. W. Norton, 1997. 1–327. Print.

_____. "Dracula's Guest." *Dracula's Guest.* 1914. Dingle, Co. Kerry: Brandon, 1990. 9–21. Print.

_____. *Personal Reminiscences of Henry Irving.* New York: Macmillan, 1906. Print.

"Stoker, Florence Anne Lemon." *England and Wales, National Probate Calendar (Index of Wills and Administrations)*: 604. Web. *Ancestry.com*. 5 July 2015.

Strochlic, Nina. "Bulgaria's Vampire Graveyards." *Daily Beast* 15 Oct. 2014: n.p. *NewsBank*. Web. 20 June 2016.

Summers, Montague. *The Vampire in Lore and Legend.* 1929. Mineola, New York: Dover, 2013. Print.

Terry, Ellen. *The Story of My Life: Recollections and Reflection.* New York: McClure Company, 1908. Web. *Hathitrust*. 19 July 2015.

"The Travels of Three English Gentlemen, from Venice to Hamburgh, being the Grand Tour of Germany, in the Year 1734. MS Never Before Published." *The Harleian Miscellany; or, a Collection of Scarce, Curious, and Entertaining Pamphlets and Tracts, as Well in Manuscript and in Print, Found in the Late Earl of Oxford's Library, Interspersed with Historical, Political, and Critical Notes.* Vol. XI. London: Robert Dutton, 1810. 218–355. Web. Penn State Interlibrary Loan. 8 June 2016.

"Ulster Home Rulers in London." *Freeman's Journal and Daily Commercial Advertiser* [Dublin, Ireland] 24 June 1892: n.p. Web. *Nineteenth Century British Newspapers*. 8 July 2015.

Upcott, William, Frederic Shoberl, and John Watkins. *A Biographical Dictionary of the Living Authors of Great Britain and Ireland.* London: Henry Colburn, 1816. Web. *Hathitrust*. 13 June 2015.

Valente, Joseph. *Dracula's Crypt: Bram Stoker, Irishness, and the Question of Blood.* Urbana: University of Illinois Press, 2002. Print.

"vampire, n." *OED Online.* Oxford University Press. June 2016. Web. 17 June 2016.

Waller, John, ed. "Irish Popular Superstitions." *Dublin University Magazine* (June 1849): 707–718. Web. *ProQuest*. 24 July 2016.

_____. "Irish Popular Superstitions." *Dublin University Magazine* (May 1849): 543–560. Web. *ProQuest*. 24 July 2016.

Walsh, Dennis. "Old Irish-Gaelic Surnames." *Ireland's History in Maps*. 1996–2009. Web. www.rootsweb.ancestry.com. 16 July 2015.

Walsh, P. G., and M.J. Kennedy, eds. "Introduction." *William of Newburgh: The History of English Affairs Book II*. Cambridge: Cambridge University Press, 2007. Print.

[Watts, Alaric]. "Memoir of the Rev. C. R. Maturin." *New Monthly Magazine and Universal Register* 11.62 (March 1819): 165–67. Web. *ProQuest*. 15 May 2015.

Watts, Alaric Alfred. *Alaric Watts, A Narrative of His Life*. Vol. 1. London: Richard Bentley and Sons, 1884. Web. *Hathitrust*. 13 June 2015.

Welsh, Charles. "Foreword." *Irish Literature*. Vol. I. Ed. Justin McCarthy. Philadelphia: John D. Morris, 1904. xvii–xxv. Web. *Hathitrust*. 10 June 2015.

_____. "Irish Fairy and Folk Tales." *Irish Literature*. Vol. III. Ed. Justin McCarthy. Philadelphia: John D. Morris, 1904. xvii–xxiv. Web. *Hathitrust*. 10 June 2015.

Whedon, Joss. "Welcome to the Hellmouth." *Buffy the Vampire Slayer, the Script Book Season One, Volume One*. New York: Pocket Books, 2000. Print. 1–65.

Wieger, Léon. *Chinese Tales of Vampires, Beasts, Genies and Men*. 1909. Translated by Derek Bryce. Somerset, UK: Llanerch Press, 2011. Print.

Wilde, Lady. *Ancient Legends, Mystic Charms, and Superstitions of Ireland*. Vol. 1. London: Ward and Downey, 1887. Web. *Hathitrust*. 15 July 2015.

_____. *Ancient Legends, Mystic Charms, and Superstitions of Ireland*. Vol. 2. London: Ward and Downey, 1887. Web. *Hathitrust*. 15 July 2015.

"Wills and Bequests." *Times* [London, England] 26 July 1937: 14. Web. *Times Digital Archives 1785–1985*. 8 July 2015.

Wilson, Katharina. 'The History of the Word "Vampire."' *Journal of the History of Ideas* 46.4 (1985): 57783. Web. *JSTOR*. 28 June 2016.

Wolf, Leonard. *Dracula: The Connoisseur's Guide*. New York: Broadway, 1997. Print.

Wright, Dudley. *Vampires and Vampirism: Legends from Around the World*. 1914. Maple Shade, NJ: Lethe Press, 2001. Print.

Yeats, William Butler. "The Celtic Element in Literature." *Essays and Introductions*. Dublin: Gill and Macmillan, 1961. 173–88. Print.

Yeats, W[illiam] B[utler], ed. *Fairy and Folk Tales of Ireland*. 1888, 1892. New York: Collier Books, 1986. Print.

_____. "Ireland and the Arts." *Essays and Introductions*. Dublin: Gill and Macmillan, 1961. 203–210. Print.

Index